A SOLDIER'S JOURNAL

WITH THE 22ND INFANTRY REGIMENT IN WORLD WAR II

A SOLDIER'S JOURNAL

WITH THE 22ND INFANTRY REGIMENT IN WORLD WAR II

DAVID ROTHBART

ibooks

new york
www.ibooks.net

DISTRIBUTED BY SIMON & SCHUSTER

An ibooks, inc. Book

Ibooks, inc.
24 West 25th Street
New York, NY 10010

The ibooks World Wide Web Site address is: http://www.ibooks.net

Editor: Dwight Jon Zimmerman
Back cover photograph courtesy J. Herbert Brill, used with permission.
Cover Design: Mike Rivilis

ISBN: 0-7434-5865-6
First ibooks printing May 2003
10 9 8 7 6 5 4 3 2 1

Share your thoughts about *A Soldier's Journal* and other ibooks titles in
the new ibooks virtual reading group at www.ibooks.net

For my wife Dorothy and daughters Betty, Judith, and Eleanor

CONTENTS

INTRODUCTION

In April 2002, I received a letter from a New York book publisher, ibooks, inc. "I read with great pleasure your manuscript and must congratulate you on your eloquence," wrote Senior Editor Dwight Jon Zimmerman. "We think this would make a fine addition to our ibooks line of military history titles. Our offer is as follows..." I immediately sat down at my computer, wrote a reply and sent it the same day: "I am thrilled to receive your letter of acceptance of my *A Soldier's Journal*. I have waited 57 years for this to happen. I was prepared to wait another 57 years. I thank you for saving me that additional waiting."

People have asked what made me decide to keep a journal of my army experience during World War II. In advance of being drafted into the Army, I reasoned that much of a soldier's spare time is spent in dreadful boredom. Gambling never interested me, nor drinking. Writing would provide me with an interesting preoccupation. I called it a journal instead of a diary because diary denotes writing every day. I used small notebooks that fit into my pocket and indelible pencils. Ballpoint pens had not yet been invented. I wrote in longhand and only when I thought I had something worth noting. At the end of one year in the Army and still in the States, I decided to write no more until I went overseas. That occurred eleven months later.

When I went home to Pittsburgh on furlough after that first year I handed my accumulation of notebooks to my father, Jacob M. Rothbart. He was an agent for the New York Life Insurance Company. He had not known I was keeping a journal. He notified me later that he had paid his secretary to transcribe my notes into typewritten pages—an intensive, laborious task. The overseas part of my *Journal* I typed myself after the war. I later made a small private printing of it and sold copies at cost to people who asked for one, usually fellow veterans.

In the process of writing this introduction, my wife Dorothy appointed herself my consultant. She told me I am too close to the subject. I miss aspects she would like to read. One example: "Even though detailed in the *Journal*, I want to see a brief, broad overview of your nearly four years in the Army." Okay, here goes:

On my induction date, February 14, 1942, I got on a metal-railed streetcar early in the morning. It delivered me to the Army induction center in the now defunct Old Post Office Building on Smithfield Street in downtown Pittsburgh. There I met a large group of other inductees. One thing we all understood. We were going to be in until we won the war no matter how long it took—two years, five, ten.... Until then our civilian lives would be on hold. Not knowing how long we would be in the Army was not a pleasant prospect. Those of us who passed our physicals marched to the Baltimore and Ohio Railroad Station by the Monongahela River. We boarded a railroad train pulled by a coal-fired steam engine belching a thick stream of black smoke. It took seven hours to carry us 100 miles to Fort Meade in Cumberland, Maryland. We entered our assigned barracks. One of our group instantly began tap-dancing expertly up, down, and across the floor. Someone mentioned later it was Fred Kelly, brother of movie star Gene Kelly. What a nice way to lead into our Army career.

Within three days I boarded a deluxe Pullman train bound for thirteen weeks of basic training at Camp Wheeler in Macon, Georgia. From there I joined the 4th Infantry Division, 22nd Infantry Regiment at the other end of the state, in Camp Gordon, Augusta, Georgia. I stayed with this outfit until the end of the war. The 22nd Infantry Regiment was formed in 1812 in response to the state of war between the United States and Great Britain. In honor of the first regular formation to defeat the superior British force, the U.S. Military Academy at West Point adopted a gray uniform based on the color and design worn by the 22nd Infantry Regiment. It is still the official dress uniform of West Point cadets.

I spent a year and a quarter in Georgia. During my twenty-three months in the states, we also moved to Fort Dix, New Jersey, in April 1943, then to Camp Gordon Johnston, Florida, in September 1943, and then to Fort Jackson, South Carolina, in December, 1943. We engaged in two months of field maneuvers in the Carolinas.

In January 1944, we shipped out from Camp Kilmer, New Jersey, heading in the direction of the ETO—European Theater of Operations. We embarked on a beautiful cruise ship converted to troop carrier, the British HMS (His Majesty's Ship) *Capetown Castle*. Fourteen days later we disembarked in England after zig-zagging across the ocean in order to outwit enemy submarines. I was seasick every minute of those fourteen days. I declined for many years after my discharge to board another ocean-going vessel, relenting only when luxury ocean liners developed stabilizers that sharply reduced side-to-side swaying.

My five month sojourn in England was mostly in Devonshire, the southern shire (county) bordering the English Channel. When I arrived in Devonshire, most of the German airplane bombing had ended. As much as it is possible for a soldier preparing for combat, I enjoyed being in England.

In the Allied campaign to defeat Germany in Europe, my regiment crossed the English Channel on June 6, 1944, to invade Normandy, France. Our assault troops landed on the shores of Utah Beach early in the morning of D-Day. As I was the regimental classification specialist, I landed with the Regimental Headquarters Company seventeen days later. Joining our regiment were novelist Ernest Hemingway and syndicated journalist Ernie Pyle. In Normandy, the rear echelon existed mostly in theory. Pockets of German army units infiltrated into fields we thought were already cleared. Guard duty at night was a deadly serious assignment at which every soldier took his turn.

Our combined tank and infantry units later broke through the hedgerow country of Normandy and swept through France, Belgium, and Luxembourg. I crossed the Rhine River on a pontoon bridge the Engineers had constructed, a remarkable achievement. Our incursion into Germany was perplexing. Why are these people still fighting? Don't they know it is over, they've been defeated? The truth is the people would gladly have stopped fighting. They were forced to continue by fanatic Nazi storm troopers who threatened them with death.

I did not personally see the death camps. I did see forced labor factories with their starving, emaciated, liberated laborers. The reports about Auschwitz and its gas chambers confounded the imagination. Germany, the most cultured of nations. Goethe, Beethoven, Schubert, Kant. We saw how low a civilized people can go.

The war in Europe ended in May, 1945. I started traveling west in June. In July, together with the rest of the 22nd Infantry Regiment, I boarded the American 10,000-ton troopship SS *James B. Parker* in Le Havre, France, and headed for home. I was awarded five Bronze Star medals. Actually, one medal with five oak leaf clusters, each cluster representing a certified Bronze Star medal. The award was for participating in five major battle campaigns. I was also awarded an Expert Infantry Badge. In 1997 I was one of four members of my regiment selected to receive from the citizens of Normandy the Commemorative Normandy Medal.

After the war I could have joined either the 4th Infantry Division Association or the 22nd Infantry Regiment Society or both. Initially, I elected to join the smaller, more intimate Regiment Society. Much later, I also joined the 4th Infantry Division Association. The 22nd is probably the most dynamic civilian organization anywhere informally representing an active-duty Army unit. At my first reunion in 1978 nearly all the members were World War II veterans. At each succeeding reunion the ratio gradually changed. Larger numbers of Vietnam War veterans showed up, a few Korean War veterans, and a reducing number from World War II. At the reunion in Cleveland in the year 2000, only ten percent of the attendees were from World War II. Twenty of us were seated together at two banquet tables, regarded respectfully as a superannuated group of survivors.

One of the noteworthy persons I associated with in the Army was John Cheever. He later became a Pulitzer Prize-winning novelist. We were both in Company E, 2nd Battalion. Private Cheever's short stories were at that time being published in *The New Yorker* magazine. We were not close buddies. We liked each other at a little distance. Our styles were different. John preferred the company of plain, non-intellectual "G.I. Joes." He hung out with them in bars and barracks. I rarely saw him at the camp Service Club which for me represented an elegant haven from crowded barracks precincts. There in a scantily patronized upstairs room I played classical music records on a phonograph contributed by some kind citizen. I found a 78 RPM record album of Beethoven's piano sonata Opus 111, the last piano sonata he wrote, and one of his finest. I listened to it over and over 'till I knew it intimately. I attributed John's choice of companions to his belief that they represented a rich mine lode of writing material.

Many years later, in one of his letters to me, John wrote: "Thanks for sending me [a copy of] your Journal. It refreshed my memory of you as a highly intelligent man who improved my IQ." One of my duties as regimental classification specialist was to administer the Army General Classification Test. The first time John took the test, he had fallen a little below the number needed to apply for Officer Candidate School. He asked to take the test again. I had no intention of letting him fail. It didn't take much to help him. I merely used a clock that showed his time was up at precisely the moment John indicated he had finished. He passed. I justified my laxity in timing to my conviction that John was a profound thinker who needed time to mull things over. Shallower minds nimble at word games often do better on tests than the likes of Cheever. Eventually, John realized he was not cut out to be an officer. By the end of 1942 he transferred to a Special Service Unit comprised of entertainers, musicians, and writers.

The veteran I feel closest to is J. Herbert Brill of Baltimore, Maryland. He was my captain in command of the 22nd Infantry Regiment Personnel Section. He promoted me to Section Leader, Classification Section, and raised my rank from private to Technician 4th Grade at Fort Dix, New Jersey, in June 1943. The T4 rank is the same as a 3-stripe buck sergeant. My job during combat was to assign replacement troops and accompany them to the meat-grinder front line. After delivering them, I returned to the rear echelon Headquarters Company which on average was much safer. Simply stated, I owe my life to Herb Brill for keeping me on that job. In addition to seeing each other at the reunions, several times a year we phone each other. Both as an active officer and as a civilian, Herb Brill is the kindest, gentlest man I've ever known.

Ernest Hemingway was another notable individual who was a part of the 22nd Infantry Regiment's history. The following report that appeared in one of the 22nd Infantry Regiment Society's newsletters highlights the deep regard Ernest Hemingway held for his association with the 22nd Infantry Regiment:

"Ernest Hemingway attached himself to Colonel C. T. 'Buck' Lanham's 22nd Infantry Regiment during the drive across France. He stayed with the 22nd through the Hurtgen Forest battle. After the war, when Hemingway was invited to one of the early 22nd Infantry Regiment Society's reunions, he always brought a smoked turkey. When he could not get to a reunion he always sent a smoked turkey to be shared, with his warm regards for the participants in the hotel Hospitality Room. After Ernest Hemingway died, the Hemingway Turkey tradition has been perpetuated as an integral part of every reunion. It appears on every reunion program as **The Carving of the Ernest Hemingway Smoked Turkey.**"

David Rothbart
April 2002

PART ONE

One Year in the Army: Stateside

Friday, 2:00 AM, February 13, 1942.

Adieus have been made, and I, Pittsburgh's Valentine gift to Uncle Sam, am off in the morning to the army, February 14, 1942. On this date, the fall of Singapore is imminent. Japan is rampantly overrunning the far cast, in an advance similar to the shocking invasion of Europe by Hitler. The bright hopes of the nations allied with the United States lie in the ability of America to produce vast quantities of war materiel, and in the ability of Russia to continue resisting the Nazi invasion forces. Such is the state of the world as I am drafted into the army under the Selective Service Act of 1940.

February 15. Fort Meade, Maryland.

I just concluded my first session of making up my bed, regulation style. Just a practice, this being Sunday, it is sorely tempting to sleep tonight beside the bed rather than disturb the prime success of the effort. Our contingent arrived at Fort Meade yesterday at 4:30 P.M. after a seven-hour ride on the B&O Railroad. Formation marching commenced at once, and I realized that I was a soldier. We filed into the mess hall an hour later for chow. I bridled my discriminating taste glands and dug in. The main compartment of the all-purpose metal tray contained beef liver. It was tender and tasty and a generous portion. The supporting fare was mashed potatoes, lima beans, shredded cabbage, white bread, butter, coffee, and tapioca pudding. Following this sumptuous repast, we were sworn in en masse and my army career was officially begun. The only dismaying incident that occurred was that one of the boys discovered last night that $15 had been lifted from his wallet as he was taking a shower. Breakfast today featured bacon and corn fritters; dinner, roast chicken that was popularly approved, and apple pie. Over 700 men arrive each day for processing at this induction center, then are diffused in a steady stream to every army post in the nation. Singapore fell this morning to the Japs.

February 16, 1942.

Today I went through the Classification routine. This included a written examination to determine both mechanical aptitude and general I.Q. (Intelligence Quotient). This was followed by a lengthy interview in which all information was discussed pertaining to job qualifications. Now "it's up to them." Next I was G.I. (Government Issue) outfitted in assembly line fashion. The clothes fit rather well—O.D.'s (Orderly Dress uniform), overcoat, fatigue suit, etc.

February 17.

I am now ostensibly immune against smallpox, typhoid fever and tetanus, having been this morning twice inoculated and once vaccinated. I reeled in a near faint following the injections of the serum, while others experienced just a slight dizziness. Later, all developed a sore left arm at the biceps. Five more "shots" are due in the next few weeks. We were read the *Articles of War*. The penalty for desertion and other serious delinquencies is death, as determined by court-martial. Most of us required little convincing to know that it doesn't pay to fool around with the army.

February 18.

Last night I was slightly feverish from the shots. This morning I participated in a calisthenics drill and was almost completely rejuvenated at the conclusion. The supervised exercises are uniquely expert. A captain lectured in the afternoon on the causes and events that precipitated the war. His views were satisfactorily expressed, I judged, but no more authoritative than a civilian observer's would be. We were shown a movie on venereal disease, and about every possible device was used to impress us with the idea of being careful in sexual relations. My name has been posted on the bulletin board among a list of men to be ready to leave for Camp Wheeler, Georgia. Most of my barracks-mates leave tonight for camps in Alabama, Georgia, and South Carolina.

February 19, 1942 en route.

I am writing as I recline on the lower birth of a Pullman. This troop train consists of six Pullman sleepers, and is transporting about 250 of us to Camp Wheeler. We left Camp Meade 7:30 P.M. and are traveling a secret and circuitous route. Before we left there was a final physical inspection, our third since induction, to catch any gonorrhea cases that might have slipped through. A band played as we lined up at the railroad station. I looked around speculatively at our company of raw recruits. They looked neat, well-clad, well-fed, and satisfied.

February 21, Camp Wheeler, Georgia.

In the gun rack by the door stands my 30-caliber Springfield rifle. On the post near my cot hangs my pack, ready with canteen, tent half and mess-kit to be slung on my back for a hike at an instant command. After a 27-hour ride from Cumberland, Maryland, we arrived last night and were assigned to First Platoon, Company D, 2nd Infantry Replacement Training Battalion. We were issued these articles, then taken through a final classification procedure consisting of an interview, a code aptitude test for the Signal Corps, and a clerical aptitude test given just a few of us. The mess hall system differs from Camp Meade. Dishes are used instead of the all-purpose metal tray, and chow is served at the table. Cooking is southern style. The weather is like the end of April in Pennsylvania, sunny, cool at night.

February 23.

Today I had on a gas mask, and, without going into the theory of chemical warfare, learned to manipulate it. Its construction is amazingly simple and can be operated by a child. On the drill grounds, we practiced elementary face movements, column formations, and the hand salute. In the army ten days and still no K.P. "kitchen police" duty.

Today I had on a gas mask, and, without going into the theory of chemical warfare, learned to manipulate it. Its construction is amazingly simple and can be operated by a child. On the drill grounds, we practiced elementary face movements, column formations, and the hand salute. In the army ten days and still no K.P. "kitchen police" duty.

February 24, 1942.

Our battalion reading room is not grand and dressy but is cozy and pleasant to relax in. Chaplain Clark is a genial host and has managed to establish an atmosphere that allows table tennis to be played, letters written, reading, the radio playing, or just dozing, without one greatly interfering with the others. This evening he had a young quintet of amateur musicians from Macon to entertain us, and the fact is, they did. The lilting hillbilly tunes and thumping jam session done in their drawling Georgian idiom was a relishing concoction.

February 25.

The general program each day is about as follows: arise 6:30 A.M., stand Reveille at 6:45, breakfast at 7:00, then "police" bed and barracks until 8:45 and "fall in" (assemble) for come what may. Dinner at 1:00, spend the day as Uncle Sam directs between 1:45 and 5:45, stand Retreat at 6:30, supper at 6:45. The bugle calls "lights out" at 10:00, though it is not required to be in until midnight. I have been retiring at 10:30.

February 26.

There is an unrelenting compulsion at this time to write: "Dear Journal, the Army's done me wrong, my arm aches from a typhoid shot, they had me–ME–digging ditches, I'm stiff all over, and what the devil's it all about anyway?" This is, I understand, an army function known as "griping," which is as staple as beans. The story goes that if a soldier has the energy to gripe at the end of the day, he is all right. I feel double all right.

February 27, 1942.

The pots are scoured, the tables clean, the floor spic and span, and everything in the mess-hall is ship-shape. It took eight of us K.P.'s to get it that way today while the two cooks cooked and the mess-sergeant chattered and fluttered about. At the proper intervals the men filed in, ate, then we started the routine all over from the beginning. The dishes clattered, the pans and cutlery set up a din as steam clouded above the wash basins. Mops and brooms went into action in a vigorous flank offensive, and the policing, done in the best Army tradition, was over for the day—the very long day.

February 28.

The normal complement of a machine gun crew is three men. In today's lesson, we simulated actual combat conditions. After a five-minute demonstration I was appointed Number 3 man in an exercise drill and found myself lying prone on the ground. The corporal gave the commands. No. 1 man snapped the tripod into place at a designated spot. No. 2 man brought up the gun and placed it into position, then I rushed up with the water container and ammunition box. Later it was my turn to be the gunner. I fingered the trigger, drew a bead, and contemplated the future.

March 1.

Macon, Georgia, is a city of some 70,000 population, with wide streets and many hotels. Yesterday was payday in camp, and being Saturday, Macon was mobbed with soldiers last night. The town seemed transformed into a Coney Island. M.P.'s (Military Police) were everywhere, pulling drunken soldiers out of saloons and ready to pounce at the first sign of a brawl. A dance was in progress at the U.S.O. service club, with six or eight soldiers for each girl.

Today Joe Rosenberg was visited by a second lieutenant from Fort Benning. He drove us into town for dinner, where the aspect was entirely changed from the night before. For the first time we observed the architecture and other characteristics of the Old South that meet the eye.

March 3, 1942.

The daily list of special assignments was posted on the bulletin board. Under "Fatigue Detail Battalion Headquarters" was typewritten: "Rothbart and Rosenberg report to Corporal Carbine." This we did, and were handed a two-man saw, an axe apiece, and led to a pile of logs.

"Trim these for fence posts," said the corporal, and left.

We went into conference. With my slight experience, Joe's subtle sense of humor, and much imagination, we found a formula and set to work. Chips and bark soon cluttered under our feet, and a neat pile of posts grew to astounding proportions. Joe and I walked home, accomplished woodsmen.

March 4.

We marched two abreast, twelve platoons strung out in a seemingly endless line. Several lieutenants were along, a couple of captains, and even the Major, stately and commandeering and accompanied by the sporting Chaplain. We were on a ten-mile hike with "light pack." Through camp the noncoms sang out the cadence, then we changed to "route step" as we entered wooded trails and by-ways. By my side strode a youth from Texas who had enlisted into the Paratroops. He told me of his bronco-busting days and his successes in rodeo competitions. In that manner the long trek finally ended. Somewhat footsore we were, but on our way out of the tenderfoot stage.

March 5.

As soon as a battalion in this camp has drawn its fill of men from induction centers, an intensive thirteen week program of training begins. Ours began today. The regimental commander, Colonel Lynch, officially greeted us. His auspicious presence lent ceremony to the assemblage that took place in honor of the occasion, and we were properly impressed with the solemnity of the undertaking.

March 7.

We came to a halt at an opening in the woods and unslung our rifles. Lt. Hodges, a mature military man with a greying mustache, proceeded to demonstrate the deploying tactics of a rifle squad. We memorized the signals, broke into assigned squads and started acting as skirmishers. The sergeant started forward in an advancing movement, I scouting ten paces to his right and riflemen lagging behind in an ir-regular line.

"Down," he motioned, and I fell flat on my stomach in shooting position.

We continued in a series of maneuvers ending in a strenuous forced march through the woods, through underbrush, crossing streams, and back to camp.

March 8, 1942, Sunday.

The soldiers are playing checkers or entertaining guests. I am perched on a balcony overhanging the main hall of the camp Service Club. Voices are subdued, and the rich tones of the New York Philharmonic Orchestra playing a composition by Eugene Goosens on its weekly radio broadcast fill the air. There is a steady drizzle of rain outside. At noon I ate in the Service Club cafeteria, a full meal costing just sixty cents. It is restful here, a retreat built away from the barracks. The structure and furnishings are severely simple in modern style. In a room at the rear of the balcony is a small library and an exhibition of drawings by one of the men. Occasionally there is a dance in the main hall, with a soldier orchestra which includes musicians who were of highest caliber as civilians and now give frequent music re-citals, both classical and popular. One of the nicest features of the Service Club is that it seems to be shunned by the cruder of our brethren. Well, maybe they'll make good battlers.

March 9.

"Gas!" came the combination alarm and command.

I held my breath, pulled out the face-piece of my gas mask and adjusted it swiftly. This was the real thing. Jets were opened and the chamber designed for the exercise filled with sulphatrioxide. I sampled a whiff, left the test chamber and removed the mask that I was rapidly growing to respect.

Next we were introduced to tear gas, this time without a mask. We ran through the chamber quickly, emerging blurry-eyed and face slightly stinging. In an adjoining open field we were treated in turn to sniffs of lewisite, chloropicrin, mustard gas and phosgene.

March 10, 1942.

Anthony Scalzo has one of the most spectacular backgrounds among the individuals I have met in the army. Tony came down with us from Fort Meade. He is now the likeliest prospect in the company to become a cook. He was an airplane bombardier in the Italian army at the time of Italy's invasion of Ethiopia in 1936. He tells vividly of his experiences in that hot, arid region.

On one occasion, while participating in ground operations he found himself isolated, and two coal-black natives sprang unexpectedly toward him. His gun jammed. Thinking quickly, he yanked out a hand grenade and flung it, managing to unbalance them; then freeing his gun mechanism, he picked them off. Quiet and amiable, Tony is an American citizen now. He still naively believes that Mussolini did much good for his country before going to war.

March 11.

The barracks hummed with activity. There was a scramble for cleaning equipment. Vague ripples on the beds were patted in an effort to give them a perfect appearance. Footlockers were straightened in line, clothes hung carefully on hangers, guns taken from the rack and vigorously assaulted with cleaning material. Today was payday, preceded by a rigid inspection. Our personal appearance too had to be immaculate, shaved, haircutted, wearing O.D. uniforms. At last the inspecting lieutenant arrived, accompanied by a sergeant. They peered closely at everything, criticized, and left, whereupon the tension eased. Later we filed one by one into the office of the company commander, Captain Allen. He sat behind his desk, returned my salute and handed me my pay envelope. I counted $11.90. The way out led past a table where quarter donations were being accepted for the Red Cross.

March 12, 1942.

The majority of men in my company were millhands and farmers before induction. They are principally from Pennsylvania and Virginia, with some among the two hundred coming from such varying points as Vermont and Utah. The cultural level is typically provincial-American, the prevailing sense of humor occasionally subtle, and always reeking of the barnyard. There is a small group of "latrine mah jong" gamblers from whom perhaps will be drawn guardhouse replacements.

In working and training, the men by and large are eager to learn, and though somewhat clumsy in marching drills, are less so with things mechanical. Officers are generally respected, as are noncoms who show fairness in meting out "gigs."

March 13.

Today marks the completion for me of one month in the army. The pace has been frenetic. Between regimented activities it requires utmost agility to perform such personal necessities as taking a shower or brushing teeth before breakfast. Orientation to this life has taken effect in a short time. It seems natural to wear leggings, drink water out of a canteen, stand at attention with heels together, toes six inches apart, and so on. Newspaper reading is a forgotten habit. Civilian news seems trite, and there is little time for more than scanning the headlines for world news. The month has not affected my physical well-being negatively; rather, the mirror reflects a ruddy glow in my cheeks and I've put on a little appropriate weight.

March 14.

My rifle is gradually and surreptitiously creeping into my life and consciousness. I all but eat and sleep with it. Today I was gigged for not having it clean, and confined to the barracks area until the cartridge chamber and ejector were demonstrably spotless. We are practicing the manual-of-arms positions with the gun, and other manipulations short of shooting it.

At the parade grounds a number of boxes with a bullseye drawn in front were set up, and we had a class in aiming from the prone, sitting, kneeling, and standing positions. Using the "coach and pupil" method one of us posed aiming at the target while the other corrected, then we alternated. Then the 1st Sergeant appeared carrying a handful of papers. He called out names and we marched to the infirmary for a yellow fever shot. It produced no aftereffect.

March 15, 1942.

"Have you seen the General yet?" asked the barber as he clipped around my head military style.

"He is a fine man. Cusses like four sailors when he's riled up," he chuckled. I added this bit to my divers store of information about the camp and prepared to receive more.

"Camp Wheeler was moved into a year ago February," continued the tonsorial artist. "It took seven thousand men to build it in a year. I opened the first barber shop on the second floor of a barracks."

He paused. "Now I own four."

He brought up a shaving bowl and sharpened his razor. "Right smart soldiers we turn out here. Keep your nose clean and you'll get to like it."

March 16.

I am listening to the band in the service club, from where it is broadcasting a camp radio program. It sounds excellent, not a bit amateurish. We spent the day learning to use a compass on scouting or other missions, and on the hand grenade court which is replete with devices purported to sharpen our skill at tossing the practice grenades through second-story windows, in trenches, shell-holes and over walls. They must be handled with quick adroitness as they go off five seconds after leaving the hand. Pretending they were active, I heaved the "pineapples" fast and far.

March 17.

At 8:00 P.M. our whole battalion consisting of four companies went on a night operation. We marched out to a wooded field area and assembled for a demonstration in the dark. The voice of the lieutenant in charge spoke out through a portable loudspeaker. He described the work of a reconnaissance patrol at night. Hazy figures appeared on the dim skyline to the left. From a distance they illustrated the speaker's remarks about how to distinguish noises, lights and movements.

At the conclusion we were given a practice problem. Each squad was presented a card on which were written four azimuth readings of the compass and a number of yards. Calculating from this inform- ation we had to locate markers that were scattered throughout the area and indicate we had been there.

At the start we stumbled and plodded into holes on a course that led through trees, underbrush and barbed wire. We came out safely, successful in solving the problem, and sang our way back to camp midnight doughnuts and coffee.

March 18, 1942.

Our drill period is carried on like this: "Platoon, attenSHUN. Dress right...DRESS; ready...FRONT; right...FACE; right shoulder...ARMS; forward...MARCH–one–two–three–four–one–two–three–by the left flank...MARCH; by the right flank...MARCH–c'mon, pick it up; column left...MARCH; eyes...RIGHT; ready...FRONT; to the rear...MARCH, to the rear...MARCH; left...TURN; platoon...HALT; order...ARMS; parade...REST. At ease. Platoon, attenSHUN. Fall out."

March 19.

On the bayonet court for a lesson in the gruesome business of bayon- eting, the lieutenant instructed us to handle the weapon with as much ferocity as we could muster. He said, "Imagine you were going to be sent to Australia and your request for a furlough was being filibustered by a mean clerk. He is coming at you...GET HIM!"

So, snorting and slicing the air, our faces twisted into a fierce fighting expression, we commenced ruthlessly to "get him."

March 20.

This time our haversacks were pregnant with "full pack." We hiked out four miles and pitched tents in a practice bivouac. A mobile kit- chen was set up and a latrine dug. Then came the order: "Strike tents. Have packs ready in five minutes. Last one is a rotten egg."

I had some difficulty putting together my envelope roll consisting of a shelter half and blanket, thus was a "rotten egg" (but not the only one). These full-field packs plus gas mask and rifle become inor- dinately heavy. I wonder that not one of our varied lot of physiques has failed to bear up under the strain. The countryside we passed is the very scene I once saw pictured in an art exhibition, the rolling hills scrubby with yellow pine trees, the ground crusty with a parched layer of sand. Ramshackle huts appear, and occasionally their parsimonious inhabitants, looking identically as portrayed by Jack Kirkland in his play, *Tobacco Road.*

March 21.

For two hours this evening a long truck convoy kept rolling in to spend the night with us. The troops had ridden for two days from Fort Shelby, Mississippi, and were mud stained and weary. They were passing through to North Carolina, part of a field artillery brigade, hauling their equipment and supplies by trailer. I walked over to "The Wheel" outside camp where some of them were gathered for sandwiches and coffee, tinkering with the amusement machines or relaxing at billiards. A pleasant-mannered chap from San Antonio asked me about our camp. He marvelled at how seriously our sentinels marched their posts. He described Fort Shelby, where he had been for his eight months in the service. He said they live in tents, that it is the largest tent camp in the country. I told him that his outfit was my first contact with a real combat unit. He agreed that he is closer to the pulse of war than we are here, and predicted that his next stop would be across the sea.

March 22, Sunday, 1942.

I have been fortunate so far to have had every Sunday free. I visited the main library, found it to be another spot of peace and serenity, and blew in a few choice smoke rings in approval. There is a nice variety of books on the limited shelves, sufficient to satisfy the fussiest erudite or thrill-seeking fiction reader. I glanced into an autobiography of the pedantic William Lyon Phelps, noted that the history section contained the recent Carl Sandburg editions on Lincoln, and that the daily New York newspaper *PM* was represented with current issues in the periodical room.

March 23, 1942.

We are in area F digging foxholes. These are three feet around, three and one-half feet deep, enough for a man to stoop in and be protected while shooting; a kind of rudimentary trench. It is sunny and beautiful this afternoon. The fresh-turned earth exudes a moist, fragrant aroma. The ground is covered with pine needles. Nearby is a clump of cactus. Tech Sergeant Bell is circulating among us, didactically passing pointers to no one in particular, but that all the distant trees and rocks and rills may hear. He is well liked—an ageless wardog with a slight craggy figure, the archetype barking sergeant of World War I renown. The whistle is blowing; the break is over and I go back to digging.

March 24.

It is four hours since we shot on the pistol range and my ears still ring from the blasts. We fired twenty rounds apiece, at fifteen and twenty-five yards from the target. My score—just a little above average—was 108 of a possible 200. The revolver was a 45-caliber Smith and Wesson six-shooter. I picked up the piece, loaded it and took a stance before the bullseye, not quite calm in anticipation of the new sensation for me of firing a deadly weapon.

"Ready on the right;" spoke the referee. "Ready on the left; for the slow-fire score, commence firing at will."

I squeezed the trigger and the gun jumped up in my hand as it went off and I flinched. But after a few shots I discovered that "after all it is nothing but a gun," as the lieutenant says, and I smoothly tried for a good "rapid-fire" score.

March 25.

Prior to our morning lecture on map reading, we "double-timed" to the obstacle course for a speed contest. "On your mark, get set, GO"—I hurdled two fences, ran through a maze, scaled an eight-foot wall, crawled under a trestle, leaped across a ditch, and sprinted atop an elevated wood structure to the finish. I came in fourth from last in my group.

After lunch we stripped to the skin and lined up for a physical inspection; then, after a snappy "dismounted drill," we rounded out the typical full day's schedule by marching to an imaginary battlefield for a practical study in the science of gun emplacements.

March 26, 1942.

The water system is out of order. We had to eat supper out of our mess kits. Now we are lounging around, munching morsels from one another's food packages from home. A pair is wrestling. One is singing a popular song, "A woman's a mean thing...." The platoon sergeant is directing the "gigs" assigned to extracurricular duties in the latrine.

Today we saw training films, and dismantled a machine gun to see what makes it tick. We are shown movies relating to every phase of work we take up and must learn the nomenclature of every gun we deal with, and how to disassemble and assemble it.

March 27.

I get less sleep than I did B.A.—Before Army, and not just because I go to sleep after "Lights Out." I can't quite get used to the snoring. With twenty-five bunkmates, it takes no more than two or three offenders to keep up a cacaphonic chorus lasting all night. I walk into the darkened barracks and navigate with practiced precision around the obstructions leading to my bed. I have developed an uncanny facility to undress blindly and arrange my wardrobe so that in the morning I can slip right into fatigue uniform without wasting a motion. I can control at least one tormentor, a neighbor I can stretch out my arm and nudge gently without waking him. Usually he stops snoring abruptly. Sometimes in his slumber he chants, "Hup-two-three-four-hup-two-three-four-."

March 28.

The Springfield '03 rifle has a reputation for kicking like a mule, causing me to be nervous as a cat while awaiting the order to fire the first round and expecting at least a dislocated shoulder. But the discharge produced only a slight recoil spasm. The myth of a kick had obviously gained credence among those who hold the gun incorrectly, loosely instead of braced tightly against the shoulder. My first shot missed the target. All the rest I fired hit it.

We also fired the Ml Garand rifle, and the Browning automatic. I did rather well, scoring a combined total of 162 out of a possible 200, including an appreciable number of bullseyes.

At a range of two hundred yards, it is said that a .30 caliber bullet can go through a three-foot tree. Yesterday we were in the target pits scoring for another company. The bullets whizzed by close overhead, landing behind us into a forest of trees which had been mown down evenly by the gunfire into stumps so it resembled a lawn.

March 29, 1942.

Army chow is frequently the consensus object of vituperatively expressed criticism. I with my epicurean palate am no exception, yet I have a high regard for the quality of the food and find the menus well-balanced. Undoubtedly, many soldiers are better fed than they were at home where their diets lacked the variety of fruits and vegetables that are served here, including apples, oranges, apricots, broccoli, spinach, and eggplant. There is plenty of high grade butter on the table.

Everyone receives a half pint of milk at breakfast, and we help ourselves to the cereal and hashed eggs or pancakes heaped on platters at the table. The main lunch dish is beef or pork except Friday, when it is fish. For supper there is usually beef stew or liver or spaghetti and meatballs. Desserts are usually puddings. White bread is served exclusively (I wonder why not occasionally whole wheat or rye). Considering all, the mess system seems adequately administered.

March 30.

A second payday has rolled around. I received $20.55. A dry-cleaning bill accounts for the deduction of 45 cents from my $21 a month allotment. Next month a laundry charge of $1.50 will start, plus any breakage for which an individual is held responsible such as careless handling of dishes, etc.

I find it is possible to live moderately well on this amount of money providing I stick close to camp. Since last payday I have a deficit of only $5.50 from having gone into Macon several times and buying toiletries and other personal items. Also, I have paid for an average of at least three meals per week, and was liberal in spending for refreshments such as soft drinks, ice cream, candy and tobacco.

April 1.

The Army is what may be called professionally patriotic and nurtures many rituals that the rookie is soon taught to observe. The bugle is a prominent symbol of these. We are awakened in the morning by the sententious notes of reveille. Midnight taps sound maternal, as though tenderly chiding the soldier who is not yet asleep. A number of bugle calls mark the routine of schedules and are more practical than sentimental; but retreat, when the flag is lowered in the evening, compels the warrior to display his most fervent devotion. Retreat inspires the bugler to invoke the maximum virtuosity of which he is capable, and the music and ceremony are passionate and nostalgic.

April 2.

At 8:30 A.M. the daily "Sick Call" was intoned. I joined a detail of other complainants and we marched to the infirmary. Two and a half hours later my turn came to see the doctor.

"What's your trouble?" he asked from behind a desk.

"Sore throat, Sir," I rasped.

An aide stuck a thermometer in my mouth. It read 99.4°, not enough to send me to the hospital. Instead, I was given pills and instructed to gargle with warm water. I returned and reported to the First Sergeant at the company Orderly Room.

"To the kitchen," he curtly directed, manifesting a conviction that anyone who goes on sick call and is not hospitalized is "goldbricking." I peeled potatoes.

April 3, 1942.

This afternoon consisted of watching a baseball game between the National League's Brooklyn Dodgers and Camp Wheeler. The Dodgers won, what with being morally buoyed by a dozen or more New York sports writers and attended by a retinue of sycophants as befits their regal major league stature. But they were hard-pressed, for the drafted soldier-players representing us are from their professional level in the baseball world.

Camp Wheeler is not lacking in outstanding athletes. I witnessed an exploit of our basketball team in which the formidable Boston Celtics were given considerable opposition. Doubtless time will reveal noted football players in our ranks, boxers, and the like. A few evenings ago we were entertained by a performance of an acrobat from the 10th Battalion. I had never seen better acrobatics.

April 4.

"Our business is picking up," quipped the Captain.

We were policing our section of the parade ground in preparation for Army Day on Monday. We ferreted for transgressing cigarette butts, burnt matches, paper, leaves, sticks, stones, virtually everything except hairpins. Hundreds of us strayed over the field searching and stooping to gather the waste, some bending assiduously to the task, others slouching indolently in the hot sun. The lieutenants had the day off and drove by from the Officers Club, womenfolk gracing their sides and attracting many a furtive inspection.

April 5, Easter Sunday.

Many of the boys got up for Easter Sunrise services, then went to Macon to dine at the good citizens' homes. Joe Rosenberg and I neglected to get ourselves invited.

The camp looks deserted, yet there is a holiday atmosphere. Planes from nearby Cochran Field are droning above us. Visitors are being shown about, the license plates of their cars denoting that they have traveled from far and near. Girls are resplendently garbed in spring finery; a goodly number of them are pretty, in keeping with the "Georgia peach" reputation.

I remarked to Joe that civilians regard our military reservation with wonderment and stare at jeeps and other vehicles that pass. We decided that while our acceptance of the army had become matter-of-fact, to the civilian public it is still new and strange.

April 6, Army Day, 1942.

Today the camp is on exhibition, with elaborate exhibits of war materiel set up throughout the post and soldier-guides to explain the intricacies of their usage. To the abashed confusion of a little old lady, one delved deeply into the technicalities of his piece. A detail of shirtless men is consigned to a conspicuous corner for the purpose of demonstrating a calisthenics drill. A Signal Corps group is demonstrating the operation of a Message Center; another infantry group is showing its skill on the shooting range. Several companies have gone to parade in Macon.

Most of us are not being used and are writing letters and taking snapshots. An accordionist sitting on a barracks step was soon joined by a harmonica player and a guitarist. Now they are rendering a lively polka. We had turkey for dinner; it was unconditionally delicious.

April 7.

After two days at ease, we resumed earning our "seventy cents a day" by harnessing ourselves into a full field pack and hiking ten miles. Before leaving, we assembled in Theater No. 2 for a weekly orientation lecture on the war, presented by an officer who spoke for an hour with the aid of world maps and slides. He seldom attempts to prognosticate future events and sticks to analyzing the current situation in the light of preceding events and other factors.

Afterward The Major instructed, "Boys, for the practice march that we shall take this afternoon have the straps of your pack adjusted so they won't cut into your shoulders. Change your socks. Fill your canteen with water but use it sparingly."

He beamed in his charming Pollyanna manner. "Help one another, boys," he continued. "We want you to be buddies. Sing! Be gay!"

I couldn't spare the energy to sing, but managed to whistle a Bach fugue. Some of my sturdier buddies, of Polish extraction from the anthracite coal region of eastern Pennsylvania, sang a colorful ditty starting with the verse:

"I've got boarder, Mike his name,
He's got ears like aeroplane,
Gee I don't know what to do,
My kids dey all got big ears too;
Yes-sir, no-sir, yes-sir, no-sir,
Sure, sure, dot's all right."

April 8.

We are a Heavy Weapons company specializing in machine guns. If
we don't know that weapon intimately yet, it can hardly be the fault
of our schedule or, instructors. We have spent hours and days on it;
presently we are "dry-shooting," learning to coordinate the multiple
actions needed to handle the gun while firing. Lt. Hodges, our instruct-
or and platoon officer, shows an infinite amount of patience as the
repetition is great and geared to the absorptive capacity of our least-
mechanical dolt.

April 9, 1942.

The two things that I most dislike have come up again: I am scheduled
for K.P. (kitchen police) tomorrow, and have just had the third in the
series of anti-tetanus inoculations. At least I'm finished with the shots
for a while, having taken the standard eight. Any hereafter will be
by special decree; mainly stimulating doses for typhoid or tetanus.
The latter reacts instantly like a bee sting.

Anticipating the insertion of the long hypodermic needle is in all
instances a terrifying experience to me, far more painful than that
produced by the antitoxin. K.P. is a marathon routine of running till
the extremest discomfiture has been reached, about 9:00 P.M.

April 10.

Many of the boys who enlisted did so to become parachutists, or
signed up for it after they were inducted. They average about twenty

years of age, are hardy, carefree, and invariably say, "I know I'm crazy but what the hell."

Here they train as regular infantrymen, then if they meet the stiff requirements of the paratroop corps they are transferred to an air base for training that demands the utmost of adeptness and stamina. In my platoon there are eight or ten, and they carry on at a lively pace, running, wrestling, crawling on the rafters and playing pranks. The platoon sergeant is not much older and participates good-naturedly, as the other night when a water battle took place in the latrine and he was not above getting soaked and pummeled with the rest.

April 11, 1942.

On Saturdays the program consists mainly of preparing for and being inspected, and marching on parade. Today the parade ground was swept by a sand storm and we came in caked with dust, our rifles white and gritty. Surely we would be exempted from inspection, we thought, until a squad leader bounded in and shouted, "Okay youse mugs, off and on; off your butts and on your feet. Rifle, barracks and personal inspection in an hour and a half."

The sergeant emerged from his private room and added, "Get that stuff perfect or you better give your hearts to God because your hide belongs to me!"

We were somehow ready at the appointed time. Lt. Hodges inspected with an air of gravity. Only a few were gigged, the terrible punishment inflicted on them being that they had to stay after hours and clean the latrine, which they accomplished in ten minutes.

April 12.

From the day I entered the army rumors have flown about indiscriminately and thicker than gossip at a women's Tuesday tea. There are rumors about everything: what to wear, where we're going, what is happening, who said what.

Yesterday we changed shirts three times before we received an authentic report on wearing either cotton khakis or woolen O.D.'s. Last week a rumor circulated that Russia was about to sign a separate armistice with Germany. Later I discovered the origin—an obscure piece in a newspaper quoting a vague unofficial opinion.

Rumors are used as a basis for burlesquing, and as a means of solacing the disgruntled who seem to derive masochistic pleasure from the more sordid ones. In the latter category the rumor that has found the most favor is one claiming that the average life of a machine gunner in combat is ninety seconds.

April 13, 1942.

Tat-tat-tat-tat-tat...the machine guns are stripping the ammunition belts in a broken series of quick bursts. We are shooting "for record" on the range. The targets are one thousand inches away—about twenty-eight yards—but constructed so that they represent shooting at a distance of 441 yards. A sulphurous aroma emanates from the guns on the firing line. I stuffed my ears with cotton and sat in the gunners position for a practice run. The coach designated the order of pasters (bullseye targets) to be hit and I fired, traversing, searching for accuracy. I didn't do well but will have one more preliminary practice run before the final that will be entered in my service record.

April 14.

I tasted guard duty last night for the first time. Our platoon was split into groups of six and driven to various outlying anti-aircraft alert posts. The "Officer of the Guard" looked us over.

"What is your Second General Order?" he asked me.

I recited: "Sir, to walk my post in a military manner, keeping always on the alert and observing everything that takes place within sight or hearing."

He asked for the last one, Number Eleven: "To be especially watchful at night and, during the time for challenging, to challenge all persons on or near my post, and to allow no one to pass without proper authority."

I was stationed near a battalion of colored troops and slept in a tent until awakened to take my turn standing guard from 1:00 A.M. till 3:00. I shook off my drowsiness, shouldered my loaded rifle with fixed bayonet and strode forth in the "military manner" to fulfill my new role as sentinel.

April 15.

This is our third day on the machine gun range. We are not overworking, unless it is work to loll about basking in the sun while waiting to be called to the firing line. The ground fairly trembles when all the guns are firing in unison. As on the rifle range, the land in back of the targets is covered with trees that have been shorn evenly by the bullets. The high scorers will be wearing a medal, but I will not be among them. My score was lamentably low, 90 of a possible 200, for which I have no alibi. My sole and rather dubious consolation is that the average in my platoon was probably not higher.

April 16, 1942.

"We're the boys from Pennsylvania—" sing our Pennsylvanians to the tune of "Battle Hymn Of The Republic".

"We've come a long way to-ge-ther," chime the Appalachian hillbillies, "and we've got a long ways to go."

The mixture of southern hillbillies and northern yankees lends a bizarre quality to army living that all enjoy. The northerners attempt to mimic the southern accents and those from south of the Mason-Dixon line retaliate by altering "th" to "d" in the style of the "dese, dem and dose" linguists. To the southerners goes the prize for the best cussing, their flavor and euphony unmatched by the northerners.

This morning after chow one of our more prolific comedians started the day cheerily, without malice, saying: "We had po'k rolls 'n grits for breakfast—yo' poke yo' feet undah the table, rolls yo' eyes 'n grits yo' teeth."

April 17.

We grouped in front of a blackboard placed in the shade of a cluster of trees for a class in machine gun firing principles. The lieutenant yielded the chalk to Corporal Wilson to discuss the Leaders and Gunners Rules which determine the points of safety at which a machine gun can fire over the heads of friendly troops as they advance toward the enemy.

"Now, Johnson, explain the Gunners Rule as we just gave it to you," he said.

That personage arose, inaudibly, paving the way for the next victim.

"Barkley, you give it to us."

Barkley didn't even murmur.

"Let's don't flub the dub on this," urged the lieutenant. "We've got to get this, it's very important," he pleaded. "Leach—."

And so was each scholar disturbed in his private reveries, and the sun wore on toward the western horizon.

April 18.

All in a day: Major Kleinman announced the transfer of Lt.Col. Hitt, our regimental commander, to a combat unit that will soon embark for "destination unknown." We returned from a baking field; Sgt. Moyer euphemistically commented, "I won't go so far as to say I'm sweating, but it's not raining," as he prepared to leave for Wisconsin on a ten day furlough. A lecturer discussed the Battle Of The Atlantic: "German Axis submarines hunt in packs, just like Company D in Macon on Saturday night," he said. With the aid of slides, Lt. Sanders introduced us to the 81-millimeter mortar gun. "This weapon is being used most effectively in this war," he said. "To clean, clear the chamber. Work around the ejector. You have to take off the extractor. One stroke of a toothbrush will wipe out the screwheads. We've been too lenient with you. We'll have to start bearing down."

April 19, Sunday, 1942.

It was about due; our platoon "mounted" fire guard in the battalion area tonight, so at last I had a Sunday interfered with—though the rupture occurred when the day was nearly spent anyway. In civilian life, the free seventh day of rest did not mean as much to me as it does now. On Sunday we are not required to make our beds, though we do; for that matter we are not required to get up at all, though we do that also. Nevertheless, the fact that we are not under such discipline on this day affords a great sense of relief.

On other days there is a constant tension in the knowledge that we can be ordered to do almost anything day or night, but on Sunday, unless notified otherwise in advance, we can if we will take a trip to China after Retreat Saturday, just so we are back for bed-check at Sunday midnight.

April 20, 1942.

The class went about as follows today: First, a reprimand from the corporal—"General, stop beating your gums and listen," he said to a private.

Sergeant Bell came on the scene. "Where is the driver of that truck?" he bellowed and proceeded on toward another group in quest of the driver, whom he found at last fast asleep in back of the truck.

The sound of a whistle came from the direction of the captain. "Take a ten minute break," said the lieutenant. "Smoke 'em up."

Boom—the reveille cannon roared once, then again, signalling a practice air raid alert. Firing it a third time would have meant a real raid. Orders snapped out right and left. Trucks scurried to the supply room for ammunition. We double timed to the barracks to grab our rifles and gas mask.

Boom—the cannon sounded the "all clear." We put everything away and marched back to resume the class.

April 21.

Area E-1 constitutes our small section of the parade ground that we use for drilling and lessons. It is a prominently located corner by the main road, close to the flag pole and the camp headquarters. The entire parade ground occupies a position reminiscent of New York's Central Park. Along its boundaries can be seen the gymnasium, three chapels, two theaters, "The Wheel," the library, Officers Club and Service Club. While we are engaged in one activity, adjoining companies are busy with a variety of others. When a woman walks by on the road, be she young or old, fat or lean, homely or fair, all eyes follow. Airplanes are a favorite distraction especially when they go through the motions of combative pursuit.

Someone is likely to whisper condescendingly, "There goes a ninety-day wonder," referring to a baby-faced second "lieuy" bearing the fresh uniform markings of a college R.O.T.C. (Reserve Officers Training Corps) and the three month course at Officers Training School.

April 22, 1942.

After work Joe Rosenberg and I sometimes commute to Macon to achieve a brief respite from our mess hall food. We eat usually at the S. and S. Cafeteria on Cherry Street where it is possible to get a good piece of roast beef. We stop in at one of the U.S.O. recreation centers, maybe have a dance or two with local damsels in their early teens, and top off the evening with a beer at the Hotel Dempsey bar.

The return bus trip is sometimes a rather depressing experience when a few soldiers imbibed too freely and overboisterously vent their spirits in lusty voices and loosely controlled movements. Even so it is interesting.

They sing, "Georgia is a helluva state, parley-vous; Georgia is a helluva state, the rott'nest in the forty-eight, hinkey dinkey parley-vous."

April 23.

Our machine guns were emplaced just enough below the crest of the hill that we would not be silhouetted against the sky. Enemy skirmishers were deploying across a long ravine on the hill opposite us. They were barely discernable.

This was our problem today: Firing at paper targets placed in the field instead of at paper bullseye targets one thousand inches away. We each fired one hundred rounds of live ammunition, endeavoring to locate our "enemy" targets by firing short bursts to see where the dust kicks up. Some tracer bullets were mixed in with the ammunition and they streaked brilliantly through the air with awe-inspiring force. No scores were kept but our perspective of the weapon was considerably enhanced.

April 24.

Captain Flom concluded the routine business matter for which he had summoned me to his office in the Camp Headquarters Complement

Building and initiated an informal discussion beginning with "How do you like the army?"

"Have a seat, Dave," he invited, and I sat down, "Have you gained much from your new associations?" he asked.

I made an appropriate reply; he nodded and proceeded to air his own ideas at some length.

"Yes," he began, "there are all types in this melting-pot. You will leave here with a new conception of life and people that will always be helpful to you later in civilian life." He leaned forward, warming to his subject. "These men will seem crude at first, but they have something right here," and he placed his hand over his heart. "Their personalities will reveal rich homespun qualities; eventually you will prefer their companionship to that of a whole barracksload of pseudo-educated snobs."

April 25.

Last night was ideal for a hike. The moon was full, the air refreshingly cool and filled with an exquisite aroma of honeysuckle now in bloom. The Captain had instructed us, "There will be no smoking. We will march out in silence. We will tread silently in the bivouac area and be silent when we return."

I walked alone with a white band on my arm marking the separation of my platoon from the next. By 12:30 we were back in the barracks and in bed. At 2:00 A.M. we were aroused by a bugle alarm. A lieutenant entered briskly and snapped on the lights.

"Everybody out!" he shouted. We snatched up brooms, mops and fire extinguishers and ran out *au naturel* for a fire drill.

April 26, 1942.

Harry would have graduated soon as a dentist in Germany except suddenly three years ago he had to leave and emigrate to America, which he quickly adopted unconditionally. He is tall, smiles easily, and his accent is gracefully cosmopolitan. As we ate ice cream in the PX (Post Exchange) he related an experience that took place in Germany: "Next to the Middle School I attended was a palace that the Nazis had taken over for the purpose of training storm troopers. I could see them marching in close-order drill. They carry their guns a little differently than we do here and their face and flank movements are slightly different; they must be perfect or they are severely punished. You can imagine how strict they were when I, just a boy in a public school, was once ordered to crawl two hundred yards when I mistook a guard command and was forced to pay a penalty. When an army M.P. approaches in Germany, both soldiers and civilians shiver; he wouldn't hesitate a moment to pull out his gun and shoot to kill for little cause."

Harry abruptly changed the topic to recounting his exploits with women, and a lascivious gleam flashed into his eyes.

April 27, 1942.

"Mail Call!"

Twice a day letters and packages are brought from the Orderly Room, the bearer inviting himself to be mobbed every time he sings out this refrain. The packages seldom contain other than food delicacies which rapidly disappear being that there is no place to store cakes, nuts, fried chicken, Virginia home-cured ham. The letters generally express an apprehensive mood pervading the civilian public which by now is completely aroused by the war and its implications.

At the time of my induction this was not the case but it has since become so, I believe, more because of the disruptive effect of the draft than for any other single factor. "It will soon be quite safe for a girl to go out alone at night," is one assessment I heard.

April 28.

The officer-dentist cleaned and filled two cavities in my teeth in about the same time it would have taken a civilian dentist just to prepare his instruments and try to convince me I'll feel no pain. The army maintains a free dental clinic in a two-story building the size of a barracks. The second floor is one large room in which about fifteen dentists operate, each assisted by a dental technician. Before I decided to use this facility I asked several fellow soldiers how they had been treated. The answers were indeterminate but rather more complimentary than not. My dentist worked swiftly and with apparently mature skill. He said he had performed 550 fillings in the past month and 100 polishings.

April 29.

The Boy Scouts would love it: eating out of mess kits in the field, squatting with the metal containers balanced gingerly on their laps, the food varieties almost overlapping one another almost forming a stew, To me it is uncomfortable, like social buffet suppers that I never enjoyed.

We line up at the chow truck and hold out our compartmented metal dish and canteen cup to be filled. Our portions received, we seek a shaded spot and juggle into an awkward eating position. Afterward we scour our metal containers in three successive deep cans filled with boiling water and hold them toward the sun to dry.

We spent today in the field practicing machine gun tactics, delving ever deeper into the science of maneuvering the weapon in simulated battle.

April 30.

For several days we studied intensively the 81-mm mortar gun and climaxed by firing it today. No other weapon that we took up was as unfamiliar in principle at the beginning as this one. The shell resembles a hand grenade, but instead of pulling the pin and tossing it, it is inserted into the muzzle of the pipe-like mortar barrel where gravity drops it to the bottom, causing it to strike the firing pin and shoot high in the air over tall hills to the unseen target on the other side.

To control the aim by angling the mortar gun properly, an observer positioned on top the hill phones back distance information and results that only he can see. The effect of a mortar explosion is devastating within a radius of twenty-five yards or more.

May 1, 1942.

"Break," came the command, and everyone breathed an audible sigh of relief. Warm Georgia weather is beginning to assert itself in earnest. I handed my canteen to a field companion.

"Thanks for borryin' me some water," he responded.

Rather than rest quietly, the boys took up in their usual repartee. Taunted one, "You're a bliffer, not a man—three pounds of air in a two-pound bag."

"Well, Big Stupe, if I'm no man I'll take his place till he comes along," parried the one addressed.

Then from another quarter, to no one in particular, "I'm like the bird that always flies backward; doesn't give a damn where he's going, just wants to know where he's been."

Our star mimic worked out on his favorite theme, Sergeant Bell castigating someone on a duty mission, "Don't bring that damn man to me for any details; I don't want him. I'm sure the Army don't want him either but dammit they're going to keep him!"

May 2, 1942.

"You and I are going to Atlanta," Joe Rosenberg declared, and I did not contradict. We traveled, as Private Johnson would say, by air—"Air you going my way, Mister?" Our uniforms worked wonders; we covered the one hundred miles in less time than we would have by bus or train. Our driver-benefactor pointed out the Georgia state capital building and advised us of a historical cemetery that he thought would be interesting to visit. After coming in by way of "the sorrier side of the city," he let us off in the heart of downtown. We walked on Peachtree Street and gazed at stores, hotels and pedestrians. We sought to get our bearings by inquiring of a short, well dressed middle-aged gentleman.

"There's a right nice hotel over there," he pointed, then counter-inquired of us and soon insisted that Joe and I come home with him for supper. We did. Afterward he took us with him to his club for the evening, and his wife gave us the guest room for the night.

May 3, Sunday.

Our host, Mr. Kinzler, had been wounded in France in World War I. He is an enthusiastic member of the Veterans of Foreign Wars and his wife works tirelessly in social organizations whose projects are presently war oriented. Mr. Kinzler entertained us with delightfully delivered tales of his soldiering days.

"Sure-shot," he said they used to call him. We departed after dinner, pleased that now whenever we leave the South it will not be without ever having been to Atlanta, and hopped a trolley to the suburb of Hopeville.

We had not been able to see the vaunted Cyclorama exposition of The Battle Of Atlanta but had managed to take in enough of the city to get a good picture of it, including the fashionable North Side. We journeyed back to Macon in the car of an "army wife," passing signs along the road that advertised guava jelly, pecans and pralines.

May 4.

Some soldiers have less taste for largely army society; they become restless and occasionally "go over the hill" for a few days. This morning, the day after payday, the sergeant at Reveille ordered, "Report."

The platoon leaders in turn called out:

"First platoon one private missing."

"Second platoon all present and accounted for."

"Third platoon four privates absent."

"Fourth platoon all present."

The errant ones come back as spontaneously as they had taken unauthorized leave and submit to a summary court-martial where they are not dealt with harshly, at least in this camp, receiving three days in the guardhouse for each day "Absent Without Official Leave."

One hillbilly lad I spoke to recently after such an incident told me, "She-ucks; I don't mind bein' a pris'ner. Ye gits good food and they don't nag you all the time like at work."

May 5, 1942.

At 2:30 A.M. the retiring guard awakened me to relieve him. I shouldered my rifle, left the tent and went to the path of "guard mount." The moon shone hazily through a mist, shedding a dull glow on the field and gun emplacements. For a moment a bird chirped at her young then all was still, except now and then when a menacing mosquito buzzed past my ear. The camp lay stretched out beneath me on a distant slope, resembling a city with her straight rows of il-luminated street lamps.

We are getting more than our proportional share of antiaircraft alert duty since a training cycle was completed in the Third Battalion. While a new group is coming in and getting organized we are man-ning their alert posts as well as our own.

May 6, 1942.

The obstacle course we were on previously was mild compared with the one we were on today which has tall ladders to climb, ropes to swing on across water-filled ditches, and winding passes and under-passes to be traversed at full speed; and no balking, what with officers standing by each obstacle egging us on. The course wound and twisted for several hundred yards. We ended with a strenuous spurt to the finish line. Most of the fellows then started over again while the rest flopped panting to the ground, prompting the Major to come over and say soothingly, "That's right, boys, catch your breath a little before you run it a second time."

May 7.

The .50-caliber machine gun was once considered an antitank weapon but is now virtually obsolete for that purpose. We are devoting quite a bit of time to studying it so apparently it is still regarded as an im-portant weapon. As with the .30-caliber machine gun, we are learning to use the sighting devices and adjusting mechanisms used to get the correct aim. Mostly we practice "dry-shooting," without ammunition. Techniques differ with each weapon but the principles are almost the same in the way they function. The firing orders are also similar; the squad leader calls out directions according to set rules, such as: "Range six hundred, enemy tanks left front, rapid-commence firing."

May 8.

"If a bullet has my number on it it'll get me."

This is the popular philosophy expressed by the boys, fatalistically but not morbid; a healthy rationalization that helps them accept their lot. They are not reckless but feel they would like to get in and fight the war and settle the matter in the shortest possible time. An attorney from Philadelphia in his middle thirties stated this viewpoint in a line of reasoning identical with that of backwoodsmen.

"I don't want to lay around camps for two or three years," he said. "I want to see action. If I am slated to die in this war I prefer not to exist in boredom until it happens."

May 9, 1942.

This arrangement is satisfactory to me: night operations on Friday night from 8:00 to 12:00 and Saturday afternoon off. Last night we hiked eight miles. The weather was right, slightly cool, actually pleasant. Carrying a light pack with rifle slung on shoulder is no longer burdensome; it even enhances a sense of power and purpose. The prospect of an extended weekend is an attraction that pacifies whatever objections one may have in working a sixteen hour day to earn it.

May 10, Sunday.

If not comparable to the halcyon days of yore, Sunday can yet be lusciously similar, as today when I awoke at noon in a fairly decent hotel after a night's sleep undisturbed by barracks sounds. Then when I went down to breakfast in a good restaurant and placed my order disdaining to consider the cost of the items striking my fancy, the euphoria of the occasion was complete. Some day when camp life is but a memory and the vicissitudes will pass before me in retrospect, surely this Sunday will be one that distictly emerges. If when that retrospection occurs I happen to be undergoing some hardship, I hope I will yet be able, as now, to enjoy crunching into a succulent piece of spring chicken, troubles notwithstanding.

May 11.

The barracks orderly is supposed to keep busy as a Dutch matron; a supposition that doesn't make allowance for the male temperament. I was given that assignment for today. I succeeded admirably in keeping the coal-fired boiler hot so there would be no complaints from the boys when it came time to shave and shower, a fault I am well acquainted with, having suffered discomfort caused by previous barracks orderlies (B.O.'s). But primping the barracks all day is a different matter; I suspect the First Sergeant does not really expect that we will strictly adhere to his instructions explained in copious detail. I followed my judgment accordingly.

May 12.

I've long known that battles are planned and fought with maneuvers much resembling those in a game of chess. The tactics we are practicing bears this out. Our machine guns are employed like pawns both as a stationary defense unit and in limited strategy on the offense. The chess knight has its counterpart in the mortar gun which is effective in getting at the enemy's hidden positions behind the front line. The object in chess is in essence to win a war. While our movements in company and battalion operations are much narrower in scope, the analogy holds true. Tactics are tactics, one might say.

May 13, 1942.

The lieutenant, a skinny flat-chested neophyte, hollered at us by way of encouragement, "Put everything into it; you'll be glad some day that you were built up to be able to handle your rifles as easily as if they were toothpicks."

We were trying something new: calisthenics with rifles. We tugged them over and behind our heads till they touched the shoulder blade, holding the gun at each end as though it were a wand. At first the rifle seemed unwieldy, until the strange exercises became familiar.

The sergeant supplemented the lieutenant with his own brand of encouragement, "Loosen up, First Platoon—ye bunch of boozehounds; get into it." We never seem quite loose enough to keep from creaking and groaning a little.

May 14.

A private's future is not settled once he has been sent to a particular branch of the army such as the Infantry, as we were. In fact he soon finds himself in a dilemma in deciding on many courses that are open to him for which he can apply.

"Shall I go to Cooks and Bakers School and become a cook? A clerk? A parachutist?" he asks himself; or, if he is eligible, to submit himself for training to become a commissioned officer at O.C.S.–Officers Candidate School. "Should I take a test to become a truck driver?" No consensus of opinion can provide a clear answer; each man must determine his own interests and inclinations. Sometimes he consults the Classification personnel, or his company commander, but the problem remains his own to resolve. A few endowed with resourcefulness, perspicacity, luck or hard work find their permanent niche in the army and are content. Most leave it to chance and are willing to muddle along.

May 15, 1942.

Firing the .50-caliber machine gun today completed our program of shooting on the firing range. We were each allowed seven rounds (bullets) to aim and fire at moving targets several hundred yards away. The gun handles nicely and the telescopic sight brings the target seemingly a few feet away. At this stage we are still far from being trained gunners; in fact some of us have not overcome some timidity towards these diabolical instruments of death. But on one point everyone is clear—that if "the Japs," as the boys refer to any representative of the German-Italian-Japanese axis, come into their sights they would not hesitate to shoot to kill.

"I'd handle these guns like I was born with them," they declare.

May 16.

Our company commander, Captain Allen, took the podium in today's orientation lecture period. It is a major task to keep an entire battalion awake and he is one who can really do it. His topic was titled American Preparedness For War.

"In the Revolutionary War we used four hundred thousand men against forty-two thousand for the British," he said. "Why? Because our term of service was for only three months. At the start of Indian hostilities we had only one trained platoon! When this war is over and you go back home I advise you to advocate a powerful standing army, navy and marine corps to keep aggressor nations at bay."

I believe this statement highlights the main difference in attitude between the army and the civilian public which thinks every war it fights and wins will be the last while the army, mindful that America has been at war every thirty years since the seventeenth century, feels wars are destined for all time to come and we should make them as painless as possible.

May 17, 1942.

The very first thing an enlisted man must do is swallow his civilian-bred pride; difficult for an American. He must obey officers, sergeants, corporals, even fellow privates acting as squad leaders. Though most are fair in their dealings with him, there are enough of the other kind to cause some troubled moments.

It is almost impossible to totally avoid being gigged, but except for a few chronic offenders there really aren't many meted out, except occasionally when the sergeant feels it's time to get tough and show his authority. Several young men who had practically stepped directly from their mothers' apron strings into the army confide they have become hardened. The only evidence I see of this is that they tend not to be altruistic at the chow table. Inferiority complexes do not thrive here, nor does obsequious behavior. In general there is good esprit de corps, and teamwork goes according to customary American tradition, superb when needed, lackadaisical when merely following form.

May 18.

War rationing of commodities to civilians does not altogether by-pass the army. Last week when gasoline rationing started in the eastern states we began carrying by hand heavy weapons into the field that previously had been hauled out on trucks. Hitchhiking, alas, is no longer feasible; all of which indicates a unity of tempo between the military and civilians. As the nation tightens its belt to provide provisions for the army, the army reciprocates with efforts to show it is also frugal; a laudable democratic manifestation implying that the disparaging term "brasshats" as applied to Army administrators may be unjustified during this war.

May 19.

The fields in which we are practicing every day are sultry and the northerners among us are discovering what inertia means, southern style. Moving itself requires utmost effort let alone carrying machine guns and mortar guns and double-timing with them. We do not entirely submit to lassitude, just enough to make it hard for our leaders by balking, or acting contrary.

"On the double!" orders the sergeant, and we drag.

"Take it easy," he says, and we run. Perspiration keeps us damp and an occasional rain shower merely accentuates the heat. Still, "You ain't seen nothing yet," we are told, "wait 'till July."

May 20, 1942.

Our squad finished our assignment and relaxed in a clandestine "bull session," keeping watch against any ambitious lieutenant.

"I'm between a stink and a sweat," said John Wood.

Suddenly it occurred to me that snakes might be in the neighborhood and I asked if anyone knew. "There are a lot of water moccasins in Florida," replied one knowledgeable in such matters. "I reckon there'll be rattlers and copperheads hereabouts," he said, and proceeded to tell some lurid snake tales.

As the afternoon wore on (or "evenin'," as they say) someone gave a dissertation on raising chickens, another on the trustworthiness of mules, and another explained why he would have been better off joining the navy.

May 21.

A week before a training cycle is finished the battalion goes on a field maneuver lasting from two to four days. These are carried on similar to the great war games the army conducted just before the war began when many thousands of troops spent two or three months in the field simulating major battles.

This morning, one thousand strong, we marched out several miles, equipped with supplies sufficient for a two-day battle, and established a bivouac area. We were explained the first day's problem, then divided into opposing forces according to elaborate plans drawn up in advance for a defending army to resist the main-line attack by forces of equal strength. Nearly everything we have been taught went into this operation and we carried out our assignments with at least great energy if not masterful precision.

At 3:00 P.M. it began to rain, then to pour, and finally hail. Thoroughly drenched, we returned to our bivouac area, pitched our pup tents and built numerous fires of pine boughs in an effort to dry out.

May 22.

We rolled our packs at 4:00 A.M. and withdrew a few miles to a new area of operations. During the night not many of us had slept much. The ground was extremely hard; also cold and wet as likewise were we so there was little affinity between us. We ate breakfast, filled canteens with water from the lister bag, and took up today's problem. Those on the offensive yesterday switched to the defense of a wide hill. After our side had completely vanquished the foe (or so we tried to convince the umpires), we assembled for a seminar analyzing the maneuver, then trudged back to camp weary, haggard, and wiser for the experience.

May 23, 1942.

Had the schedule been followed we would have the day off; but there is the small matter of generals and such that schedules fail to reckon with so when it was announced that our camp is included for inspection by a touring international party of high-ranking officers we had no choice but to turn the camp inside out cleaning and dressing up the most obscure corner or unruly blade of grass. We were informed later that they came and visited mainly the Fourth and Sixth battalion specialty schools. A private of the Fourth Battalion told us he saw a portly Netherlands East Indies general, a Russian general and a couple of English and American generals. Why should Camp Wheeler merit such attention? Because, I learned now for the first time, it is the largest "infantry training replacement center" in the United States.

May 24, 1942.

Again the question anxiously presents itself—where do we go from here? The previous time for me was at Camp Meade when the all-important question was which branch of the army would I be in as determined by the type of camp I was sent to. Our basic training period is nearing the end. Twenty men from each company in the battalion are boarding a train tonight for somewhere. Within two weeks we will all be scattered to the four winds. We have stopped sending out our laundry so we'd better leave soon or (perish the thought) I'll have to start washing clothes.

May 25.

They are in khaki uniform now and thus as I, common clay: Bart Anderson as a civilian had traveled in Europe doing research in historical archives; a professional pianist who had barnstormed between New York and Argentina; William Batt, son of the metals division director of the War Production Board; a Columbia University history professor; Henderson Morrison, a Scotch attorney whose job now is reviewing cases for court-martial; Jack Ruppert, a Broadway producer now putting on variety entertainment programs in camp, for talent drawing on a plentiful supply of former vaudeville performers; a former newspaper reporter from Philadelphia named Taylor; a Chicago Symphony Orchestra French horn player. These are some of the men I have met at Camp Wheeler. They are trying to maintain their grasp of assiduously-cultivated civilian skills while adjusting themselves to a new way of life.

May 26.

I am not familiar with the historical evolution of the custom known as Dismounted Full Field Inspection but judging by the exacting niceties involved in this ceremony of displaying equipment I'd say it is a very old and cherished one. Last night we had to clean our equipment and make sure we have the articles pictured on page 78 of Soldiers Handbook # FM 21-100.

This morning we marched to the parade ground bearing our field packs and there performed "by the number." At the given signal we lined up, "covered off" to the front and sides, pitched tents and laid out our equipment for display precisely as prescribed: mess kit knife with cutting edge to the right, gas mask with strap vertical, shaving brush with bristles down. When the inspecting officers started walking through the aisles we stood between our tents in ranks as straight and orderly as a checkered field of corn.

A bugle sounded and we pulled out the tent pegs from one side but held up the tents by hand. At the next bugle call down went the tents in one mass motion and each platoon vied with the others to see which would be repacked first and ready to leave.

May 27, 1942.

The bugle blew First Call. I heard it and turned over on the other side. When it blew Reveille I still didn't budge, nor did the others. Today, in the middle of the week, our group had been given the day off while the rest of the camp went to work.

At 7:00 we were served a late breakfast, then I went to the reading room and in the barracks a few card games were begun. When I returned to wash for lunch the games had recessed and the evidence of casual occupancy was manifested in rumpled un-made beds, newspapers strewn around carelessly, trash cans filled with orange peelings and empty pretzel boxes; a scene of untidy abandonment obviously affording the boys profound relief from the usual daily inspection requiring the place to be immaculate.

May 28.

Many of our problems call for lying still in the woods while action takes place in other sectors. It may take an hour or two before my squad is called on to make a move. Previously this was a welcome interlude in which I could doze, dream, marvel at the wonders of nature, or contemplate a more effective course to hasten the conquest over Hitlerism. But now suddenly all the negative features of the outdoors have come into play. Houseflies have increased in numbers, poison ivy has become unavoidable, poison oak has ripened alarmingly and mosquitoes have not failed to perform up to their reputation. But worst of all are chiggers, which I never heard of before and the knowing woodsmen among us describe as tiny ticks that emerge from the ground to penetrate the skin of their victims, leaving a swelling larger than those of mosquitoes and infinitely itchier.

May 29.

In the few extra days we are remaining here we are kept busy mainly with reviewing, especially some of the subjects we had glossed over rapidly. The officers contend that we are slackening our efforts so they are sternly accelerating the pace of activities in an effort to get us "on the ball," as they say.

The past two weeks have seemed the hardest of the whole time that we have been in basic training. We have marched oftener than before at an unnaturally quick pace, led by a lanky cadre-man who "steps off" at longer than the standard thirty-inch step which is easiest for marching. In the increasingly hot sun there is cause for a legitimate gripe; but we are quite "on the ball."

May 30, Memorial Day. 1942.

"You looked better than ever before," said the Captain after we passed in review in our final parade. "I am very much satisfied with your work. I ask no more than that every future training cycle I conduct will maintain your high standard of performance." Today was our last day of scheduled training. In the morning we assembled in the theater and were addressed first by the regimental commander, Colonel Goodyear, who said he considered us better trained than some of the combat units he had seen lately. Then an officer from Intelligence spoke on the need to guard military information by weighing carefully every word before speaking, followed by a training film titled "Prisoner of War" which stressed that a military prisoner is legally required to reveal only his name, rank and army serial number, and his captors will not threaten physical injury as a means of persuasion, though they may bully some. I recall reading a newspaper report recently stating that so far the Japanese have not intentionally harmed their prisoners for fear of retaliation in kind, indicating the training film is not indulging in mere wishful thinking.

May 31.

I went to Macon to get a last look and bid the town farewell. Though many soldiers complain it has little to offer, for me it has tried its best to provide diversion and what more can I ask? The hospitality of the townsfolk is magnificent; their daughters are beautiful to gaze upon, the beer is good, and I've had excellent roast beef. At the service club in camp where I've spent much of my leisure hours I enjoyed entertainment programs ranging in variety from vaudeville to the best in classical music. Yes, there is a possibility I will long for Camp Wheeler, especially if I am ever at a camp that does not have nearly its facilities.

June 1.

It is nearly midnight. Within an hour we will line up to receive our pay, and at 3:30 A.M. our first large contingent of men will march to the railroad depot. We already turned in bedding and working equipment to the supply room except gas masks and mess kits which we packed with clothing and personal effects into two barracks-bags for each man. We went through a dozen or so different inspections. Supper had been a celebration, with company officers joining us and pitchers of beer on the table. The Chaplain staged a program of entertainment for us, out of doors in the center of the battalion field area, and we heard all sorts of speeches in honor of our departure expressing all the sentiment of a college graduation.

June 2, 1942.

The boys regretted separating from one another. I watched the large groups that departed at intervals during the night. At 10:00 A.M. I and four others were called to report for transfer and assembled with small numbers from other disbanding training battalions until we were forty-six in all. We went by bus to the Macon railroad depot where, escorted by a sergeant and a lieutenant, we boarded a coach. At Millen, Georgia, our coach was sidetracked for five hours during which we went to a movie (*My Gal Sal*) and ate a T-bone steak supper. It was 1:30 A.M. before we were delivered at Camp Gordon, Georgia, fifteen miles from Augusta, one hundred thirty miles northeast of Camp Wheeler, and went to sleep.

June 3, 1942.

THE ROLLING FOURTH, they call it. I am now in the Fourth Infantry Division, 22nd Infantry Regiment, Company E, 3rd Platoon; 2nd Battalion, too, but in broadly identifying the unit he is in one would say, "22nd Infantry Regiment." I am told that the Fourth is a parent division from which other new divisions are formed. There is a constant turnover of personnel composed largely of men who had been taken from the ranks, trained as cadre and sent out with various ratings. The initial and most persistent rumors I have heard are, first, that all furloughs will be stopped before the end of June, the last having just been granted; second, that the division will go on field maneuvers for the two months of July and August. Till others come along, I will moan along with these.

June 4.

I am equipped with an Ml (Garand) rifle, mosquito netting, and a steel helmet with a lightweight fiber insert that we use while performing general duties on the post. It is round-shaped the same as the steel helmet giving the first-seen wearer a ludicrous gnome-like appearance. This afternoon I was initiated with a ten-mile hike carrying full field pack. Before gas rationing this was a motorized division with the title Fourth Motorized Division and hikes were rare. We passed radio companies, engineer, artillery, and intelligence outfits with their vehicles, and a flock of tanks that stirred up huge clouds of dust in racing over a stretch of bare sand.

June 5.

Essentially the army is the same everywhere, if I can judge from this change. At Camp Wheeler we often heard that details (chores) and inspections would be much less strict in a combat outfit than in a camp for raw recruits. This is not so. There is as much here of "policing" (cleaning), guard duty, inspections and gigs meted out as at Camp Wheeler. There are of course variations but the theme is the same. The chow served here is no more palatable than there, and made of similar menus and ingredients. Camp Gordon is handsome in appearance; it is laid out well, with the same gym, service club, chapel and post exchange that I've become accustomed to seeing.

June 6, 1942.

The First Sergeant intercepted me at breakfast and instructed, "Report to Regimental Headquarters. You are to be on special duty from now on. Let me know how you make out."

I reported as ordered to the sergeant-major at the regimental personnel office. He called over the corporal of the Classification Section and I went to work under his supervision in the capacity and title "Classification Specialist." This was the first official intimation I received that I would actually be assigned to do the work for which I had been classified in tests and interviews at the induction center when I entered the army. I spent the day studying pamphlets, forms, systems and other data pertinent to performing on the job.

June 7.

Many of the soldiers I have met here are from New York and have been in the army about fifteen months. They say proudly that they are in one of the truly crack fighting outfits and have personally been seasoned in two great field maneuvers, one in Louisiana, the other in the Carolinas. Most had been drafted and, expecting to be released after one year in the service, had not tried to get ahead. But since the start of the war on December 7, 1941, many started "bucking" for non-commissioned officer ratings and other advancements. Most New Yorkers talk fast, some in Brooklynese with all the "Toidy-Toid Street" trimmings; they angle (pull strings) for the best jobs, "sweat out" furloughs, curse the war, and work very hard though they would have everyone believe they are the best "goldbrickers" in the army.

June 8.

Never before did The Rolling Fourth put on such a parade. All her materiel including thousands of vehicles was massed on the huge parade ground. Pugnacious "half-tracks" carried arrayed in full war dress every man who could be spared from routine duties. Row after row, jeeps, trucks, motorcycles peeled off and rode in orderly procession past the dignitary-laden reviewing stand. As flags and banners were raised and lowered by the passing units, they were saluted by the high officers in the stand including Army Chief Of Staff General George C. Marshall, and Lord Mountbatten of the British naval fleet. Their presence augured big things to come in their estimate of the division's might.

June 9, 1942.

More and more the Classification Section is being utilized in placing soldiers into positions for which they are best suited. It is a relatively new setup in the army and promises to replace the usually hit or miss methods used previously to evaluate a man and list his qualifications for various jobs. The present system incalculably increases the effectiveness of such appraisal and in addition raises morale, for a man will work more willingly at his assigned task when he knows that some sincere effort has been made to place him where he is best fitted.

June 10.

I watched them tread in—a weary, mud-caked, unsmiling bunch barely dragging themselves into the barracks from the most trying in the series of proficiency tests, a two-day affair in which they marched thirty-five miles, mostly in rain, and spent the night in a swamp. "The mosquitoes were like dive-bombers," described one. "We waded a wide creek of mud that came above the knees. At 3:00 A.M. we went into attack. The 'enemy' fired live artillery shells that landed two or three hundred yards behind us. One of our lieutenants nearly made a mistake that would have led us directly into the line of fire. A corporal discovered it just in time or we would not be here now."

June 11.

"Hey, got a story for me, kid?" Izzy Goldstein asked as he flitted by. He is a reporter for *The Ivy Leaf*, the four-page weekly newspaper of the Fourth Motorized Division which chronicles local news and gossip of the military community. Since the Division settled at Camp Gordon, the publication has flourished as a popular institution matched in interest by only one other—our service club hostess, Miss Sue Curtin. She is a poised Hollywood-beauty type for whom everyone avows almost fantastic, yet plausible adoration. Under the near-celibacy circumstances, she would probably achieve the same effect with half her pulchritudinous endowments.

June 12.

Every company has its Day Room, located at the rear of the building that houses the Orderly Room in front and the Supply Room at the side. It serves the same purpose as the Battalion Reading Room at Camp Wheeler except on a smaller company scale. In an average evening it is used for playing billiards and ping-pong, or for writing letters, lounging. For three nights or so after payday, however, one of the pool tables is cleared for an epochal crap game which determines who will come out on top of the capitalistic system for the rest of the month until next payday and who will have to order credit Canteen Coupon books that become available for issue on the 10th of the month. Except for these few days the Day Room is homey enough, with its big fan stirring the air and the radio playing music and bringing war news.

June 13, 1942.

A batch of soldiers is congregated, the girls are ready, and the U.S.O. "Break In" dance begins in which any male is permitted to cut in: "Hello; nice evening. What's your name?" "Magnolia May." "Pardon me, may I cut in?" "Yes, see you later."..."Taking over, Pal. How d'ye do?" "Fine; how do you do?"..."Here y'are, buddy."..."What's the matter, soldier, don't you talk?"..."Mind if I cut in?" "Sure I mind, but go ahead."..."Good evening. My you have pretty eyes. So long."..."I bet you tell that to all the girls!" "I don't know all the girls."..."This place is decorated nice; you from Augusta?" "Yes; Oh! Thank you."..."Here I am again. What were you saying?—ouch—these jitter-bugs. Goo'by."..."Cuttin' in, friend."

June 14.

It is four months to the day since I entered the army. I am satisfied with my lot as a conscripted soldier whose sole interest is the successful end of this war inasmuch as during this time I have seen satisfactory progress made toward that end, including: Japanese navy defeats at Coral Sea and Midway Island; German frustration in the Caucasus, Kharkov, and at the vital northern Russian supply port of Murmansk; the burgeoning and full development of American war production; the Rhineland city of Cologne almost leveled to the ground in a single night by thirteen hundred British Royal Air Force planes;* also the splendid morale I see here in the service and wherever I speak with a civilian or pick up a newspaper, even journals whose editorial aim is to root out flaws which they scream to the public in a frantic effort to get them corrected and in sum seem trivial complaints. "The turning point of the war;" that is the phrase that is on everyone's lips, embodying the spirit of a Joe Louis knockout punch that his opponent knows with dead certainty is due.

June 15.

A civilian coming unnoticed among a group of soldiers might sometimes think them excessively profane and perhaps a little depraved, forgetting their need to compensate for living abstemiously with pent-up desires and energies.

"Few of us wanted or liked to gamble," explained Sid. "but when we were at Fort Benning, Georgia, we were located far from a service club, theater or any other recreation center, so what happened? We started gambling. Money meant nothing to us, and we had nothing else to do in our time off."

Swearing is so pervasive that expletives have become diluted of sting, blasphemy, or ill will and there is actually less bawdiness in this Eve-less society than might be expected.

The first 1,000-bomber attack in WWII. Approximately one-tenth of the metropolitan area was destroyed.

June 16, 1942.

Supper finished, we stood outside waiting for Mail Call.

"Any good rumors today, Jack?"

"Naw—except the Supply Room collected our extra blankets today so maybe we are going to South America. What do you hear?"

"Well, they say we might go to Washington and guard the President."

"Who says?"

"Someone heard a colonel ask his wife over the telephone if someone they know in Washington, D.C. is still there, which sounds like he expects to see him soon."

"Baloney. What's at the movies?"

"A cowboy picture, wanta go?"

"Do I look crazy! Well all right, if you want to. You coming, Kep?"

"Sure, and I'll wind up with a Section Eight" (Medical Discharge specifying mental aberration).

June 17.

The Regimental Personnel office is a clerical nerve center providing coordination of personnel matters with the action needs of Command Headquarters. It is one very large room lined with several rows of desks, each manned with a company clerk and his assistant, their job being to maintain the constantly changing roster of their company, the service record of each man, and to make out the payroll. The place functions like a stock exchange. At intervals the Sergeant-Major calls out, "At ease." The typewriters stop clacking; he reads out information and instructions, then—tumult, rush deadlines, noise, transfers typed up—and in no time the new matters are integrated, dispatched, and order again reigns in the regiment. At the controls is Captain J. Herbert Brill who is capable, knows his work and the men under him.

June 18.

Augusta, Georgia, with a population of seventy thousand is about as large as Macon but has a longer main business street, brighter lights, and more restaurants and shops. The many new shops that sprung up to accommodate the expanding army (and the shops' entrepeneurs) have given the town a metropolitan air. The interaction of Military Police and revelling soldiers is less noticeable. Certain estaminets and shady establishments are forbidden territory posted with military "Off Limits" signs which are usually obeyed. It is on Saturday night especially an "army town," meaning an urban place to go for a change of scenery, to eat a steak, say hello to other soldiers, walk up one side of the street and back on the other, repeat this once or twice, drop in at a U.S.O. center complemented with benevolent civilians, leave early enough to get a beer before the midnight Saturday army curfew, perhaps eat another steak, then get in line for the Camp Gordon bus.

June 19.

The regiment went out on a hike—a "ripper" I would say if I were English. It was a twenty-five miler with full field pack which weighs upwards of eighty-five pounds. Anyone who could be spared went along including clerks and cooks. By a kind stroke of fate I and a few others were narrowly exempted this time. The sun beat down intolerably and hundreds literally fell out along the way. Trucks and ambulances went out looking to pick up those who had the sense to drop out before they fell as well as the ones who continued on until they dropped senseless. There was at least one sunstroke fatality; also thousands of blisters, but that is not unusual. Everyone including gnarled veterans said this was the roughest hike they had ever been on.

June 20, 1942.

He was a by-the-book "G.I." staff sergeant with gold wavy hair and cherubic peaches and cream complexion that belied his well-advanced youth. "I've been in the army fifteen years," he said. "What was it like in peace time? First of all we had permanent barracks with all the comforts of home installed in them. Our Day Room was furnished with a thousand dollars worth of furniture. We seldom hiked or had an overnight problem. The big thing we had to worry about was inspection every Saturday morning. Every inch had to be perfect, brass polished to a high lustre, shoes you could see your reflection in like a mirror; then we had off from noon until Monday morning and were permitted to wear civilian clothes. I didn't care for the army the first couple of years, then it kind of grew on me. I'll be pensioned off in only fifteen more years."

June 21.

Summer has brought with it a large influx of visitors. Wives, parents, and sweethearts are trekking into camp, mostly from the north. Some stay in the Guest House at camp for as long as five days at a nominal fee while others find quarters in town, usually with difficulty. Their visit to camp is very revealing for them and they have many tales and new viewpoints to take back home with them, not that which should remain secret military information but about matters few fellows care to discuss in letters; things that in a letter might shock or mislead, but seen in person are calmly taken as normal facets of camp life.

June 22.

There is a lull on the battlefronts of the war. Not a real lull, for important campaigns are in raging progress throughout the world. In fact, yesterday the Libyan port of Tobruk was taken by the Germans after months of desert fighting Sevastopol, Russia's; last stronghold in the Crimea, goes into its nineteenth day of defense against a desperate onslaught by Nazi panzers who apparently consider the objective worth the sacrifice of a million lives—of their own countrymen! But to the soldiers here in camp, defeats don't count and good news that inspires elation lasts about as long as it takes for everybody to hear about it; therefore, between times there is a lull.

June 23, 1942.

In Brooklyn, New York, Jack Zencheck would be pale, clownish and tempestuous. Here in Georgia he is crispy brown, clownish and tempestuous, expressed with a detached theatrical air that only a New Yorker can manifest.

"They can't put me down," he declaimed to all within hearing distance. "I'm a soldier. I'm not looking for special jobs. Give me straight line duty. They haven't made the bullet that can put me out."

His light satire and quick humor have lifted many a shroud of gloom afflicting his Company. This evening he walked over to me and unceremoniously gave me an assessment of my spare-time project: "What can you have to write about; what happened today? What did you do? I'll tell you what you did: you ate like a horse, smoked cigars, drank soda at the PX—what else is there to say!"

June 24, 1942.

A few mornings after I arrived here I awoke as usual for reveille and, as usual, it was very early. Bleary-eyed, I found an inconspicuous place in the rear rank, responded stiffly to "Fall in. Report. Fall out." fell out, and sauntered over to the chow line. Returning from breakfast, I started stripping the sheets from my bed and stopped abruptly. A bedbug was creeping nonchalantly toward a crease. Horrified, I cog-i-tat-ed a brief moment then mashed the creature on a floorboard.

"Sergeant," I later said to the First Sergeant, "I want to go on record as reporting that I am plagued with bedbugs."

"Me too," he retorted; "—can't get rid of them."

Yesterday when I came in the mattresses and bedclothes were disheveled and smelled of disinfectant. They had been sprayed and I went to bed rejoicing. This morning I awoke as usual for reveille and, as usual, it was very early. Skeptically, I lifted the covers and there it was, a plump bedbug.

June 25.

Though I am on Special Duty and not required to stand guard duty or perform KP and some other chores, I am considered nonetheless as a full-fledged member of our rifle company. Nothing irks a company commander more than Special Duty men such as cooks and clerks who appear unmilitary and are inept at handling basic weapons. This afternoon a number of us Special Duty men were gathered together and hauled out to a rifle range. We adjusted our guns, walked to the firing line and without further ado proceeded to shoot forty rounds of ammunition apiece. We then piled back into the trucks, came home, cleaned and oiled the weapons, took a shower, and for the time being the company commander was appeased.

June 26, 1942.

"Steadfast And Loyal" is the Fourth Division slogan, and the slogan for the 22nd Infantry Regiment, "Deeds Not Words." While browsing through books in the Day Room I found histories of these units giving a detailed account each played in wars and battles. There are photographs on the wall of past commanders, officers, enlisted men and group convention pictures. In World War I the 22nd Infantry Regiment is reported as having spent most of its time guarding the industrial plants in Hoboken, New Jersey.

June 27.

Several of us sat on the barracks steps. It was midnight, Saturday. A full moon shone overhead and a soft breeze soothingly caressed. There is always a breeze here no matter how hot it gets. We conversed:

"Where are all the airplanes and munitions that we are supposedly producing? Why don't we hear of them being in action? I think it's all a pack of lies and rotten politics."

"A few months isn't much time. The Nazis have been preparing war for years. Wait a while."

"I have been waiting. Sixteen months in the damn army."

"Would you rather we jumped in half-cocked? For my part I am willing to wait. I say this: build a half-million, no, a million airplanes. Send them over Germany and Japan and bomb them off the map. Forget the infantry except as an army of occupation because in a short time of such bombings we will be able to walk right in to Berlin and Tokyo without firing a shot from the ground."

"Well, I'd like to see it happen, and those supermen deserve whatever we give them."

June 28.

It was early in the evening when we met him or rather when he accosted us while we were walking aimlessly around town. Now we were in his hotel room where he had invited us for a drop of good cheer (liquid). He was a traveling salesman; also a highly religious man with a keenly analytical mind and a sparkling conversationalist.

"What is the soul?" he asked rhetorically, and proceeded to answer himself. "Here is a light bulb. Screw it into a socket and the electricity passing through its body causes it to light up. But what if its filament should burn out? Then as we know the electricity goes all the way back to its source, the generator. And so it is with a human being; when the filament burns out—lungs, pancreas, heart—the body dies, but the body is not important, only the soul is, which, like electricity, goes back to its Maker."

June 29.

Next week we will leave for field maneuvers in North and South Carolina. We think but are not sure that afterward we will come back here. There is little we are sure of, such as whether being in the Second Army Corps but attached to the Sixth Army is for maneuver purposes, or that we have been transferred into the Third Army Corps which is about to become divorced from the Fourth Corps Area and sent overseas, or that we are still part of the Second Army Corps. Those of us working at Personnel Headquarters do not know more, perhaps less, than the others. I doubt that our local low-echelon officers are better informed. It is more than a trifle confusing, and I suppose that's what the Army wants.

June 30, 1942.

At noon Tucker the cook lay prone on his bunk taking a nap, a white apron surrounding his portly midriff. Into the barracks walked a vision also named Tucker, and he bore an amazing likeness to Tucker the cook: the same wide grin, paunchy cheeks and oversized "breadbasket." We all gawked at Tucker the cook and then at Tucker the vision and finally conceived him to be not illusory but the real identical twin brother of Tucker the cook. Then and there we formed a kangaroo court and unanimously accused the pair of deceiving the government; that Tucker the cook would go on furlough whenever he pleased and his brother, a civilian, would take his place in the kitchen. We couldn't, however, verify whether or not Tucker the civilian could cook.

July 1.

In army camp towns all over the country there will be the phenomenon tonight of thousands of men, down to the lowliest, walking around each with forty or fifty dollars in his pocket he can spend. Today was payday, the first since the recently enacted law passed by Congress authorizing fifty dollars per month to be the base pay for soldiers. Out of this most soldiers are allotting some deduction for life insurance, dependents or war bonds. A $25 war bond costs $18.75 and matures in ten years. It may be cashed in any time after sixty days from date of purchase.

July 2.

Between now and maneuvers our Company is predominantly occupied with "Cleaning And Care Of Equipment." Preparations for leaving are thorough as though anticipating not returning here afterward. All the literature, games and miscellaneous items in the Day Room are packed in boxes, as will be the dishes and pots in the mess hall. The Supply Room, Orderly Room and barracks will be cleared out "lock, stock and barrel" when we depart. Already stored are our winter O.D. woolen uniforms, packed in barracks bags sprinkled throughout with naphthalene against moths. Our haversacks, cartridge belts, and leggings, have been dyed green to blend in with the terrain.

July 3, 1942.

"For a modest fellow I certainly am showing off a lot," remarked my coworker Harold Needle. We had been on parade, this time on foot, to greet our new Division commander, Brigadier General Barton. Afterwards we assembled, he drove up in a jeep, stood up on the hood and, half scowling, half smiling, gave us a pep talk.

"I am your leader," he said. "I want you to know what I think. In the not too distant future we will be in battle. When bullets start flying your minds will freeze and you will act according to habit. In order that you develop the right habits, training discipline must be strict. I know ninety percent of you want to cooperate. I will take care of the other ten percent."

July 4, Independence Day.

In the holiday interlude interrupting the Fourth Division's myriad of preparatory activities, nearly everyone made ready to go into town. A neighbor, Private Cserepes (pronounced Cherapus) stared lugubriously into space, a pipe clenched between his teeth.

"Brooding over your sins?" I asked.

"I'd never have enough time for all of them," he replied.

The news of the day is focused in Egypt where the Germans have thrust to within four score miles of Alexandria which protects the Suez Canal. From there to the oil fields in Iraq is a short step and if Germany takes control of that region the Allies will be in a sad plight. Germany needs oil desperately. Once attained, and securing a route to Iran, they could then look to India sandwiched vulnerably between themselves and the Japanese in Burma. From tiny Iran the German-Japanese Axis would have easy access to all of Asia and Africa.

July 5, 1942.

Pre-maneuvers talk; first, a novice speaks: "On maneuvers we'll be moving by truck every four or five days or less and every time I've had to travel in my life it has made me sick."

From a more seasoned recruit: "The 22nd Infantry Regiment is the sloppiest of all the three infantry regiments in the Fourth Division yet in all field problems we outperform the 8th and the 12th."

From an old-timer: "If you get lost from your company out there look for a mobile kitchen—any outfit's kitchen—and stick with it or else you might go for days without eating."

The boys are tired of staying in one place and are happy to be moving, even to maneuvers.

July 6.

It came time to pack and face the question: what does one take along to live in the wilderness for two months? A flood of suggestions produced little and since even those with previous experience could not agree on what constitutes bare essentials I purchased according to my own urban intuition. A box of cigars now resides defiantly in the protected center of my one bulging barracks bag. I ate a steak, took a shower—God knows when the next one will be—and am off in the morning to maneuvers.

July 7, 1942.

We crowded our equipment and selves into trucks and rode off in convoy. Left behind were barracks guards, orderlies, hospital patients and A.W.O.L.'s. Now we are bivouacked outside Jefferson, South Carolina, a few miles from the North Carolina border. It took us nine hours to cover the distance of 168 miles from Camp Gordon. Each platoon carried one portable radio. We stopped to stretch, et cetera, every two hours for ten minutes. For supper we had liver and peas; we were ravenous enough to have consumed anything remotely edible. The first bugs we encountered were gnats the size of a pinhead which zigzagged in front of our eyes while we ate. They are mostly a nocturnal nuisance.

July 8.

I needed a jackknife from the moment I got into the woods. Previously I could think of no use for one except fancy whittling which I wasn't planning to do, therefore didn't buy one. We did not put up a tent last night, just spread a blanket under a gum tree and gazed at the stars in lieu of sleep. In the morning I picked myself up, bone by bone, and bathed in a canteen-cup of water. When I got to the chow line for breakfast it was long and slow. In the army we are always standing in line for one thing or another. Several civilian barbers had followed us from Camp Gordon; they are camping near us and for this meal they tacked themselves onto our chow line.

July 9.

Everything is set up in the field to approximate the facilities of a permanent camp. Telephone wires are strung connecting one headquarters with another. Our Personnel unit is set up in two large tents with typewriters, tables and folding chairs. The regiment is strung out along both sides of a dirt road, each company taking up much more living space than it would in barracks. From one end of the regimental area to the other is about three miles. All around are woods and farms. Last night some of the boys went looking for ripe watermelon patches and farmers' daughters. They found a few of each. At night a companion and I put together our shelter halfs forming a pup tent and placed a mosquito net over the opening. In the morning I hung my tin mirror on a tree branch and shaved using a canteen cup of cold water. For those with very tough beards a cup of hot breakfast coffee does nicely.

July 10.

The companies are taking it easy for a few days, sort of getting into the mood. There is a field PX for refreshments and twenty-four hour passes are being issued on request. Personnel Headquarters, however, is working as usual. We smoke a lot, as it seems to repel some of the insects, and what an assortment there is: at night our kerosene lamplights attract June bugs as big as bats, inquisitive moths and burly bumblebees, something with long wings, another with blunt horns, and spiders. Somebody brought along a chess set and in the evening some of us are pitting our powers of ratiocination against one another in mighty chess jousts.

July 11, 1942.

Soldiers went into the town of Jefferson, population 600, of whom 169 are said to be in the armed forces. The citizenry sponsored a dance to which mothers brought their daughters for dance partners then sat around and watched. The soldiers beered up, grew annoyed with the protective outer ring of mothers and began tossing empty beer bottles at their feet to see how they could jump. A riot ensued and several soldiers were locked up in the local jail which they proceeded methodically to tear down. Rumor has it that as one repercussion of the case the town's jailhouse will hereafter be "Off Limits" for soldiers.

July 12.

Apparently it is possible to get used to anything. I've been sleeping like a babe in primitive fashion, falling off to the dulcet chirping of crickets and awakened by rays of sunlight shining through the trees. In this bucolic setting the war seems far away, guns and jeeps notwithstanding. Green lizards wriggle swiftly through underbrush. An adjoining field is planted with cotton and a few short rows of ripe tomatoes.

Three hours later: our Personnel section is now ten miles behind the battlefront line, a fact determined when an order came through announcing that the first maneuver problem is about to begin. The plan for these maneuvers calls for twelve separate problems with rest days in between. At the sudden order we had hoisted our equipment into trucks in a jiffy and traveled south away from the designated battlefield. Partly concealed in the brush along the road were tanks readying for the fray, their goggled drivers pouring gas and making a final checkup. Our new bivouac area is in a thicket of saplings and underbrush three miles from the village of Kershaw, South Carolina.

July 13.

We were to have eaten supper last night with a Fourth Division quartermaster company to which we are officially attached for rations. Instead, as soon as we unloaded we put on our dirty khakis and walked to Kershaw. There my greatest pleasure was not eating in a restaurant, which I did, nor taking a showerbath, which I didn't, but walking on paved sidewalks without having to push aside brambles or stumble on uneven turf. It is now 1:30 P.M. We are still waiting for the Morning Reports which the Message Center was to have delivered from the companies last night. A messenger just dropped in and asked to see the officer in charge regarding information he had for us about the "enemy." He said he had been looking for us since 4:00 A.M. and the information is probably useless by now. The 22nd Infantry Regiment seems to be lost, he said; nobody knows where it is.

July 14, 1942.

The Morning Reports came through at 2:00 A.M. but the whereabouts of our regiment remains undetermined. Thirty of our men are said to have been captured by the enemy whose identity we still don't know though we've been told they are employing cavalry in their attacks. Our side is the Red Army wearing red armbands, the opposing side the Blue Army. The towns Jefferson and Pageland are reported captured by our enemy, the Blues, and there is fighting in the streets of

Lancaster. A mile from here we found a lake and went swimming. Next to it is the Haile Gold Mine which we inspected from a safe distance being it is well guarded. It is the biggest gold mine in the South and appears to be working overtime.

July 15, 1942.

The first problem is over, there is one day's rest till the next, and only the high command knows what happened. We hear that of the three infantry regiments in the Fourth Division, the 8th and 12th were captured by the Blues who outnumbered the Reds three to one while at the same time the 22nd held off three divisions in a delaying action. Ostensibly four divisions were engaged in the problem. I experimented eating from three different company kitchens billeted nearby. One at breakfast served scrambled eggs made from powdered eggs, another had real eggs fried sunny side up and the third offered boiled ham for the fifth consecutive meal. The temperature is high; yesterday I drank possibly six Coca-colas, six cans of fruit juice, six bottles of beer and a hogshead (63 gallons) of water.

July 16.

To take up new positions our line troops marched thirty miles, on their day of rest, and stopped near Monroe, North Carolina. Our personnel section has not moved pending orders to do so, which leaves us presently close to the "enemy" 2nd Armored Division, reputedly one of the toughest tank units in the American army. They seem peculiarly prideful of their dangerous work in tanks which in summer are exceedingly hot, in winter very cold. Almost every day we are furnishing a few men as Cadre and transferring them to units outside the division. Some also leave for Officer Candidate School at Fort Benning, Georgia, after passing physical examinations and interviews before a board of officers. "Griping" goes on without end, which is as expected; at best army life is hard and men age fast under rigorous conditions. In discussion a few of my buddies argue that morale among the troops is poor, that many are disgruntled because of real injustices and sometimes stupid demands made of them. I refute and say morale is relatively good, that "War is Hell" and I can visualize living in far worse conditions than we are presently—which doesn't stop me from griping as much as anyone.

July 17, 1942.

Our section moved north fifteen miles, forty miles distant from our line companies where a new "battle" has begun. I don't know how communications are for tactical command posts; for us, we are at a range of having some administrative difficulties. Our bivouacs are no longer in selected cleared fields or even between widely spaced trees; we plump right down in the middle of a jungle of underbrush, push some of it aside and unload. Blackouts are enforced at night, but even in daylight were I to walk ten paces from my tent and turn around quickly three times I might not find my way back for an hour. Brooklynite Sergeant Landau comments loudly and frequently: "Struck a home didn't you, you guys; ye never had it so good, playing cowboys and Indians at government expense!"

July 18.

The fighting front extended perhaps sixty miles in a problem that ended in two and a half days while our section near Lancaster, South Carolina, was hoping to get into town for a Saturday night blowout. Instead we heard the non-secret Army code signal: "Let's go!" and in a few seconds we went, following the procedure one learns to expect—"hurry up and wait," meaning load up swiftly then sit in the truck for up to four hours waiting for your contingent of caissons to roll. The convoy must have been fifty miles long. Our section reached an assigned destination after nightfall. I have no idea where we are except we crossed the border into North Carolina after riding about sixty miles in seven hours. En route we stopped near a farmhouse and while waiting for the convoy to resume helped ourselves uninvited to water from a bucket-drop artesian well. There wasn't very much mud in the water; not enough for a thirsty man to question.

July 19.

I washed clothes in my steel helmet. Our Captain did, too. When we left Jefferson last week we left our barracks bags to be transported separately. I brought with me a pair of khakis to wear in town should the opportunity occur and at night used them as a pillow. We got permission and went into the town of Monroe, North Carolina, population 8,000. After washing in a rest room and enjoying the luxury of a modern commode, my companion and I sought to eat. So did fifty thousand other soldiers. By 7:00 P.M. nearly every restaurant sold out of food and had to close. We found a place, sharing a table with a newly-drafted veteran of World War I, aged forty-one, and his wife, and had a meal priced special for soldiers—higher than for local civilians. The South is being economically rejuvenated. On the day we received our first pay increase every menu in Augusta restaurants showed printed prices crossed out and in handwriting increased ten or fifteen cents for each item.

July 20, 1942.

Nine of us returned to our camping area last night and no one was there. All our equipment, too, was gone. We began walking to Service Company five miles away when one of our trucks returned for us. We hopped on and joined the rest of our crew at the motor pool near Service Company. In the morning we traveled in convoy entirely on dirt roads to a spot 22 miles south, arriving with a half-inch layer of dust on everything including ourselves. I washed quite effectively in a puddle of a nearly-dry stream. The Captain advised we may "stay put" for a whole week for the reason that the line companies have been working in loose coordination and would have to take some time off to review basic principles; a project that in fact had been scheduled in advance for sometime during the maneuvers.

July 21.

Supplies are keeping up with us very nicely. We haven't yet missed a meal. As soon as we arrive anywhere a chow truck is right with us and in a half-hour whips up a cooked meal. We are again eating with the Service Company of our regiment and what a difference! With Quartermasters we had ham almost three times a day, every day. The men in Quartermasters say they work hard drilling, standing guard and performing other details just as those in the Infantry. This morning a four-foot black snake intruded on us. He was more scared than we. I am told they are not dangerous, even beneficial in keeping rattlers and copperheads away.

July 22.

We're plied with rumors again. Allegedly our regimental commander Colonel Tribolet sent down word that he is pleased with the outfit's performance; also that our next destination will be thirty miles distant and north of Monroe, for which we are now packed and ready to leave. Any of us will soon be qualified as assistant sheik in a tribe of nomads. The boys in the line companies tell as they have been doing a lot of hiking on maneuvers. Company E claims as usual to show up best on problems. Now we are about to board our vehicles to rumble o'er the Carolina prairie at ten miles an hour with only dim blackout lights to steer by.

July 23, 1942.

There are times when one can't fall asleep even in the fresh woods and after a four-hour ride in back of an army truck. Then he gets up from his "bed" and without dressing, for he hadn't undressed, takes a walk to look over his new surroundings. From what he can see in the dark, he likes the layout. It is spacious and well padded with leaves and pine needles. Romantically he whistles softly a bit of Brahms' Violin Concerto. Approaching his tent he makes out some yellowjackets hovering over possibly their home. Suddenly one blunders into his armsleeve and stings him. His whole arm seems to swell and the pain is dreadful. He goes back to bed determined that come hell or high water he'll smoke out the damn yellow jackets first thing in the morning.

July 24.

A problem is beginning. Here is the picture: The Fourth Division is defending a line in the vicinity of Charlotte, North Carolina. Two Red armies are attacking at the flanks. The Fourth's 8th and 12th Infantry Regiments are at the defense line and the 22nd is held back in reserve. Water is being rationed, a canteenful every twenty-four hours as a lesson in conserving the precious liquid. We in the rear echelon must be ready to fight in case there is a breakthrough by the enemy. Who would have thought we'd be clerking and soldiering at the same time? Now I must go dig me a foxhole.

July 25.

Among us are older drafted men who had never married. Most have regrets, some because marriage and children would have saved them from being drafted. In the main they seem to have come around to the conventional idea that when they are civilians again they will marry and live the simple life á la Walter Pitkin, author of the book *Life Begins at Forty*. One man, a teacher in his late thirties whose life had revolved around studying to advance in his teaching specialty, stood to lose more than others by being taken into the army. When "caught in the draft" he had been on the threshold of harvesting the fruit of his academic endeavors. Not marrying early was the biggest mistake in his life, he says. "I could have pursued my career and at the same time had the rich benefit of a family life. Now when I get out of here I must forget about trying to advance. I will be too old, and will be better off marrying and settling down to straight teaching and raising a family."

July 27.

After breakfast "The Man" said we should drop everything and line up for calisthenics. As the boys say, "we dood it." "Now double-time," he ordered, and no one contradicted. Round and round the field we ran, and had the field ears they surely would have been burning with the sound of curses heaped upon it. Next we did deep knee-bending; "like a bunch of Bowery bums," asserted "The Man," and no one contradicted. After a couple of simple arm exercises the twenty minute harrowing session ended, like a tornado, as abruptly as it began and notwithstanding a full day's work ahead of us. We were "hurtin'."

July 28, 1942.

We moved only six miles, in the direction of Charlotte, North Carolina. This time our division will take the offensive in a four-day problem.

On the spot where I established residence a different battle took place, between ants and a juicy grasshopper. For some reason the grasshopper had already become immobilized when a huge red scout pismire espied it, ran over for a quick reconnaissance then went away. In a few seconds he returned, accompanied by a superior officer. The two tugged frenziedly at the carcass. Soon they were reinforced by four others, some pushing, some pulling, all in unison. Meanwhile a whole community had sprung to arms; in every direction there was action in anticipation of a feast. A fresh crew relieved the first in dragging the grasshopper. At this juncture I heard Chow Call and left the arena. When I returned a few ants were marching around (on guard duty no doubt) while the rest gorged on the meal their alert scout had obtained.

July 29, 1942.

Presumably because the enemy was too close, our section picked up again and started southward. The convoy moved spasmodically, speeding for three or four miles then stopping for a half-hour. On a residential street in Monroe someone from our stopped truck asked a nine year old boy passing by: "What's the latest news over the radio?"

"I heard at 8:00 this morning that the Germans are near a town at the Don River; I forgot the name of it," he replied.

We continued on to a woods that was the jungliest of jungles, sojourned there for just a few hours and spent the night further south in a park-like glen.

July 30.

Today is a rest day for the division. A heated discussion just ended on the issue of drafting eighteen- or nineteen-year-old boys (presently it is twenty-one). Those arguing the affirmative were possibly a shade more convincing. I have practically solved the problem of chiggers (tiny red bugs). A yellow powder called Flower of Sulphur, dusted on the skin from neck to feet has effectively deterred them. One soon becomes used to the smell of sulphur. Otherwise nature has not been more than moderately unkind; I have yet to see a rattlesnake or copperhead. The boys often compare this with their experience with maneuvers in Louisiana where deadly bright-colored coral snakes only a foot long abound. Here in the Carolinas there is more civilization, they say.

July 31, 1942.

The Rolling Fourth unexpectedly and inexplicably rolled back to Camp Gordon, Georgia. We made very good time, averaging thirty miles an hour. We moved into the same barracks, which were just as we left them. There are numerous conjectures as to why we suddenly withdrew from the Carolina maneuvers, and rumors are having a field day. The dirty laundry we had sent out before we left was back and waiting for us. Now for the first time in more than three weeks I am clean both in body and attire. The popular tune of the day is "Over the Waves," as a predictive theme.

August 1.

It is not difficult to readjust to a real bed with spring and mattress. Clean white bedsheets add a much-appreciated bonus. Today, Saturday, is payday and also an extra day off. If ever a two-day vacation came at the right time, it is now. The boys are rarin' to bust loose, and doubtless will. Maybe I will, too.

August 2.

Several of us took off for Savannah, Georgia, 135 miles away, a very old city of 100,000. Unlike most towns its "main drag" is the dingiest part and peripheral neighborhoods are attractive—like an apple with good flesh and a rotten core. We had expected to see many sailors and marines from the Parris Island training base, but there were very few, and soldiers from the Coast Artillery training center at Camp Stewart ruled the roost.

In the lobby of a large hotel, a fracas took place when an M.P. blackjacked a soldier and the husky private fought back. Blood ran from his head as he held off three M.P.'s with his fists. One of the M.P.'s drew a revolver and changed his mind when a crowd gathered. From what I could learn coming upon the scene late, the attack by the M.P. had not been entirely justified in its severity and the gory incident could have been avoided with a little tact by the M.P.

M.P.'s seem endowed with almost limitless powers which as exercised by an occasional bully makes one feel cheap to be in uniform. Once, in Macon, Georgia, three of us walking to the bus station near the midnight curfew hour paused to answer a question asked by a civilian. Promptly a jeep pulled up, a red-faced M.P. got off, ran toward us with his club poised menacingly and in an abusive manner ordered us to keep walking. Such unnecessary provocation makes me wonder if there is sufficient supervision of M.P.'s.

August 3.

The turnover in camp is more than we realize. Our division is the largest but not its only occupant. When we returned from maneuvers we saw many new insignia worn hereabouts, some apparently denoting units just forming in Field Artillery, Signal Corps, and Quartermasters. One Signal Corps private I met has been in the Army only three months and is now in a small company of one hundred specialists.

"At present our work is basic line duty, which I find congenial because the men are a matured lot and easy to get along with. Our cooks are masters and apologize when rations are not as they should be," he said. "Our officers are real gentlemen and show genuine interest in every man."

August 4, 1942.

Before maneuvers the training schedule had been extremely hard on the line companies. This seems now to have eased. Tomorrow they are scheduled to march twenty miles with light pack, which isn't easy either, but much better than the twenty-five miler a month ago with full field pack. At that time many hikes and strenuous problems were imposed to test the sturdiest constitutions. It might have been necessary for developing a rugged army, but many a man complained bitterly that his youth was being burned out.

August 5.

A couple of hundred men came into the regiment today, transferred from Camp Wheeler, Georgia, and distributed among understrength companies. One chap from my basic training Alma Mater reported that some battalions there had been sent directly to a point of embarkation after only six weeks of basic training. He had personally completed the full thirteen weeks. The incoming group is fairly standard in composition. One or two individuals were outstanding in business or profession before coming into the Army. Several more are lesser lights, as artisans or students, and the rest semi-skilled and unskilled farmers and laborers.

August 6.

It is evening. Some of the soldiers have gone to town, some to the service club in camp. The latter, unlike the service club at Camp Wheeler, attracts a varied crowd and is less restful, at times resembling a noisy "juke joint." An organist seeking repose found it in the regimental chapel which has an organ. I can hear him as he plays it softly and whiles away the twilight hours. The inevitable dice game is on in the Day Room. There is a long line waiting at the movie theater for the second and last show. Two men are in the barracks cleaning their rifles. The PX is jammed with patrons drinking beer. Now it has become dark. A bugle is blowing "Lights Out." The recreation hall is empty and a soldier gave up in disgust trying to put through a long-distance telephone call to his home in Scranton. In a cubbyhole-sized room in back of the "rec" hall a serious-looking youth working on a scholarly treatise titled "Ethnological Phenomena In Nature Study" succumbed at last to nature and fell asleep.

August 7, 1942.

It is undignified for a company clerk to run around the office with one shoe off and one shoe on but his personality lends itself to it and besides, he reasons, he is only a Private First Class and when his foot hurts he "don't make no bones about it." Coming from a backwoods farm town in Maryland it is rather odd that he developed a talent for company clerking, and thankfully it is so for he exudes an unadorned, refreshing exuberance. Asked a question that is over his head he exclaims: "It beats the hell out of me!" When asked, "How is everything?" he hitches up his trousers and replies, "I'm happy. I have nothing to worry about. I get three meals a day. My girl will wait for me. What the hell!"

August 8, 1942.

"Amazing," muttered the soldier sitting neat to me on the civilian bus.

"What is?" I asked.

"Up north there would be a riot," he continued, unheeding my question. I looked in the direction of his gaze and caught what he meant. The bus had stopped for colored passengers. As they entered the driver held them back while white soldiers sitting in the rear moved to the front. We stopped again in the next block where more colored soldiers waited for the bus.

"Six seats left," the driver told them.

"How about standing room?" pleaded one meekly. The driver drove on without replying. He stopped at the next corner and allowed whites to enter and stand in the aisle.

"Amazing," repeated the soldier sitting beside me.

August 9.

"Camp Shows Presents—." Tonight's presentation, "direct from Times Square," included The Roxyettes, tumblers, comedians, and voluptuous Harlem rhythms. The New York boys especially "ate it up." For months they had been living inextricably with hillbilly music. They went to sleep and rose to it, worked by it and try as they would could not escape its dolorous strains. Now they were on Broadway again, shouting gleefully for more and even applauding an act or two that were clearly "ham." For a moment they had rapturously glimpsed 125th Street at Lexington Avenue, Little Italy and Grant's Tomb. They gloated at shimmering feminine limbs displayed as only Broadway can do it and carried back to the barracks with them a lingering spirit of The Big Town and Bright Lights.

August 10.

We were sitting on a long bench, waiting. Another fellow swaggered over. "Plentya chairs here," someone offered and moved over to make room on the bench. The newcomer puffed on a cigarette, pointed at a cut over his eye and said, "I had a little rumpus last night. Two guys attacked me. They knew they were in a fight though; I ain't snowin' you—they were hurtin."

On questioning he admitted he'd had a few drinks in advance of the fracas. "I'm not mean," he said, "but I never could stay away from a good fight. I used to carry brass knuckles, only they were made of aluminum."

"You know what's good?" broke in a young soldier eagerly, "a blackjack." They discussed this and some other vital bits of information at length and spiced generously with gory details of their exploits.

August 11, 1942.

Probably every outfit in the country is in the same position ours is now in. Everyone reports hearing rumors that the Fourth Division is getting ready to "pull out," meaning for overseas. Every day new General Orders come in from the War Department giving directions on loading troops aboard ship, proper comportment on trains, etc. We are "salvaging" our equipment—turning in for new those items not in the best condition. In addition we are issued articles we haven't had heretofore. At each sign of change interpreters begin conjuring plausible explanations which soon convert to circulating rumors. One rumor holds that officers who train an outfit rarely go overseas with it; this in precaution to hatreds developed that might cause an officer to be shot in battle "accidentally" by one of his own men.

August 12.

We went out again to the rifle range to fire "for record." The gun is second nature to me by now. I stepped up to the firing line, pulled back the bolt and inserted a single cartridge into the chamber for a practice shot. Crack!—the shot exploded with startling force. A bulls-eye. Today's shooting was "jawbone." Tomorrow we try to qualify formally as Marksman. The last time on the rifle range I adhered strictly to prescribed form and came away with an aching shoulder. This time I chose my own position and shot as well without the ache. In all practice shooting positions there isn't a one that permits resting the muzzle on a solid object. I imagine that in combat one would try to get a steadier aim by doing so.

August 13.

I "boloed;" or in other words, failed to qualify as Marksman, failing by four points to reach the minimum qualifying score of 198. The maximum possible is 300. Still I did above average. Someone remarked that if he were shooting from a foxhole he would raise the gun over his head and shoot blindly in the general direction of the enemy. He couldn't say what system of protection he would devise if ordered to "go over the top." Whatever our scores, none can say that his training with the rifle had been inadequate. Being a Sharpshooter might sometimes be an asset, but I think in modern battle conditions we are proficient enough to hold our own.

August 14, 1942.

Marking my six-month anniversary in the Army is a new development on the rumor front: empty crates issued to the companies are ostensibly for the purpose of packing equipment to send aboard a transport ship, with ourselves to follow....

The United States has launched our first land offensive action of the war, in the Solomon Islands. Our Marines are showing themselves as powerful as the famed British Commandos. I wonder how the cannibals are faring....

It is hard to make do with only two summer khaki uniforms. The laundry takes a week to return one and in this weather, in three days the shirt collar smells like vinegar....

Mike bought himself an ashtray; a drastic move for Mike and requiring his careful reasoning: "Why should I get up every minute to drop my ashes in the wastebasket?" he pondered aloud. Hearing no rebuttal, he made the purchase after consulting Dun and Bradstreet and *Consumer Reports*, and registered the pedigree....

Now to conclude the celebration of my anniversary I gotta go help clean the latrine.

August 15, 1942.

Jimmy had befriended a young recruit at Camp Wheeler and showed me this letter he received from him:

"Dear Jimmy, Well, we actually landed at Camp Shelby, Mississippi. And you should be thankful that you didn't come here with us. I don't like it here one bit. Camp Wheeler was a palace compared to this place. We sleep in tents, eat out of our mess gear. And it rains here all the time, and we're always in the field walking through swamps and getting eaten alive by the insects. I am in a rifle company here and the work is much easier than that at Camp Wheeler. We were on the rifle range last week and I made Expert Rifleman. Now that we've been here a month I am getting used to it and don't mind it so much. However, I am feeling fine. You were lucky to stay in Georgia, Jimmy. Here's hoping that you're in a better outfit than I am in. Your friend—"

August 16.

The line of soldiers waiting for buses back to camp being figuratively a mile long and my companion and I in no mood to "sweat out" the line as we did coming into town, we picked up an acquaintance from the camp finance office and went to one of the few restaurants open all night, run by an opportunist who slung hash that glistened with grease. Calculating that he has a large turnover in coffee so it won't be too stale, we ordered some.

"How are things at the finance office?" I asked our friend (in the Army when you speak to a man twice his status changes from acquaintance to friend).

"So-so, but we're shorthanded," he replied. "There should be thirty-five working with us, instead we have only fifteen. A ruling has come out that only those who are physically unfit for line duty may work in Finance. I'm not up to par so I'm still there but if the Fourth Division goes overseas we will too."

August 17, 1942.

Speaking of morale: Last night everyone participated in a field problem from 9:00 to 12:00. As we entered the woods it started raining and we were soon drenched from head to foot. Our staff sergeant platoon leader happened upon my squad in the dark and said, "This storm is sure to keep on; now you can use your own judgment, if you want to you may go back in, or continue on to your objective."

He left; my squad leader turned to us and said, "Well, what do you want to do, boys?"

No one spoke, then someone said: "Aw let's go on, it can't get any worse."

No one dissented and we kept going. In places the hillside gushed with thick streams of rainwater. It kept coming down and again our squad leader put the proposition to us and got back the same response. We sloshed through a swamp. A little farther the sergeant squad leader stopped, about-faced and led us home on his own initiative.

August 18.

Our personnel statistical expert stopped by to chat. "How did you make out on your three-day pass?" I asked.

"Good," he replied, "I went to Columbia, South Carolina, to catch the 9:30 'Streamliner' train for New York. The train was full and a thousand soldiers wanted to get on and couldn't. I ran over to a porter as the train was about to pull out. 'Hey porter, where are my bags?' I yelled and pushed a dollar into his hand. 'Up there,' he pointed to the train and I jumped on the car past the conductor. Later he came through collecting tickets. 'Your ticket is O.K.,' he said, 'but what's the idea of getting on without a reservation? You'll have to get off at Washington.' In Washington I locked myself into the washroom. The conductor pounded at the door. When the train started moving I came out and sat down, 'Wise guy, aren't you,' said the conductor. 'Look,' I told him, 'the Army gave me just three days; I've got to get home;' I told him to stop the train and let me off if he wanted to.

"Yea," he concluded, "I had a good trip."

August 19.

The thing that keeps the routine and repetition of camp life from complete boredom is that the next day or next hour may bring something interesting or exciting. Today brought Secretary of the Treasury Henry Morganthau to camp for a visit. We were issued an additional khaki uniform and other clothing items. The Allies used tanks in a raid on the French southern "invasion coast." heralding the approach of "Der Tag" when we will be ready for our all-out invasion. We had baloney and cheese for supper, steak for lunch. The General lectured the newly-trained cadre who are leaving in a few days as a nucleus in forming a new division in Texas. And the day brought new rumors, including one that is the most appetizing in weeks.

August 20, 1942.

Our division has drawn heavily from replacement training centers and we are now overstrength in the companies. A bunch just came from Camp Croft, South Carolina, among whom were a higher number than usual of men whose civilian occupations fitted them for jobs requiring special skills. Few openings exist here for them. An artist from New York's Greenwich Village protested that he would be far more useful in camouflage work than in carrying a rifle. He showed us photographs of his paintings that are hanging in Washington art galleries. They looked good.

Our Classification Section is not developed enough in status or authority to recommend that such men be transferred to an appropriate outfit; but I believe that a little personal aggressiveness goes a long way in the Army and a man with special skills can sooner or later get himself into the job he wants.

"Classification" in our regiment means mainly maintaining a record of each individual's training, and on that basis supplying personnel requisitions for cadre and other special jobs. In that we do a good job. We are often criticized for lacking the authority to help someone who really deserves the transfer he seeks, but we are not a warmongering nation and thus have not evolved a system in which millions are turned into soldiers almost overnight at the same time placing each individual in the position for which he is best qualified.

August 21.

The nickelodeon blared Irving Berlin's "Oh How I Hate To Get Up In The Morning" in the crowded, beer bottle-strewn P.X.

"That song still hits the spot, doesn't it," observed a soldier in green fatigues, then drained the last bit remaining in his bottle in one effortless gulp.

"You wouldn't remember," he went on, "in the last war they needed martial music to steam us up. I'm forty-three now, and married, but was drafted anyway. I don' understand how in 1917 they got five million men into the Army when the draft age was only between twenty-one and thirty-one.

"Funny," he rambled, "how there is so much written now—magazine articles, newspaper reports that are not just propaganda but real honest stuff. In the last war it was all propaganda and parades."

August 22.

Almost every night for the past two weeks, E Company has been restricted to quarters for an hour or two after supper. One night a notice posted on the bulletin board reads: "Company restricted till barracks are cleaned and inspected by First Sergeant;" next night: "Company restricted till all salvage equipment has been turned in to the supply room," and again: "Restricted till all clothing and equipment has been marked with initials and serial number."

E Company hastens to comply, and everywhere the order is carried out with one urging the other: "Get on the ball one time; Let's Go!" The Colonel let it be known that a week ago this division was scheduled to pull out for overseas duty but the order was rescinded at the last minute.

August 23, 1942.

Our shop-talk was all infantry and the soldier with the blue insignia on his sleeve squirmed impatiently. At last we mercifully permitted him an opening.

"From Daniel Field?" we inquired.

"Yep, been there a month. Did my basic in Oklahoma. I'll be a ser-geant-technician soon and head a gunner crew on a B-25 bomber. That B-25 is a sweet boat. It's a two-engine job and—" He continued describing in tiresome detail every last nut and bolt that the plane possesses and climaxed triumphantly with: "This is the plane that was used most in the raid on Tokyo."

"Isn't it dangerous up in the air so high?" we challenged his enthu-siasm.

"Isn't it on the ground so low?" he countered. He won his point.

August 24, 1942.

I've been granted a ten-day emergency furlough and am on a train tonight bound for home in Pittsburgh. Now I know what they mean when they say "sweating out a furlough." I had first to present myself to the company commander, offer my reason for requesting an emergency furlough and furnish proof that the need was urgent. After receiving his approval the company clerk typed the proper form and bade me take it to the Battalion Personnel Adjutant for approval and signature, then to the Regimental Adjutant who, after a brief discus-sion, applied the final signature needed on the form. I turned in my rifle to the supply room, stored my bedding and footlocker in the upstairs storage room in the barracks and ran to catch a bus out of camp.

(*Note: Presently, it is my recollection that there had been no real emergency; that the Army was willing to grant a small number of furloughs and did so on an "emergency" basis. In effect there was a moot conspiracy between Army and soldier to accommodate soldiers whose desire for a furlough was truly sincere, as evidenced by their painstaking efforts in producing proof of an "emergency" that needn't necessarily be severe in nature.*)

September 3.

Train connections on the return trip were good. I arrived back in Augusta twenty-seven hours after leaving Pittsburgh, where the weather had been cool all summer. The war went into its fourth year the other day since England and France declared war against the German Axis after Germany had invaded Poland and the Netherlands "low country." Few military uniforms are seen in Pittsburgh, but the common subject of conversation is the draft. The army is scheduled to more than double in the next year or so. About four million are said to be in now. One girl canceled her plans to marry when her boy friend was physically classified 4F. "If he isn't good enough for Uncle Sam then he isn't good enough for me," she declared.

September 4, 1942.

Nothing momentous occurred with my outfit while I was away on furlough. A program of routine training had resumed and evidence of brisk preparation for moving died down. I expected there to be millions of new rumors but instead heard only a few thousand, none very stirring. I am afflicted with "after-furlough blues," consisting largely of brooding about how long it will take to finish the war and return to civilian life. I venture a prediction—and consider it optimistic—that the war will be won by us in a year and a half. President Roosevelt said yesterday that "it will be a long, hard war." Anybody's guess is as good as the next man's but facts do not lie, and the facts are on the debit side still, with a long way to go unless shortened by some miracle that could happen only in ancient mythology.

September 5.

A lieutenant who is not afraid to joke a little can work wonders with the men. One of the second lieutenants who just joined our company (his orders were first to meet us at the boat, then when that move by our division did not materialize he was sent here) led a session of instruction on marksmanship. This instruction and dry-firing was exactly the same as the company had practiced many times before and the men, not a little bored, were going through the motions half-heartedly, their interest centered only on the ten-minute break given every hour. The short chunky lieutenant sized up the situation, assembled them away from the simulated firing line and began lecturing. He entertained them with stories, kibitzing (joking), then explained logically why the repetitious exercises should be taken seriously. In the end they were sold both on him and his reasoning.

September 6.

Movies coming here these days are not very good so I haven't bothered seeing many. Most are well-meaning but inartistic war propaganda. I saw an interesting one today, however, *Mrs. Miniver* from the book by Jan Struthers. The all-soldier audience bought tickets (fifteen cents) and popcorn, then sat down on the wood benches. The picture began and the comic sequences evoked their easy-to-please laughter. Soldiers are a great audience. Once when the laughter went on too long someone yelled "At ease!" and they slacked off. In tragic scenes they were empathetic enough, but if the tragedy is played at a pitch to instill horror the soldiers will have none of it and simply laugh. We have our own troubles.

September 7, Labor Day, 1942.

The Motor Pool sergeant wore a happy look on his face ever since the new half-tracks came under his dominion. When the old ones had been taken away last June the truck yards were empty and his men, noted for both their mechanical ability and expert goldbricking, were sent to drill and hike with the company. "Things are clicking," he said, "all I need now is to get home next month. My wife is having a baby." "While you are in the Army?" I asked innocuously. "She wanted it," he explained. "We got married after I was drafted and she could see no reason for not starting a family until the war is over. This suits me, and I'll even get to see the kid when it's born. I thought by that time I'd have been in Tasmania or somewhere else far away."

September 8.

Persons like Cy have a right to gripe—it would be a shame if he didn't, for he does it so beautifully. "Smiling Cy" he is called, so nicknamed for the constant expression on his face of pathos and outrage. "I don't know what I am," I heard him vociferate, "in this Army they make me a bugler, then I'm a cook, and suddenly I'm outside swinging a bayonet." A Tennesseean cannot be taken seriously—well, maybe some can, but not the ones I've met. "Another three years of this life," muttered Cy, his forehead creased in thought, "and I won't even want to get out of the Army; I wouldn't know how to act outside." A whistle blew, someone shouted "Let's go!" and Cy walked out stiffly with an air of oppressed dignity.

September 9.

A log of current happenings cannot but include a recount of the present intrigues concerning furloughs. It was officially announced that furloughs will be granted. All well and good; the boys have worked hard all summer and deserve them. Then a notice was posted stating "Conditions of Preference," allowing fifteen percent of each company to leave at one time. Another condition: the company is penalized for its AWOLs; for every AWOL three innocent men will be cut out of the fifteen percent and will have to hope that their delayed turn comes up before all leaves are canceled. Lists were made and company clerks prepared the furlough papers for the first group. Still well and good, except suddenly a new notice appeared reducing the quota to ten percent of the company permitted to be gone at one time, and no furloughs authorized for those who had one within the last six months. This struck like a bombshell. In addition the powers that be proclaimed that only those living a thousand or more miles away are allowed ten days, the rest seven or five. So in the ranks there is perplexity, and indignation, and talk (mostly in jest, some serious) of going "over the hill."

September 10, 1942.

Chow tonight was rough so I said, "Jake, let's go eat at the Service Club." Jake replied, "I'd like to but today we had a retreat parade and when the company commander inspected he ordered me to spend two hours tonight and tomorrow night practicing to stand at attention. Another fellow is in the same boat; we were told to teach each other. The C. Q. (Charge of Quarters) is to supervise." Jake went resignedly to the barracks and I walked to the Service Club cafeteria for a short-order steak. It took me weeks to realize that the "Large" steak at eighty-five cents is essentially no larger than the "Small" steak at sixty-five cents. The difference is that the "Large" has bone and fat which the "Small" doesn't have. Live and learn, they say.

September 11.

Practically a citizen of this state by now, I couldn't help but notice the local crisis taking place in Georgia in the form of a bitterly contested gubernatorial campaign. For weeks the newspapers have been championing the challenger, Ellis Arnall, over the incumbent governor Eugene Talmadge who has adopted White Supremacy as his main appeal for votes. The Georgia newspapers do not oppose him on that score, but on his policy toward the State University in Athens, Georgia, which they accuse the governor of trying to subvert for political purposes to the detriment of its accredited educational standing. At any rate the election was held and Ellis Arnall, with the moral backing of President Franklin D. Roosevelt, won; thereby, it is said, Democracy has recovered another bastion in America.

September 12, Rosh Hashana.

Because there are many New Yorkers in this camp, there are more Jewish boys than average for the general population. Today they are excused from regular duty for several hours to attend Rosh Hashana services—"New Year" according to the old Jewish calendar. The large gymnasium is being used for this purpose, the religious rituals and ceremony conducted by Chaplain Frank of the 22nd Infantry Regiment, the only Jewish chaplain in this camp. No ethnic people in history have suffered as much persecution for their religious or cultural independence as the Jews. Therefore it is understandable that the High Holiday observance is especially significant during this world war, when Jews are more than ever singled out for brutal treatment, and in some places mass extinction.

September 13, 1942.

Almost every soldier has at least one brother or brother-in-law or close friend who is about to be drafted into the Army. Whoever is not yet in at this late date usually has some problem that has kept him at home. Federal pressure is gradually solving all the problems.

Over a heaping ice cream sundae a soldier told me of his brother's predicament which he doubted could be solved, "My brother is a lawyer," he said, "and has always managed to make a living without doing anything more strenuous than using a pen or lifting a telephone receiver. The telephone was never more than a step away. He would call a taxi to go just one block away. My mother was dependent on us and when the draft came only one of us had to go. My brother insisted that he be the one. Everyone felt that would be ridiculous so I enlisted before he had a chance to protest. Now he has to go into the Army. He's willing, but we all know that he is simply allergic to exercise. Is there a place for lawyers in the Army?" "Sure," I replied, "there is an empty cot next to mine."

September 14, 1942.

Jack Zencheck heard that a friend of his is in China teaching the Chinese a military skill. "My God," Jack exclaimed, "The war will take as twenty years to get started while we learn to talk Chinese, teach the Russians to eat hot dogs, the Greeks to jitterbug and the Solomon Island cannibals to say grace before eating!" Jack was in a high mood, He had recently taken over the job of company mail orderly which is not very hard work. "After all I'm not young any more," he justified, "I've made all the hikes. I'm tired. I asked the First Sergeant for the job and he gave it to me, I go out in the field with the boys once in a while just so they won't think I'm lazy or stuck-up."

September 15.

The Drum and Bugle Corps contingent marched and played ahead of the guard detail it was leading to the main post for evening guard mount. All the clerks left the Personnel Office except myself; I remained as Charge of Quarters for the night. The telephone rang several times during the early part of the evening with long-distance calls for enlisted men. I referred the operator to the unit where they might be located. It is now ten o'clock and the PX next door is turning out the lights. There is a bunk with a bare mattress on it handy to the telephone. I am entitled to sleep on it between phone calls.

September 16.

Recently many of my co-workers have been transferred out of the regiment to pursue their careers elsewhere in the Army. Now John is leaving to become an Air Cadet. "I really want to fly," he said gravely, "It's not just for the novelty, though I am tired of pounding a type-writer." He paused to say goodbye to a friend then continued, "Well, maybe we'll meet again some day—say, what have you there," he interrupted himself to address a passerby, "a new hat? Aren't you going to hell with yourself?" He resumed to me, "You know, I'm not trained in anything outside of office work and I don't want to do that when I get out of the Army. Aviation will be the thing when the war is over. I want to get in on the ground floor and this way I'll at least get to know what it's all about. Now I'm leaving for good, 'patch,' so long."

September 17, 1942.

The headline in tonight's paper reads: "Fighting In The Streets Of Stalingrad." The report says that the Battle of Stalingrad is the bloodiest in history. This is the twenty-fourth day under siege, the Russians not yielding a step in their effort to save the great industrial city which is sometimes called the Detroit of Russia. The law of self-preservation is apparently disregarded as a military element in this battle in which the defenders hold with maniacal tenacity and the attackers persist demoniacally with bulldog fury. Here we have an eloquent preview of what the projected second front in Western Europe will be like. No one sees a prospect that the Germans will be defeated without a second front which, when it comes, must transform us, too, into veritable demons.

September 18.

Izzy Goldstein decided that his energy and talent were not being utilized to the fullest as a reporter for the Division weekly newspaper, *The Ivy Leaf.* He organized a staff and began a regimental publication. He named it *Double Deucer*, for "22nd" Infantry Regiment. By the second issue the paper received a hearty commendation from the Division commanding general, Major General Barton. By the third issue the weekly had become virtually a tradition in the regiment. One reason is the pithy cartoons by ex-civilian professional cartoonist Lin Streeter. Another is the writing of fiction writer John Cheever, renowned for his stories in *The New Yorker.* Izzy himself supplies the spark and balanced continuity, expressing an anti-Nazi motif in German-derived words and sayings such as "Ich hob dir in bod."

September 19.

Like many other enlisted men, I have submitted my application to attend one of the Officer Candidate schools. Today I was called before a board of interviewers consisting of a major, a captain and a first lieutenant. In my best manner I saluted, sat down in a thespian pose designed to reveal the qualities I believed would impress the interviewers: poise, self-confidence, alertness. "What is the purpose of contour lines on a map?" began the lieutenant while the major peered at me sideways, studying intently. "Sir," I replied, "I'm a little rusty on that, would you mind if I guess?" "No, go right ahead," he said and I groped for the right terminology. Then it seemed I was plied with every question ever asked anybody at these interviews. "What does lewisite smell like?" asked the lieutenant. "Why do you want to be an officer?" flung in the major. "Where is Port Moresby?" chimed in the captain. At least I got that one right.

September 20, 1942.

Saturday night and Augusta teemed as usual with pedestrians and autos whose small gas rations had been hoarded for the Saturday night event. But tonight the cars had to detour away from the busy part of Broad Street to make way for a big war bond rally led by Hollywood celebrities, actress Jane Wyman, Jinx Falkenberg, and actor John Payne. People danced in the street to the music of a camp orchestra and stood in line for autographs. I hope withal bonds were sold; and why not, where is the sacrifice? How many guaranteed investments are there today that will pay three percent interest? For a change there were a good number of civilians to be seen among the soldiers. As John Cheever put it, "there is plenty of hospitality in the South but these towns are embarrassed by our numbers." After the usual rounds I returned to camp and got off the bus at 23rd St. and

Sixth Avenue. Walking down the company street toward the barracks a soldier who also got off the bus hurried past and said: "Now b'jees I'll go sweat out the bulletin board."

September 21.

There are some civilians who receive a questionnaire asking, "Do you want to join the Army?" and the answer is invariably yes. These are the "enemy alien" refugees. Here and there in camp one hears accents of varying thickness, usually German or Czech. Fritz and Kurt and Rudy await the day their application for citizenship is approved and they are notified to appear in court. They bring along a sergeant and lieutenant or captain as witnesses to their loyalty and character. Those I met here are pleasant, humble and eager to become American citizens. In their anxiety to please they conceal their anguish for loved ones in Europe who couldn't get out—relatives and friends they had lost all hope of seeing alive ever again. Here in America they find a new world and new life for which they want to fight even before they are granted the rights of citizenship.

September 22.

A new Table of Organization has come to the Fourth Division which is tantamount to a complete reorganization, with companies changed both in number of men and the types of weapons they employ. By now the men who have been in the division for a year or more have seen several new Tables of Organization come and go and are versed in the ways of more weapons than some outfits ever heard of. Now the men have to experiment, learn new tactics and are assigned changed duties adapted to the new guns and trucks that are coming in. Soon they will start a series of proficiency tests showing whether the division has mastered its techniques and is ready for combat.

September 23, 1942.

Several of us came into the Day Room and there sat Baden, smiling and nonchalant. "Hi Baden, what's cooking?" we greeted. "Oh I just dropped in to see if I have any mail," he chuckled. Baden had been on "French leave" and came back this time of his own will. He'll probably break Arrest In Quarters though and be gone in the morning. He is one of the classic delinquents who fears neither man, beast, nor regulations. The guardhouse holds no terror for him either; he prefers it to straight duty. A few nights ago, after he had just been released from the guardhouse we sat outside the barracks and Baden, looking at the moon, related stories of the stockade, incidents that occurred while he was there and anecdotes about his fellow prisoners. He spoke shrewdly and seemed to divine the tragic and comic nuances of the matter yet remained personally so carefree about mere rules that one could not possibly regard him as a common criminal.

September 24, 1942.

It is autumn, and though not chilly as the autumns in Pennsylvania it has become a little cooler and once we even walked out shivering at reveille in the morning. Things are rather quiet, with hardly a rumor of either latrine or quasi-official variety rippling an engrossment with routine happenings within the regiment. I believe the soldiers show more interest in general news of the day than before. Most can discuss intelligently current events throughout the world. But few know much about what is going on under our noses concerning diverse units moving in and out of camp, and what they do while they are here. It is a booming military city, with fifty-thousand things happening of every sort imaginable: commerce, training, art, crime, romance, mystery, construction, entertainment and whatnot.

September 25.

A runner walked over from the company compound and notified us at Personnel that all Special Duty men should be ready to leave at 6:00 o'clock to join the line troops on a night problem in the field. We protested that the only night problem we wanted was with female blondes or brunettes, but to no avail. We left the office early, changed to fatigues and leggings, ate supper in the field then teamed off in squads to go out on patrol. Our squad leader led us to a trail we were to cover and we discussed plans and women until the problem started at nine o'clock. Then we crept and crawled phantom-like through the dusky woods and remained motionless when light flares were shot into the air. Some men approached.

"Halt—surrender," we ordered and clicked our rifle bolts to let them know they were surrounded.

"Georgia," said one.

"Law," we responded with the countersign and let them pass.

For an hour it was still as we lurked behind bushes waiting for business. We got it. A skillful enemy, Company H, infiltrated our position and we were captured. They started to take us to their Command Post in the rear.

"Halt," we heard from one of our patrols led by Lieutenant Claing who captured our captors and released us. A green flare went up at midnight and the problem was over.

September 26, 1942.

At last—the General! I met him (accidentally on purpose) in the lobby of the swank Hotel Bon Air outside Augusta where I spent the weekend. Coincidentally there was a dinner-dance for the officers of the 12th Infantry Regiment which the General attended. Espying him, I walked over casually and said, "Good evening, General."

"Hello," he smiled through his brushy mustache, "having a good time?"

"In a passive sort of way, Sir," I replied, glancing at the lustrous two stars (denoting Major General) attached on his right collar-wing. "This is the first time I observed officers at leisure, Sir," I volunteered; "it is interesting to see how they comport themselves."

At this he smiled wanly, turned stiffly and slowly trod away.

September 27.

My companion and I accepted a soldier's offer to ride back to camp in his car instead of the bus. "It'll cost you two bits, only a nickel more than the bus and you ride in style," he proposed. So we rode in style—fearfully clenching the seatcovers around curves.

"I'm gittin' me a drink tonight or bust," he declared, which on Sunday seemed a determination unlikely to be fulfilled. But he drove past the camp's main gate, continued about two miles and pulled up at a dark farmhouse. He got out of the car and said he'd be right back. A soldier walking alone up the dark lane ahead turned off behind a hedge. Our man followed him, came back in a few minutes, voiced a long-drawn "ah" and drove back to camp. We asked no questions, he offered no answers, and who cares; "live and let live." Judging from the odor, I think his brand was Scotch.

September 28.

Our rising hour is 6:30, just at break of dawn. It is except when there is a special program on the day's schedule; then, someone (I never discovered who) turns on the lights at an ungodly hour.

"Up and at 'em," shouts he who has never known the better things in life such as breakfast in bed at noon. That day Reveille is omitted; instead a whistle is heard, then "Chow."

We of the Special Duty corps tunnel beneath the covers.

"Last chance," shouts a Paul Revere type lustily, "Get it or starve till lunch time—delicious fried eggs sunny side up."

"Make mine sunny side down," I retort and run almost dressed to the mess hall. John Seabright doesn't.

"Bring me an apple," he mumbles.

"Ye damn fool, you'll have to get up anyhow in ten minutes," I say to him.

"It's worth it," he grunts, and burrows deeper.

September 29, 1942.

It was cold enough to make the furnace. And still only September. In Georgia!

"Every day," said Harold, "the boys in my barracks get up in the morning immediately when the lights are turned on, jumping up like one man. This morning not a one got up right away."

We were walking to the PX, dressed in warm field jackets. As we entered the juke box was blaring "I've Got Spurs That Jingle Jangle Jingle."

"Doesn't that ever go out of style?" I complained.

"What's wrong with the song? It's nice," Harold defended.

"It ain't Beethoven's Quartet Number 15 Opus 132," I countered.

"What do you want, egg in your beer?" said Harold.

September 30.

Pay day.

"Blankety blankety blank damn blank," expressed D Company clerk Sergeant Mamrosh, "seven men were red-lined and won't get paid today because they couldn't sign their names right on the payroll. He set about making up a supplementary payroll for the offenders so they could be paid on the 10th. Two hours after they were paid one man won a hundred and fifty dollars at dice; another won two hundred and thirty. Fantastic but true. Others were left without a dime.

Part of this afternoon was taken up with mass athletics, mostly football. "Time" was called at 3:00 o'clock and everyone ran to a radio to listen to the first game of the World Series between, I think, the St. Louis Cardinals and New York Yankees. My hobby is war, so I'm not quite certain.

October 1.

We all moved, from one barracks to another and from one squad and squad leader to another. The company shuffled, my erstwhile bed-neighbors scattered, I found myself in a new home upstairs in the next-door barracks building. I accomplished in all of ten minutes the transplanting of all my belongings and set up my household in a far corner away from the noisy stairway. Next to my bunk, twelve inches away, lives a red-haired lad whom for all his flaming top I hardly noticed before. He had hardly been around before, being an habitual over-the-hiller recently returned from his latest trip to the "other side of the hill." A corporal came over and informed me I am now a member of his squad, from which I am conditioned to infer that he is endowed with authority and I'd best be cooperative Or Else.

I said, "Glad to meet you," and placed my helmet on my shelf.

October 2, 1942.

"High Card Wins" must be the what-the-hellishest card game there is. The players simply each pull a card from the shuffled deck and, well, the high card wins.

"What you got, Jaffee?" asked Jasper.

"King."

"Ace," said Jasper, and scooped up a dime. Jaffee shuffled the cards, split the deck and drew a card.

"Five."

"Three" said Jasper and gave up the dime.

"Match two cards at a time," proposed Jaffee.

"Shoot," agreed Jasper, thus raising the stake to twenty cents.

"Ten and Jack," quoth Jaffee.

"Two queens," Jasper returned.

The game went on mechanistically, dimes going from one side to the other as regularly as ping-pong. Smitty came over, watched a while and broke into a loud, convulsing laughter. The players looked up, looked at each other, smiled, then broke into laughter like Smitty.

"We'll get it yet, that Section Eight discharge," commented Jasper.

October 3, 1942.

Meeting an officer socially in the home of a civilian, it would seem a breach of etiquette to "Sir" him as in camp. So in meeting this captain, a medical officer, we set him at ease for the evening by treating him as an equal in every respect except we addressed him as "Captain," but much in the same way as saying "Bill" or "Joe." Later he drove us home.

"How do you like your setup, Captain," I asked.

"I hit a bad break," he replied, apparently pleased to freely discuss the lot that befell him when he volunteered into the Army. "I was commissioned a Captain and sent to take basic training," he elaborated. "They immediately threw me in with a group of young newly-made second lieutenants, none of whom were doctors, the oldest of them twenty-six. On the second day my commanding officer, a major who had no right to do so, sent me on a difficult field problem under the supervision of hard-boiled noncoms. For three months I was made to go through a training that few other doctors my age had to take. In the end the Major admitted he had been wrong. I didn't like it and still don't because of my age and the fact that medical doctors do not have to carry side arms. Even so, I am a soldier now and know what the men I treat have to go through."

October 4.

Sunday, and for soldiers still in the United States but not near home the ways in which it can be spent are limited; limited, that is, for all except some who chase around seeking excitement, who will run to New York and back on a three-day pass or in some other fashion "knock themselves out." For most soldiers there are letters to be written, and when but Sunday? They may desire restful entertainment, and movies help in that. The USO centers in Augusta are really a boon to many soldiers. The largest one is in a big well-appointed building on Telfair Street, The main hall combines the luxurious features of lounge and dance floor. Upstairs divides into a table tennis room, a library room, one with a phonograph and classical music albums and another where Sunday evening suppers are served. All summer one could participate in swim party outings and hay ride picnics. Today the boys were invited to the Spear plantation for a barbecue and cotton picking contest on the three thousand acre tract, one of the most famous in the South. These are limited diversions for men who require a thousand other stimuli for their adult needs, but without them the desolation would be a thousandfold more severe.

October 5, 1942.

The kid had just dropped in to see his company clerk about requisitioning a pair of glasses. It was the first time he had been here in months and by all sound reckoning he should have returned right away to his company for his customary routine. But that's not how it went. Here is what happened: "Division" telephoned requesting we search our records for a stenographer and when we find one send him up to be interviewed. We found a likely prospect, walked over to consult the clerk of the company he was in, and there he stood, the kid, dressed in grimy work clothes. We hustled him into a jeep and drove him to Division Headquarters where a tech-sergeant gave him a brief shorthand test. "Go back and pack," directed the sergeant;

"Be ready at 8:00 P.M." The kid is on a train now, bound for some-where.

October 6.

Murray is a thirty-five year old former businessman with little hair left between his neck and forehead and is a storyteller supreme. To-night his narrations were of his fellow trainees at Camp Croft, South Carolina. "There was Goiber The Goon," he began itemizing the characters in his platoon. "He was a great one for gadgets. You could find anything in his locker or hidden behind his clothes hung against the wall: an orange squeezer, a crystal set, a small printing press. Once we went on a hike and Goiber had taken along a thermos bottle. Then there was a fellow we called Dental Hygiene. He hadn't a tooth in his mouth but claimed his gums were hard as wood and could chew anything, until he tussled with a steak in the mess hall that was more than a match for him. There was a platoon sergeant in the next bar-racks that everybody hated. At the end of every thirteen week cycle he got beaten up and hospitalized just before the men moved out. He was meaner than a lynx; our crowd left him with his usual souvenirs, a lip that required four stitches and something else that permitted him to stand or lie but not sit for quite awhile."

October 7, 1942.

We have presently in this regiment of some thirty-five hundred souls a full-blooded Indian of the New Mexico Zuni tribe. Red Robin had been a researcher and educator on Indian culture at the American Museum of Natural History in New York. The other day on a radio broadcast featuring soldiers of the 22nd Infantry Regiment, Red Robin recounted this legend he had heard as a child from an old patriarch of his village: "It began many, many years ago in the days of the Ancients when all was but air and darkness. Awona Wilona, the all-beholding life-giver, cast a thought into space. Impregnating the thought with a seed of its own being he created our grandfather, the sun. He cast another seed into space evolving the waters, the all-be-holding sea which is our grandmother. Our Sun-father with his warmth and grandmother with her warmth caused a scum to grow over the waters and from the surface rose a vapor—rising higher and higher—and a new being was born, our Father the sky. As yet there was no life in the universe. Thus to create a mate for Father Sky, Mother Earth was conceived from our Grandmother, the waters. We are the children of Mother Earth and Father Sky. All the animals and plants are our sisters and brothers."

October 8, 1942.

We are bivouacked near Stapleton, Georgia, sixty miles east of camp. "The supper menu," announced Sergeant Dorst, "is corned beef hash, peas, bread, coffee, canned pears and cookies. The reason I'm telling you is that you are going to cook it yourselves."

So after we dug our slit trenches, our squad of nine grown men proceeded to prepare our individual rations using as a stove a small No. 10 tin can which we filled three-quarters with sand and saturated with gasoline according to S.O.P. (Standard Operating Procedure). I alone amongst all these swashbuckling soldiers had a pocketknife and I became the dining room orderly, cutting the bread and opening the cans. It is a beautiful Indian summer day, just right for the three-day problem in which the whole division is participating. Our object, we are told, is to defend Panama City, Georgia, from a German invasion task force which had succeeded in landing after crossing the Atlantic Ocean.

October 9.

After a cold night's attempt to sleep we returned to within ten miles of camp in what is called Artillery Impact Area, which is where the shells land when the field artillery practices. Getting there we rode through back dirt roads and woods in a half-track, which is a little different from making the same trip in a regular six or eight wheeled army truck. The half-track with its odd chain-track rear and two-wheeled front is built low and wide, with armored wagon-like sides and no roof. It smashes through woods, blazing a trail by pushing over trees up to seven inches thick. An enemy might be cowed just by the sight of it.

We dug in; it seems the problem consists of maneuvering into position and every man cooking his own grub. Every farm we passed showed evidence of the cotton harvest. Here and there I saw patches of sugar cane, or citrons resembling small watermelons, muscadines which grow on trees and look like large black grapes, or pomegranates which some call Chinese apples (everything is blamed on the Chinese).

October 10, 1942.

3:30 A.M.. "Git up now, hurry, we're moving in a few minutes."

I opened my eyes at the softly-spoken order, sprang up and rolled my pack. There was no moon but the stars were brilliant as we moved from our outpost and gathered in line before the chow truck. I wiped my mess kit with a handkerchief and held the kit out for fried eggs, bread, butter, coffee, and took a bag of sandwiches for lunch. Then—what is an infantry problem without walking?—we walked eight, maybe ten miles through sand, hills, swamps, and waded Boggeygut Creek.

Nearing the "battlefield," we approached cautiously and by daybreak had all our positions ready for attack, machine guns on the flanks, mortars to the rear, automatic rifles and rifle platoons distributed for offensive strategy. A "walkie-talkie" radio kept us in touch with companies positioned on either side of us and through it received orders from battalion headquarters. The Division had spread out on line for miles. At Zero Hour the General rode through inspecting to see how well the outfit had coordinated and poised to strike at the enemy. That concluded the problem and we returned to clean up and go to town (Saturday night).

October 11.

The night man at the Dispensary is Corporal-Technician Jake Brill. "Some job," said Jake, "but I don't mind it any more and I learned enough already to be almost a doctor. Payday night three sergeants came in bleeding, slashed by knives. They were in South Carolina and six civilians opened up on them. I took care of them. A private came in, shot accidentally in the arm by a revolver he was loading to be Charge of Quarters. I fixed him up, then gave out three prophylactics. A soldier was brought in very drunk and disgusted who had tried to commit suicide and failed because he thought the heart is on the right side so that's where he shot himself. He's getting along all right."

Jake is a Polish refugee, twenty-eight years old. He had been a private for eighteen months in the Polish army and is in America three and a half years, two of them in the Army. "I helped a few mess sergeants," concluded Jake, "and they invite me to eat at their places any time. I eat like a king."

October 12.

When the problem ended Saturday Captain Ledbetter, my company commander, and a few other officers sat in the field awaiting further orders and engaged in an officer "bull session" on the event. Lt. Colonel Williams, the battalion commander, came over and carried the main current of the conversation, which he would have even had he been of lesser rank.

"This is about the best problem we've had yet," he said. "We all knew what was going on and the job we had to do. When the General came to our section he was well pleased. He pointed out some companies and said their commanders should be commended. As he said it a captain emerged from the woods, 'You too, that's a nice job you're doing,' said the General, and added, 'Say, I want you fellers to help me write some nice flowery letters of commendation. If I write them myself they'd sound like a country lawyer,' and he laughed." Lt. Colonel Williams is renowned for his wit and personality.

October 13, 1942.

Every so often I bump into Sergeant Mike Silensky, a thirty-three year old ex-restaurateur who runs the Classification Section of "Station Complement," the Camp Gordon headquarters.

"Let's have some coffee," Mike invited tonight at the Service Club.

"Oh, one of the coffee boys, Mike? Suits me," I accepted, and in the way of coffee drinkers we settled into a table for three or four cups.

"Well, Mike, how goes it?"

"Busy, very busy."

"Anything special?"

"Right now an order came through that in five days everyone who is physically fit must be transferred to a combat outfit. I have to transfer several master sergeants and many other high-ranking enlisted men."

"Well, that is as it should be. Say, that will leave open some high ratings; maybe you'll get a master sergeant rating yourself."

"Could be, could be," he beamed. Such are the breaks in the Army; buck private today, sergeant tomorrow or never. Then again maybe it's wonderful just to keep out of the guardhouse, what with all the regulations.

October 14, 1942.

In five minutes a round table discussion among soldiers can touch on every topic and still follow a logical sequence. Something like this:

"Where did you register for the draft?"

"Florida, but my home is Boston. There is the best combination there is, Florida in winter, Boston in summer."

"I differ; Southern California in winter, New Jersey seacoast in summer. But not now. You'd be surprised how much oil there is floating on the surface of the water near shore. An awful lot of ships are being sunk. German U-boat submarines are thick as fish."

"The papers say we are beginning to get control now. Say, can a soldier sue the Army if he gets injured?"

"He can demand a hearing for a Medical Discharge and a disability pension, but you can't buck the Army. You have to go through 'military channels.'"

"When I get out I want a stateroom reserved on the train, a bottle in one hand and a 'tomato' at my side. That's to start life fresh with; then-"

"G'wan, blow it out your stacking swivel. You are going to die naturally like the rest of us—by a bullet."

"Good, I love nature, did I ever tell you about the pigeons I used to raise?"

October 15, 1942.

With sneaky suddenness the General went on an inspection tour of the barracks in which his division is housed. He apparently found the conditions of cleanliness far from the standard he sought; his trained eye saw through the superficial neatness, and a little scraping revealed filth and vermin. And truly, the elementary practices we were taught at initial training centers have become lax. It used to be a cardinal rule to sweep and mop the floor every morning; now we merely sweep, and not very thoroughly. In the past we took out our bedding to air every Tuesday; not lately. But starting today the crusted soldiers of The Rolling Fourth will revert to policing their living quarters as when they were "yardbirds," spurred by a daily Battalion checkup and twice a week by both Regiment and Division.

October 16.

Frank kissed his wife goodbye and bade her, as an obligation to home and hearth, to have chops for supper when he returned from work. That was Tuesday; today is Friday and it will be at least ten days more before Frank comes home, for Frank is a soldier, a private in Cannon Company. It happened that someone in his company had contact with a civilian in town who came down with a case of spinal meningitis, consequently quarantining the entire company though no signs of the disease had shown up in camp. I went over to visit Frank Winer and spoke to him at a distance from his barracks.

"Bring me some magazines," he requested, "and call up my wife. Tell her I still love her and to have the lamb chops ready when I get there."

October 17.

I read that it takes five years to train a coal miner and the army might release some soldiers who were miners.

"How about changing my classification to coal miner," proposed the H Company clerk as I worked on an assignment to list names of former coal miners in the regiment.

"I'm trying to find a way to change my own," I replied, expressing that half-serious passion of all civilian-soldiers—a lovely Honorable

Discharge from the Army. The question raised a flurry of excitement among those who came from mining districts.

"Who is from Pennsylvania?" asked one in a latrine group. "If you are you know what a joy loader is. It is a machine that picks up loosened coal and loads it into cars. I can replace twenty men. I blasted the coal with sticks of dynamite and the joy loader did the rest."

October 18, 1942.

Bernie Pearlman came into the Army an accomplished artist and scholar and now occupies a "studio" as a member of a detached chemical warfare battalion that found his artistic ability useful. Delighted at the privilege of retaining his brush and easel, Bernie produced some paintings in his spare time that are now being placed on exhibition at the Augusta art museum.

"Above all I want to develop my art," Bernie said to me. "Though the Army is confining I am grateful for one thing, and that is living among common people, 'the common clay.' I like these people, rubbing elbows with them at the same time I am unjustly intolerant of their small town ways and lack of sophistication. I realize they are more genuine and representative of the world than many polished scions of sheltered communities. I feel the only way I can be of some use to humanity is through my art. I like the simple, unaffected style of painting rather than the mystical. I am looked upon a little as a physical weakling, but we have some gym equipment and the boys are going to be shocked when they see what I can do on the crossbars and ropes."

October 19.

The youth in question was 26 years old; the argument, between an ex-social worker and two clerks, concerned how best to deal with him.

"He went over the hill several times," said his company clerk, "and always returned whining and penitent. I think it is an act, especially when our First Sergeant, who is rare as first sergeants go, gave him several chances to change and make good. He gave the fellow a private first class rating and an office job, and he disappeared again immediately after. Now it's time to stop catering to him."

"Don't you think the boy should be handled by a psychologist" said the social worker, "rather than be put behind the eightball?"

Said the other clerk: "I don't want to minimize the value of psychologists but from your description this fellow is not neurotic; probably the best thing for him would be a kick in the pants. Placing him in the hands of even a competent psychologist would be more traumatic for him than punishment for breaking rules. I think he will grow out of his adolescent behavior easier being punished rather than making him out a mental case."

"Bosh," said the social worker, peeved with the primitive methods the Army employs.

October 20.

Because for several days there has been nothing but cleaning of literally everything inside and outside the buildings, there is talk that the Division is changing to a passive garrison outfit role—which is absurd and not taken seriously given the common knowledge we are at war and a division like the Fourth is anything but destined for passivity. At any rate there is no end to the present campaign against untidiness. The General even came to our Personnel Office.

"Atten-SHUN!" barked a clerk nearest the entrance, ignoring the usual informality in the office where officers of lower rank constantly come and go. He minutely inspected the latrine, typewriters, files and general orderliness. His manner was firm and brisk, but not sour or stiff. The rank and file are strongly impressed with the ability and energetic leadership he has exhibited in the short time since he took command of this division.

October 21, 1942.

Two privates tiffing: "That is not correct; in the hand salute you raise your arm at a forty-five degree angle in front of you and bend it straight at the elbow."

"No sir, your arm goes straight out at the side; wanta bet?"

"I never gamble."

"Don't you drink, either?"

"What has one to do with the other, drinking is a Bacchanalian function, like women; but not gambling."

"Well, I'm positive I'm right. Let me show you: bring your arm straight up; now bend your elbow."

"You see, I would have to tilt my head to bring my hand correctly over the eye."

"Wait, I'll find a picture of someone saluting. General MacArthur should be in one of these magazines; here's one, but you can't tell much from it."

"Sure you can, see how he has it?"

"N-naw; see you later. I'm going back to the barracks and look it up in the manual."

October 22, 1942.

The gym—or Sports Arena as it is justifiably called for its vast proportions—was packed. The occasion: a boxing exhibition. Contenders from various units fought and punched as they would back home in amateur tournaments. Typical of sports enthusiasts anywhere, the audience applauded well-placed blows, cheered aggressiveness, gameness against bigger adversaries, and disparaged foul blows.

"Sport? Sport, hell," commented a smoke-enshrouded gent who looked sideways at the ring. "They bounce around hitting each other in the face with their fists; what kind of sport is that?"

No one audibly responded to his query.

October 23.

Upon returning to the company area today after work, just after Retreat, I joined the men crowded around to hear our new company commander, First Lieutenant Alcorn. He comes to us from Battalion Headquarters where he had been the officer in charge of range detail. Months before that he had been a harried second lieutenant in Company E—my company; now he is the Big Chief, and that's what a company commander is, liege and lord over the lives and fate of ten score men. Yet it is the first sergeant, the "S–1" executor, who actually manipulates personnel in the company. His recommendations are foremost in the company commander's decisions on who shall be appointed noncommissioned officer, who shall be "busted" for inefficiency or rule infraction, and severity of gigs handed out. Our new boss did not make a big speech, only advising that he expected his orders to be carried out promptly, efficiently, and that he would try to be fair and impartial. That was wise; some of them try to explain all their aims and methods and wind up twisted into a knot.

October 24, 1942.

Making the trip from camp to Augusta on a busy night, and back again, the men go through a series of adventures that in future memory they will no more forget than they will experiences on the battlefield. Going in, buses leave from a station a mile and a half from the company area. A long shuttle bus is supposed to go through camp and shuttle us to the station, but its reliability is such that it is healthier on the blood pressure to walk than wait. From the station to town is usually all right. The return trip finds all the soldiers trying to return about the same time, at midnight. We get in line, often behind a drunk who may or may not be well behaved or able to hold his liquor. Back at camp, we unload and pile into the waiting shuttle-trailer bus. We are packed in tight.

"Pour in oil and can us like sardines," someone yells. The driver is not in the cab; he seems unaware that his vehicle is filled and waiting. At last he deigns to get in and pull out. The clumsy vehicle scrapes the road with its weighted bottom as we round a curve and are on our way down Sixth Avenue.

"Hold it one time, hey!" goes a chorus of shouts and shrill whistles at the driver who negligently passes up the first stop, causing those who wanted off to walk back a block. Further on where most get off there is a rush for the exit and one counts himself fortunate not to be kicked or have his uniform disheveled. Finally we manage to get off at our stop and stand breathlessly watching the monstrous carrier go on.

October 25.

It was a late hour, as late hours go in camp. The lights were out on both floors except the latrine, in which inner sanctum a conference was in session. Tom, with his thick Scottish brogue, stood steadfastly intent on talking while three or four others alternated between talking and preparing to retire.

"It is the sixtieth day and the Russians are still holding at Stalingrad," said Tom, "and I see the British are opening a drive in Egypt against General Rommel. Maybe this will be the second front instead of across the English Channel."

"Yes," took up another, wiping his face, "it looks pretty good all around. The Marines are holding out in the Solomons—what is that island, Guadalcanal? The Japs are putting up a stiff fight for that one."

"What gets me is the United States keeping quiet," said Tom. "We have airplanes helping out over there, and once in a while we hear of big convoys of troops landing in Ireland and supply units reaching other parts of the world. It's a good many months now, and I think that one of these days we are going to break into something very big."

"Well, I'd rather have it that way," spoke a voice from the shower room, "than just puttering around with little scrapes here and there."

October 26, 1942.

There is time for parties too; nice parties, that is, at a YWCA where nothing stronger than unspiked punch is served. Chaplain Carlson astutely arranged a party for the end of the month when everyone except a few skinflint sergeants could be counted on to be too broke for other soldierly diversions. The affair last night at the Augusta YWCA turned out a consummate success, beginning with the fact that we were fifty men boarding the bus in camp and strangely, according to the good, experienced Chaplain, we were the same number when we got off and entered the hallowed environs of the female haven. At sight of the shapely welcoming committee a military chorus sang out: "Range, two hundred, enemy front, ready—FIRE!"

We were received in the luxuriant garden in back. We had arrived a little early, or maybe they were a little late; regardless, we were deferentially presented with marshmallows to roast at an outdoor stove.

"There's a badminton court here," announced a cute matron, "anybody want to play badminton or, uh-"

"Let's play UH," boomed a soldier helpfully.

The girls at last ready inside, we were permitted to enter the converted house a few at a time. Inside we came upon an elaborately arranged Halloween House of Horrors. Further inside the place blossomed into a pair of open chambers replete with maidens, sweet apple cider and suitable ornamentation. Someone activated a record player and dancing commenced. Dave Jaffee corralled for himself a well-stacked brunette; a lanky lad from First Battalion Headquarters surrounded a very impressive blond, and Sergeant Needle took unto himself a bright red apple and discussed with the mature official hostess the social conditions of poor whites in backwoods hamlets of eastern Georgia. Toy horns enhanced the festivities—one frisky girl startled every G.I. passing by with a loud toot in his ear. Finally the hour called for Auld Lang Syne.

"Had a good time?" I asked friend Levine of Company E.

"What do you think, with three dates lined up," he replied.

October 27, 1942.

Sergeant Lawson Durden from the post office came into Personnel Office to use our locater file in finding the proper owners of poorly addressed mail. Among that component of Regular Army men who are interesting, Durden is a distinguished representative. He is the chief mailman of the regiment and has been known on occasion to alleviate the rigors of his responsibilities with hard spirits. Any Saturday night he may be seen hobnobbing with cronies of lesser rank in town, greeting and joking with passersby on the street, thus helping to bolster the general morale.

"You fellows," he would say to his low-rank buddies, "finest in the world. I don't pull my rank on nobody."

The genial Georgian has never been known to "screw up."

"Division Headquarters says I'm the best mailman they've got," he said to us. "Nope, ain't had a drop of spot-ball all day. 'Course, everybody will say I'm stewed anyway so I might just as well be." At all times aware of propriety, Durden would wait until Sunday morning when only a few are in our office to observe his unsteady condition. Then, he opens the door, declares "At Ease" as though a high officer were entering, pauses for dramatic effect and says softly, "What time is it?"

October 28, 1942.

A private in a 12th Infantry Regiment was griping. It sounded like this: "It doesn't make sense; we walk into the mess hall through a narrow door and get into the chow line. When we are finished eating and bring back the soiled dishes others are still coming in. We are all squeezing through the same door going in opposite directions instead of using another door to exit through, which would make it easy.

"Last week our first sergeant said: 'Throw everything into your barracks bag; everything!' We figured this is It, we're on our way. 'And be ready to fall out at 10:30,' he added. Promptly at 8:30 the whistle blew and the first sergeant yelled, 'Can't you guys ever get out in time when the whistle blows?' We were away all day and found when we returned that the barracks had been fumigated. All our clothes and toilet articles were exposed. Look at this wool shirt; it's almost ruined. Some fellows had jars broken and ink splattered over everything. The clothes won't get over it in five cleanings. We have the best officers there are, but our First Sergeant—that's where it hurts. I guess most of these first sergeants have had little education; they've been kicked around a lot and have developed an attitude as if to say, 'You guys aren't going to put over any horse manure on me.'"

October 29.

Private First Class John Cheever was on K.P. duty for three days. At mealtime I held out my plate over the counter. The head cook portioned out the meat, the next cook piled mashed potatoes on top, then John, standing shirtless behind a salad pot, smiled at me and extended his long-handled ladle of salad to my plate. In the evening he came into the personnel office to work on a story. He finished typing it, borrowed a couple of stamps and sent it off. We went to the PX next door for a couple of "brews."

"There must be something wrong with all mess sergeants," remarked John. "The one I had at Camp Wheeler was okay."

"What's wrong, doesn't this one treat you right?" I returned.

"Well, it's not exactly that he keeps on our tail, but it is as if we were dirt under his feet."

We walked back to the barracks.

"I don't mind working in the company on straight duty," he continued. "I don't like K.P., but it doesn't come that often. The thing I want most is to write. I like to write; it makes me happy. All I ask is for some time and the use of a typewriter."

Cheever, a man of thirty, is slim, of medium height but for a mere hint of a stoop seems shorter. He retains somewhat of a New England accent. His friendly, shy grin quickly made him popular with everyone in the company. Today he came over with a letter in his hand and said, "That story I sent has been accepted by a magazine. They liked it very much and asked for more; and if you'll look in the October 17 issue of *The New Yorker* magazine you may care to read a piece I sent in previously. It is titled, 'Problem Number Four' and its setting is Camp Croft, South Carolina."

I read the story and found it interesting and written with professional craftsmanship.

October 30, 1942.

Army beds are easy for me to make; at least I have the knack down pat. Today I shook out the covers, spread them smooth and tucked in the flaps. Simple as pie. But then came the footlocker, and that is a different story. It was not in good shape—the bottom compartment a heap of seldom-used fatigues tossed wildly together with odds and ends and the top compartment a jumble of toilet articles, towels, and stationery.

"You'd better straighten out that junk," observed my neighbor, and began explaining how each article should be placed according to regulations.

"Whoa, hold up; I don't intend making a career of this footlocker,"

I protested, and proceeded to straighten it my way by swiftly veneering the surface appearance purported to give the impression of neatness throughout.

"Okay, I warned you; I wish you luck," he concluded. Now for the rifle in the rack. I lifted it out, ran a patch of dry cloth through the bore, brushed the dust off the exterior and that's that, I thought, and went to work. I returned for lunch, but first visited my boudoir.

"How is it, any gigs?" I inquired expectantly of the boys. Inspection had not yet taken place. As I started to leave a lieutenant entered.

"Atten-SHUN!"

"Rest," he ordered as he walked to the rifle rack. He got to mine, looked inside the trigger housing and was about to tell the corporal his findings when I spoke up, "Sir, the Charge of Quarters forgot to unlock the rifle rack this morning; I was going to clean my gun now." He graciously handed it to me and the day was saved. There are ways to get along in the Army, though sometimes by the skin of the teeth.

October 31, 1942.

"Shoot six—c'mon, Six." The dice heard not the plea and showed up eight. The winners scooped in their greenbacks, making way for the next round of bets.

"Hey, Six, one time—shoot 'em six." Hardly ten minutes had elapsed since pay envelopes had been opened and already the game was going strong, crisp bills changing hands faster than I could keep track.

"How is this game played?" I asked Kappy who watched intently but did not participate. He explained the mechanics to me.

"Sounds complicated," I commented.

"All right, let's do it this way," he continued. "We'll pretend that you are in the game. Now you place, let's say, five dollars."

The dice were thrown: a four.

"What happened?" I asked.

"You lost; now suppose you bet eight dollars."

Again I hypothetically lost.

"Try four dollars." The throw produced a winner.

"You are nine dollars behind. Now suppose you are betting seven dollars even for the next five minutes—let's see what happens."

In quick succession I won seven dollars, lost seven, and another seven, then won a round, lost two in a row, won one, then lost four straight. It's a good thing this was a "dry run" for at the end of the five minutes I would have been out a total of thirty-three dollars.

"Well, you just had an off-day," Kappy rationalized.

"Yes, and I would have been starving for a whole month," I noted.

November 1, 1942.

A sergeant walked over to Josh Rackovisch and said: "Djibish yeva smolle dobrash," or so it sounded.

"Ah, djej meh yod sklal furlough!" responded Josh exuberantly. "Dzi sie lomir esn kreplach good time."

"As you were," I intruded, "what is that, Russian, Polish, Slavish?"

"Some of each, but mostly Russian. Don't mind us, we're just trying to keep in practice."

"Yea," said the sergeant, "and you can't tell when we'll be putting it to practical use. It's a good thing some of us have parents or grandparents who were born on the other side so when we go over there a few of us will know how to ask directions; at least we'll be able to talk with the girls."

"Who wants to talk with the girls?" said Josh, emphasizing the word talk.

"Oh it will help," replied the sergeant, "besides, the word 'no' is the same in any language so there's no use playing dumb."

They labored the point a bit, as gentlemen will, then the sergeant ended with, "Well, gotta be off. Yonya trompa gai tzum teivel."

"Okay" Josh concurred, "yakvi maki juj dodo bist a hunt."

November 2.

This war is commonly called a war of attrition, which sounds distinctive even though almost any war was probably so regarded by its participants. There is another kind of attrition at work in the war, affecting the men engaged in it and not necessarily of a negative nature: the psychology of becoming a soldier—to act, think, breathe like one. Thus from last June when I joined this outfit, to the present, a marked change is noticeable in the men. A better harmony than ever seems to exist, exemplified by the fact that fewer go over the hill now. Many factors contribute to this, not the least the granting of furloughs and extra effort at providing diversion and entertainment, but much should be credited to a mellowed attitude shaped by living the life. Time, the great healer, has balmed the initial wounds of fitting into a new form of existence; a process sometimes called war weariness. If such it is then so be it, for it is a necessary conditioning that enables the men to carry on.

November 3, 1942.

One was tall, curly haired and could not be more than twenty-two. The other, stocky and a little older, leaned thoughtfully on the table.

"You would expect it of the Japs," Curly was saying, "they always have been backward culturally and their economic structure was medieval until fifty years ago, but how in the world can you explain the Germans? How is it that a people with so much culture—the greatest artists, poets, musical composers—can repeatedly show barbaric traits and instigate wars?"

His companion shrugged his shoulders, drew a cigarette and said nothing.

"I know what it is," Curly went on, "it's bullheadedness. Germans are the most bullheaded people there are. My father is a German. He is as smart a man as they come, but once he gets an idea he's like a stone and nothing can crack him except dynamite. There were a lot of German kids in the neighborhood where I grew up. They were the fightingest bunch you ever saw. No matter how badly they were getting licked you couldn't stop them till they were beat up so they couldn't move. Germany never won a war. They often fought though, till they were beaten senseless."

Curly paused thoughtfully a moment, then aired his conclusion, "The only way we can win an absolute victory over Germany is to break them up. Scatter them. In any case, they should not be allowed to continue as an individual country because they would lay low for a few years, be as nice as you please, then one day tear loose again and grab the world by the horns."

November 4, 1942

Scene: the company orderly room.
Time: any time in an ordinary day.
Place: any company in camp.

Most members of the company are out on various details, some to the rifle range, some painting a latrine, others attending a lecture by their platoon leader. The First Sergeant sits with his feet planted discreetly atop a waste-basket instead of on his desk—since war began there is no allowance for tomfoolery. The Company Commander comes in and right away goes to his desk in a partitioned cubicle.

"Sergeant, get a detail to dig a garage under the mess hall for our new antitank gun," he directs the First Sergeant.

"Yes Sir. Corporal, get your squad and start on this. Draw whatever tools you need from the supply sergeant."

The corporal nods and departs. The orderly room is neat in fact as well as in name. A sign on the door instructs visitors to "Knock or Stay Out." A knock is heard at the door.

"Come in" says the top kick. A private enters meekly.

"Go inside, the Captain wants to see you."

Their voices are heard from the Captain's office, "The doctor at the infirmary says I am to be on light duty, Sir."

"What's wrong with you?"

"My knee is weak, Sir."

"You've been goldbricking around here for a long time. Sergeant, put this man on K.P."

"Sir, why should I be punished, I can't help it if I'm not able to do regular duty."

"Put him on K.P," repeats the Captain emphatically to denote the conversation is ended.

The Charge of Quarters comes in.

"Go around to every barracks and take the name of everyone there and find out why he's there," directs the First Sergeant. The CQ leaves on his mission.

"Sergeant," says the Captain, "we have a few Private First Class ratings to give out. Who do you know that deserves one in the third platoon?"

"There's Delassy; he's a good soldier. Barker is on the ball lately, Sir. Pillucci is doing some darn nice soldiering, too."

"All right, I'm going to give this fellow Baden a PFC rating."

"But Sir, he just came out of the guardhouse. Some of the boys who have worked hard and never miss a formation are going to be pretty disappointed."

"Well, maybe it will encourage him to change his ways."

The mess sergeant comes running in.

"A couple of majors from Medical are inspecting the mess hall; they want to see you."

The Captain and First Sergeant get up and leave.

"Whew," sighs the clerk who does the paperwork for the first sergeant, "maybe now I can get this report typed for Battalion S-3."

November 5, 1942.

The editor of the *Double Deucer* asked me to write an editorial. This is it, titled "About The Draft:"

> One of the jokes making the rounds presently is how we might be walking down a company street one of these days and run into our old man marching in with a barracks-bag on his back. It "ain't funny McGee," because there are cases where it actually happened. Also, our older brothers are leaving their families to join up. Soon our kid brothers will be in, and the kid sister graduating high school this year will be taking our old job in the factory.
>
> In the days before Pearl Harbor a fellow would be drafted and his friends would say, "Have a good time, Jack, make the best of it. You'll be back in a year." It was like seeing him off to college and the only ones who worried were his parents. Jack felt cheated because he began training hard and soon realized things that many of the people on the outside could not see.
>
> Then last December the fireworks began for us in earnest. Slowly the country got steaming mad. Production was geared away from making luxury automobiles; instead, tanks started rolling off the assembly lines. Arguments arose about who should be drafted into the fighting forces and who remain on the home

front. Congress decided that sooner or later every man from 18 to 45 would be drafted. Jack felt gratified; his buddies in uniform no longer complained of having been shanghaied. The war effort became truly democratic and every soldier knew at last that everybody's sacrifice was as great in one way or another as his own.

November 6, 1942.

Leo Levine has obviously "been around." This is seen in his firm step, poised carriage and sureness and self-confidence in his speaking voice. More than merely having been around in the usual local sense, he is widely traveled in most countries of the world, beginning with Argentina where the first Standard Oil Company freighter that hired him was bound. He must have been quite young, for he is now no more than 27. Russia, France, China, Finland—there is hardly a place from which he cannot tell tales of his experiences. In England he met Willie Gallagher, renowned Communist orator in the House of Commons.

"He introduced me to many people in London," said Leo. "We corresponded for a while after I left. When he got up to speak the other members invariably razzed and heckled him but soon quieted down and listened with rapt attention to his brilliant speech. It is very peculiar for an American witnessing a session of Commons; in fact anyone but an Englishman would be highly amused. Cliques are organized amazingly fast for each new issue that comes up; not established cliques—at one time or another Tories will side with Midlanders, or Laborites with the Old Guard.

"Once I rode in a cab to an outlying district of the city. Bumping along a rough road, an intense biological urge took hold of me and I hollered to the driver to stop.

"'You cawn't stop here,' protested the Cockney cabbie, 'this is the king's property.'

"'Take your choice, either you stop here or I do it inside the cab.'

"'No, no, oy'll call a bobby on you.'

"So he left me with no alternative and the king's property remained undefiled."

November 7.

The long awaited Ballet Theatre sponsored by S. Hurok finally came to Augusta and performed in the spacious Municipal Auditorium. No art medium could have been more escapist than this terpsichorean drama. The dancers leaped and pirouetted with graceful precision and wafted ethereally off the stage. Back in the barracks Tom's soul also leaped and pirouetted. He was drunk, thoroughly drunk, limp as a rag so that he had to be dragged in and heaved into bed by a couple of less inebriated samaritans; but somehow he was able to sing, and he sang lustily. "When Irish Eyes Are Smiling."

Sunday morning we stood in line for pancakes, known also by other names such as saddle blankets and concrete weights.

"Ah feels like ah been drug through a sick cow and whupped wif its tail," said Tom.

A voice in back said, "It looks like the beginning—the radio says our forces have landed in North Africa and opened up a second front there."

This news came exactly eleven months after the United States entered the war on December 7, also a Sunday.

November 8, 1942.

There are more than all kinds in the Army, there are also the impossible. These are men, if men they are, who are known hereabouts as Section Eight material. Section Eight is the regulation by which the mentally deviant are discharged from the service. The person in question need not be insane. Odd behavior, a congenital misfit, renders one a candidate for the discharge. Sometimes a man comes along who acts "strange" on purpose, prompting the boys to say he is "bucking for a Section Eight." The fact is, a man who can keep up a pretense of abnormality for an extended time is likely to become victimized by his own morbidity.

Such a case came up recently of one who looked every bit the character he chose to play. From the first, this hillbilly from Tennessee, whose education showed on the records as two years of grammar school, kept entirely to himself. He was surly and unkempt. Even the noncoms kept away from him for he was strong as an ox and might turn violently on anyone, sergeants included. One day he was ordered to join a group of illiterates to learn how to write his name. He refused to go and was arraigned before an officer for disobeying a "direct order," than which no offense in the eyes of the Army is greater. Apparently a court-martial was not to his liking; he showed up the next day with a page on which he had written his signature fifty times. The writing was more than legible, it was handsome. Nevertheless he was given a Section Eight discharge two days later, probably for his inability or unwillingness to adjust rather than for the fraud discovered later: he would have others write letters for him and when they misspelled a word he corrected them with the right spelling. No one regretted his departure.

November 9.

Today big, jovial Jules Alderman transferred to an Engineer outfit in Kentucky. Only recently he had come here from an Infantry basic training camp. Now the Army will have the advantage of his civilian expertise as a construction foreman, which Jules naturally desired but one rarely changes outfits without misgivings. Before leaving he had been attending a three month regimental radio operator class. He was way ahead of the others in learning code. A few days after it started he reported taking four words a minute while everyone else still worked on two, then every few days he advanced to six, eight, ten words as the rest either lagged behind by several words or dropped out. At the last he was doing sixteen words a minute without an error; the next closest did fourteen. While making a reputation for himself in company and regiment, other authorities weighed his usefulness as a lawyer and construction man, and finally selected the latter.

November 10, 1942.

Jack Zencheck returned from furlough and in his best burlesque manner entertained his New York chums on the subject of the current American military thrust into Africa.

"Why don't you come home and stay for good," he mimicked. "The war is over, practically; Hitler is holding out just long enough to build a legal case so he can plead insanity."

This appraisal is far too optimistic, but the events of the last few days are of major importance. Germany's Afrika Corps under General Rommel has been swept backward in headlong retreat toward its west Libyan bases, its recently proud organization decimated by the British under Montgomery. Concurrently the Stars and Stripes landed in North Africa, occupying Algiers, Casablanca, and driving eastward to Tunisia in a race against German reinforcements.

At this point in reading the report I had to stop and get a map—what a marvelous thing, a map! On it I located Germany's present position in Africa, then studied the points of possible vulnerability in its European stronghold. Germany appeared threatened principally along the English Channel and North Sea coastline. Russia she could hold off for the time being. Now with the Allied conquest of North Africa, Germany will have to face potential invasion not only on her west coast but—if we succeed in the African campaign—on the long Mediterranean coastline as well.

November 11, Armistice Day, 1942.

The hillside curved into a huge amphitheater which easily contained the whole division assembled today to celebrate the signing of the armistice ending the war in 1918. An impressive seventeen thousand dressed uniformly in green field jacket, khaki trousers and overseas caps presented an attractive subject for the cameramen who shot pictures from many angles. A bright sun heightened contrast among the pastel colors, providing a dimension of excitement lacking in the typecast format of the program. The division chaplain opened with the invocation. A member of the commanding general's staff, himself a brigadier general, then paraphrased Lincoln's Gettysburg Address in remarks preparatory to introducing the main speaker, Major General Barton.

"Men," said General Barton, "you are in the finest division in the United States Army. You have a fine record; no trucks anywhere have been greased and cleaned better than yours."

Widespread laughter.

"Seriously, you have taken the training in excellent spirit. We know how tough the hikes and double timing are that you do. The reason we do them is that we have to be better fit, better prepared than the dirty yellow-bellied sons of b-s who would slit all our throats if they had a chance. My only ambition in life is to lead you men in battle. I know someone will say, 'Yea, the old man will lead us into battle—from ten miles behind the line.' Well, I want to lead you men in battle wherever it may be—from ten miles behind the line."

There was loud applause at this bit of wry humor. Nobody, I believe, doubted his sincerity. The band concluded with the "Star Spangled Banner," we saluted the colors and were dismissed.

November 12, 1942.

My editorial in *The Double Deucer*, titled "Thanks, Leathernecks:"

> After all these months of riding the bus to Augusta our editor, Goldie, suddenly discovered the billboard which hits you just as you enter the city. "Tell it to the Marines," it reads. He came back inspired and now this issue of *The Double Deucer* is dedicated to the Marines. We think the gesture is timely because from now on the Army is ready to take the spotlight in the war. The Marines deserve our highest praise and thanks for the wonderful start they made for us. They have been our shock absorbers, giving us time to develop a tremendous battle force. Since the Marine Corps was activated 65 years ago, with a major at the head, the Marines have always worked in harmony with the Army. A year ago a friend of ours decided he wanted to join a service that was most nearly like the British Commandos. He chose the Marine Corps and went for a physical examination. It was a tough one, but so was he, and the next we heard from him came in a letter with a return address, Parris Island, South Carolina. He didn't have much to write while in basic training but he did convey full enthusiasm for the program. Upon completion he shipped out for duty on islands near Australia. We received one letter from there; in it he expressed serious foreboding about coming events. Soon after, the Marines landed in the Solomons and our friend undoubtedly with them. We knew then that there could be no rest until we followed up this brave little force and took over the opening they made for us against great odds, and with confidence that we would not let them down.

November 13.

Just as when we returned suddenly from maneuvers in August, a new flurry of rumors has sprung up. The current crop is inspired by the building of crates. Crates are being built for everything—guns, field equipment, kitchen stoves, books, office supplies, footballs. The job is going on around the clock to produce the enormous number required soon for whatever purpose. Amphibious jeeps have appeared on camp streets. They are already absorbed in the Motor Pool as standard vehicles. In this division, when a new and strange vehicle or other piece of equipment is here two weeks it has lost its novelty and become S.O.P.—Standard Operating Procedure.

Training in the past few weeks has stressed double-timing. It built up gradually, running first a mile, then two miles carrying a rifle and stripped field pack, By now almost every field problem includes double-timing a distance of six miles in one hour. The normal walking pace is two and a half miles an hour, On such phenomena were the rumors based.

November 14, 1942.

Again troops are seeping into the division to fill gaps left by outgoing cadre. A number came today from Camp Butner, North Carolina. They ranged in age from 17 to 55. The process of assigning each man to a company was worked out both before and after their arrival. Before, we surveyed the companies for shortages in their allotted strength. Next we determined their shortages of specialists according to the Table of Organization. When the men arrived, they marched from the station and assembled outside the personnel office. Their leader handed us a folder containing each man's service record. We studied the information contained in the Soldier Qualification Card, Form 20, while the men stood outside with gas masks, waiting quietly and smoking. Having carefully considered skills attained as civilians and in military training, we then made appropriate assignments, riflemen to rifle companies, radio technicians to headquarter companies, former merchants to Service Company, clerks to where they were needed, machine gunners to heavy weapons companies, and held out a teacher for Division Headquarters.

November 15, 1942.

Everyone goes to the Service Club the first evening in a new camp. Tonight a friend and I met one of the new arrivals, an older fellow trying to get the lay of the land from old-timers by virtue of several months' residency. We tried to give him an inkling of the kind of outfit he had come into. He was enthused with the brand of people he met. He wondered if he could bring his wife down to live in Augusta. Many men do it, we told him; no reason he couldn't.

"I don't want to overextend myself; if married life will interfere with my army career I'd rather leave my wife at home," he said.

Many married soldiers have found it feasible and a big boost to morale to have their wives in Augusta. The soldier felt heartened at hearing this.

"You know," he said, "I have learned that an older man in the army must shake off all the worries he is accustomed to, and forget the losses he suffered by being drafted. I, for instance, lost a twenty thousand dollar business and broke up a home. I'm not complaining, because others have done likewise. To make a go of it a man has to free himself of such burdens and concentrate on getting along with his sergeants."

November 16.

He is called Soapy the Scribbler. For a fee, Soapy will ghost-write a letter for anyone. His customers are mostly lovelorn youngsters who manage to get a girl's address and want to "snow" her in blind faith that she is good-hearted and beautiful. His introductory letter starts about as follows: "Dear Sue, I've heard so much about you from our mutual friend Aloysius that I thought it a good idea to write and get acquainted."

It is not until the second or third letter that he lets his imagination run free, and on behalf of his client writes: "My dear Sue, how good it was to hear from you and realize there is another living person whose thoughts are so much like my own. My mind was AWOL to celestial realms when—"

As he writes, his client stands by with mixed feelings of elation and dismay at the use of flowery language that will be attributed to him. Once, the correspondence arranged a home-town meeting with the girl and the client when he went home on furlough. Soapy's enticing words had fired a synthetic romance between them. The fellow entered the restaurant where they had agreed to meet and looked around. There was no one in sight but a girl of about thirty, thin, hooknosed, pimply and wearing thick-lensed eye-glasses.

"You are Herman?" she suggested.

Caught, he couldn't back out, but on returning to camp he found effective self-expression by which Soapy learned to restrain his rich flow of endearing adjectives, at least for a while.

November 17, 1942.

The recreation hall was being renamed MacArthur Hall in honor of the general, Douglas MacArthur (Jack Zencheck thought the company day room should at the same time be renamed Zencheck Hall). To mark the change the boys put on a show, led by Goldie, He produced, cast, directed and publicized, whipping it into shape just an hour before the performance with the audience already beginning to gather.

"Let's do it up good, some big shots will be here," he encouraged. "Now bring up a table. Put it over there. Lin wears this raincoat in the hypodermic needle gag. Bubbles, you'll go on the program last with your burlesque dance; the best act is always last to sweeten the taste of any rotten acts."

"How do I open this stage door, Goldie? Red went to pick up the girls in town and took the key."

"We'll dig up a skeleton key. See that the light and microphone are in good condition."

Soon, with little apparent effort all was ready and the curtain was pulled. The Master of Ceremonies walked out before the capacity crowd. It was Goldie. He set the pace of the program and managed to vitalize acts that threatened to become dull. For the little trouble he had taken the show provided an unbelievable variety of fast-moving entertainment.

November 18.

Working in the office means being a little distant from everyday training activities. To keep current I ask the boys what they are doing. I met Al at the PX.

"Hello Al, haven't seen you in weeks" (probably wasn't more than four days).

"How are you?" he greeted.

"Well, what's new, Al?"

"Oh, same thing; we were on the combat range today."

"Machine guns?"

"No, '03 rifles. We operated in squads and were scored by squad team instead of individually. They have everything figured out; we move forward in skirmish formation as if actually on a battlefield. We hit the ground on signal and roll over into shooting position to shoot at the targets in the distance."

"Sounds interesting."

"It is more so when we go out in company units and mortars and 75 millimeter artillery fire over our heads as we move forward. The operation is very realistic and shows up the knowledge and stamina of officers and men. A battalion commander umpires and observes every move that is made. He judges if the company is taking advantage of protective cover, how long it takes them, and counts the number of hits they make on the targets."

November 19, 1942.

As the pace of war grows swifter a nightly forum is held in the latrine before retiring, to interpret the news and express personal attitudes about the prospect of being in battle.

"I'd hate to go with this outfit; we always screw up and get lost in the woods."

"Don't you believe it; this is as good a division as any and maybe better. No army is ever perfect. If we knew we were going to be in battle and had a month's advance notice we would learn fast enough. One month of training overseas is worth six months here, 'cause everyone takes it seriously."

"I'd hate to be out there with the bullets flying, but I know that in this war you can't just duck yourself in a deep foxhole and wait till

the shootin's over. A Hun would sneak up and stick you with a bayonet before you could move."

"I admit I'm afraid; anybody who isn't ain't normal."

The American spirit of gamble and fair play is reflected in the
symposium. The majority believe war is a lottery in which they want
to be winners by returning in good health. At the same time they
adhere to the classic creed (Hamlet): "but being in, bear't that the
opposed beware of thee."

November 20.

Camp plans for any weekend begins with cleaning the barracks Friday
night for the unfailing Saturday morning inspection. This week there
will also be a division parade on Saturday morning. A few men apply
in advance for a three day pass while several poor suckers are stuck
with weekend details such as K.P. or guard duty. Saturday afternoon
is given to a sports program which ends early, and the weekend starts
4 o'clock. Some of the boys have learned it is not wise to hang around
the barracks longer than necessary in case a sergeant happens to nab
them for an impromptu detail; somebody might become sick and can't
do guard duty, in which case the Charge of Quarters may substitute
with any private he can find. A certain number are always around to
become victims; usually they couldn't afford to leave the area, having
blown their pay early on booze or dice. That about sums up planning
for a weekend—as much as one can plan in the Army.

November 21, 1942.

Jerry White was formerly a vaudeville comedian, and Eddie Lane a
Broadway nightclub performer. The two are the prominent entertainers
in camp. One or the other appears at nearly every camp show or local
USO event. They are attached to the Special Service unit in their respective outfits, Eddie in the 12th Infantry Regiment, Jerry in the 4th
Field Artillery, To deny them this privilege would be unfortunate,
depriving soldiers of the entertainment they are well equipped to
provide and damaging to their own future careers. A few minutes in
either's company leads to this conclusion. Eddie is the older showman,
His every word and gesture divulges how completely his past, present

and future are enmeshed with performing. Jerry is younger and no less infected with the acting bug.

November 22.

It was past midnight, time to turn in, but Addis preferred to talk awhile so we sat on the barracks steps and talked. He had attended the Infantry Officer Candidate School recently and finished the course with a grade not high enough to be commissioned an officer.

"I am satisfied to have had the experience of attending," he said. "I don't regret it, and anyway there are disadvantages to being an officer."

That is so. Many of the young lieutenants are lonely for the plebeian companionship of enlisted men. They must always carry themselves with officerial dignity and cannot easily indulge in the luxury of griping. Henry likes being in Company E.

"Many men have passed through the company since I first became a member," he went on, "it has been my pleasure to live and work with them, study them and watch them develop. There is something in every man, maybe some personal problem, that he has to work out. He reserves his confidence for someone he likes and looks up to. You often find one with little worldly knowledge who becomes broadened in the Army. Avenues open to him of education in things he never dreamed existed. Chick Williams was like that. He started reading. He got hold of the best books, read them and intelligently discussed with me things he found strange. He corresponded with me after he left. His letters were marvelous. In the few months he had been exposed to literature his ability to express himself in writing improved beautifully; also his understanding of the world, which might never had occurred without being in the Army."

November 23.

The men dragged themselves and their mudcaked equipment off the half-tracks and into the barracks. The hour was 7:30 A.M.. They would not have been in yet except the two day problem had to be stopped at the end of a day and night or there is no telling how many would have been stricken with pneumonia. As it is they were a "sorry-looking" lot. The weather had been sunny and warm for two solid weeks, then the very minute they started out yesterday there came a heavy downpour of rain that settled into a cold penetrating drizzle that lasted all night.

"We were freezin' forty ways to Sunday," said Pat as he crawled under the covers in his bunk with no thought of going to the mess hall for breakfast. He told how they had shivered all night in open half-tracks, and by the small hours of the morning it became almost unbearable. It reminded me of our two-day problem at Camp Wheeler last spring when we at least were permitted to build fires. The advanced training in this outfit would never countenance such a lapse in the first principle of night maneuvers—the strict blackout.

November 24, 1942.

Arthur laid his rifle in the rack, hung up his rifle belt with attached bayonet and we went to dinner. Just eating steadily without hurrying, an Army meal is finished by most in half the time than elsewhere. We lingered longer than usual today, to the annoyance of the KP's who like to start cleaning up early and get it over with. Arthur poured himself a second cup of coffee.

"This bayonet drilling is coming out of my ears already," he remarked, "wish I was back in Minnesota where I've got the nicest five hundred farm acres you ever laid eyes on."

It is not hard to visualize him as a farmer; his sturdy build and tranquil disposition are compounded of years spent in corn fields and with domestic animals.

"I would be twice as useful to the country remaining at home," he stated factually rather than in protest. "They would not have drafted me now—farmers are too valuable. Too bad I couldn't have been deferred a few more months."

Many men are in camp who would have been exempted from the draft under new regulations reflecting changed circumstances.

"I guess though," he added, "I have no more right than the next man to stay out of uniform in this war, even if I can be more productive at home."

November 25.

Her age was hard to judge. The wrinkled face suggested sixty but her springy step and lithe movements said forty. She was waiting on the corner for a bus. We had been introduced once, and she recognized me.

"I would like your advice," she said, "you remember the Chevrolet I had?"

I didn't, but nodded affirmatively.

"Well, I loaned it to some soldiers a couple of weeks ago. They went to town in it and had a flat tire on the way back. Instead of fixing it they kept riding on the rim until it twisted, then they removed it and rode on the disk wheel until it also caved in, and they abandoned the car on the side of the road. They didn't notify me until four days later. I went to look at it and what do you think—the car was stripped clean. All the tires were gone and everything else of value. The boys promised to stand good for it but they haven't called me for two weeks. Should I go to their company commander about it, or the Colonel?"

Here's a howdy-do: the lady comes to an army camp, gives her car to G.I.'s to hell around in then wants to know the best way to go about getting them in dutch. Her bus came into view as she waited anxiously for my advice. Fearing she would pass up the bus rather than miss my response, I hastily advised: "Whenever in trouble speak to the Chaplain."

She boarded the bus without comment.

November 26, 1942.

My editorial in the *Double Deucer*: "What Price Thanksgiving."

It was obvious that Thanksgiving could not pass without an editorial about it in the *Double Deucer*. We thought up all kinds of ideas that would fit the occasion but somehow none seemed good enough. This Thanksgiving is different and the usual things that are said every year seem a little trite. It occurred to us to ask the boys in the regiment what they thought about it, so we got our notebook and pencil and went around interviewing. We talked to everyone from private to first sergeant, and even to a lieutenant.

To begin with everybody agreed that the turkey dinner was worthy of thanks; that Mrs. Mess Hall can do a pretty good job when she sets her mind to it. Several expressed regret at missing some good football games, but who knows—maybe next year. Most of the opinions, though, were on bigger issues. The modern soldier is a philosopher—or maybe only the men in this regiment.

We are well on the way to victory, was most commonly expressed, and there is plenty to be thankful for in that. We read about the way battles are being fought which shows that our leaders know what they are doing and can be relied on to use superior judgment. As soldiers we are not separated from the country at large, because civilians are as much a part of the war machine as we. There is just cause in our fighting; we are fighting to save from the ravages of diabolic monsters everything that is human and decent. These are the things that count most in the way we regard Thanksgiving this year. That is what the men of the 22nd Infantry Regiment had to say.

November 27.

They were waiting to go on guard mount.

"Who's going to make Colonel's Orderly tonight?" asked Pat.

"Why you are, Patty. Look at him there, all spiffed up."

He was, too; they all were, for that matter—uniforms pressed, shoes gleaming, ties clean and straight. All wanted to be Colonel's Orderly, a coveted post where all one has to do is sit in the Colonel's office during the evening and take phone messages. In addition he is reward-ed with a twenty-four hour off duty pass. 'Runt' Sterling, sitting on a footlocker in the corner commented: "Hell, I ain't been out of the guardhouse long enough to pull prison-chaser."

"Well when they ask who's been in the stockade within the last six months just yell out and they'll send you back."

"I'm glad Joe LaCarta isn't on tonight. That man shoots first and asks questions later."

"He must have been on last night then; remember there was a whole string of shots?"

"Oh that was only an old car backfiring."

The incident came freshly to mind; at about 2 A.M. a noise started sounding like a barrage of rifle fire. At that hour, and in an army camp, I was startled out of my sleep half-convinced that a real conflict was taking place outside.

"There goes the whistle, let's go," announced Pat. They made last minute adjustments to their uniforms and went out.

November 28, 1942.

Mandy was once a floral designer, but that was incidental to his main profession as athletic trainer in Houston, Texas. In the Army he quickly became accomplished in bayonet fighting and trench knifing and has gained recognition in the regiment as an authority. He and a lieutenant put on a demonstration for the Colonel. The lieutenant is a big brawny former wrestler. Mandy is small. They clashed first with trench knives. The lieutenant rushed at the diminutive corporal. Mandy stepped aside nimbly, stuck out his foot and the lieutenant sprawled on the mat.

"Did I hurt you, Sir? I'm sorry," said Mandy.

The lieutenant got up and rubbed himself. In their bayonet contest the lieutenant went through the set drill maneuvers starting from the Rest position, to on Guard, then Vertical Butt Stroke and so on. Mandy stood still a moment, then suddenly parried one of the orthodox blows with a quick upper motion and pushed the lieutenant in the chest with his hands, again sending him to the floor.

The Colonel walked over, picked up a billiard cue stick and put on a little demonstration of his own.

"Some of you officers go too much by the book," he said, "you've got to remember that in the final analysis a soldier will fight and think according to his own mind. All that the set drill does is get him accustomed to handling the bayonet."

November 29.

We were taken to eat "real southern cooking" at an exclusive board-inghouse in Augusta. Our hostess, an old, bewigged, rotund woman sat hunched in a square lounge chair, one of the many antique furnishings in the living room.

"Excuse my cold," she whispered in a low hoarse voice, "I guess my time is nearly up. I've lived too long already; I've seen too much, heard too much, and have done entirely too much talking."

There were other diners besides us, including two soldiers and their wives, a spinsterish beautician in the company of two elderly gentlemen who might have been bookkeepers in an aging business concern and a proletarian gent wearing a sweater who possibly manages the fruit counter in a large grocery store.

Soon the sliding doors were opened that separated us from the dining room. My companion and I went in and took the small table supplementing the round family-size table in the center. A colored maid brought out platters of food and passed them around. There was a choice of steak or pork chops, biscuits, fresh vegetable salad, sweet potato pone, and hotcakes. It was nicely served, but if an example of "true" southern cooking, nothing to write home about. The fried steak had an unsavory smell of lard grease. The coffee was very, very bad.

November 30, 1942.

Here we are, the indomitable Rolling Fourth, haunched on our backside in the midst of a great war waiting to be used. While waiting it is natural that some men marry, bring their wives to a neighborhood near camp and weave about themselves a quasi-normal mode of life, much as traveling salesmen establish homes though their journeyings are irregular and their wives never certain of their plans. All men in camp, largely confined within the pale, settle into a mold of their own manufacture that extra-duty interruptions fail to disturb.

Presently a basic training program is instituted for veterans and novices alike. The training proceeds on the theory that every man has just this day entered the Army and must be taught elementary lore. A lieutenant lectures on military courtesy.

"The hand salute originated in the Middle Ages," he recites, "when it was customary for knights in armor to raise their visors and stretch out a bare hand to show their peaceful intentions. Buckley, tell us, why do we render the hand salute?" he asks an old army man who in his hectic career has been a private, corporal, staff sergeant, private, private first class, sergeant, tech sergeant and private, in that order.

So it goes—tomorrow will be taken up with the rudiments of close order drill, and the day after with how to put on a gas mask.

December 1.

Harry Miller chewed the end of a cigar. The shuffle had left him in Headquarters Company where in a short time his presence among the men was profoundly felt.

"They finally got me in a uniform," laughed the forty-five year old recruit, "it's a good thing, too, or the fellows would never get out of bed in the morning. I pity them though, they're young and burning for romance. That stuff doesn't matter much to me anymore."

His grey head and pugilistic nose showed a marked resemblance to Louis Wolheim in the movie about World War I, *All Quiet On The Western Front*.

"Would I take an honorable discharge if it was offered to me? No sir. No sir, I would not, and I'm not an army man any more than you fellows. What would I do on the outside—say I was too old for the Army and they didn't want me?"

He exhaled a cloud of smoke. "When this is all over I have a nest egg that will last me for the next twenty years. After that I don't worry."

December 2, 1942.

Only Jack Zencheck could have thought up such an alibi for coming back a day late from three day leave.

"Why?" asked the First Sergeant.

"I forgot," said Jack.

"Huh?" asked the First Sergeant.

"I forgot," Jack repeated.

The Sergeant was not equipped to handle such a reason; he could quickly squelch a plea that the train from New York had come in late or he had suddenly become sick and couldn't travel for a day. But this one floored him and rather than admit his slow-wittedness by putting off his reaction till he could think up a suitable objection he merely grinned and let Jack go scot-free.

About his visit home Jack later observed, "Two years I'm in the

Army and still waiting for something to happen. I'm afraid to go home on furlough any more. People whose sons trained for six weeks and were shipped overseas look at me queerly as if to say, 'What! You're still in this country!'"

Then he launched into his usual satirical cadence, "When I become a civilian again I'll join the War Veterans and the American Legion. Every time there is a parade I'll be in there marching and bragging about how I was a soldier in the war. Only one thing I wouldn't have the nerve to do, and that is go on a march to Washington asking for a soldier's bonus."

December 3, 1942.

'Rip' Chandler is not known for deep concentration or severe mental exertion. He has, however, taken to a hobby "so my mind shouldn't go stale": poetry writing.

"What's your latest, Rip?" I asked.

"Just a second and I'll finish it," he replied, taking a piece of paper from his pocket. He scribbled the last two lines of his poem that had no title and showed it to me, as follows:

Hey it's great to be in the Army
Under a Georgia sky,
Oh I feel so hale and hearty
It almost makes me cry, Why—

I wake up in the morning,
Zip right out of bed,
Everyone's still snoring
Laying there like lead, I—

Yell out Squad AttenSHUN,
Where d'ya think you're at,
Any o'youse on pension?
Blow it out your hat, And—

It was great to be in the Army,
Just up until now, then
The boys said I'm getting snarty
So they hoop'n yupped how pow, WOW!

December 4, 1942.

Today is the 25th anniversary of the Fourth Infantry Division. Lt. General Ben ("Yoo-hoo") Lear, commander of the Second Army, dropped in by airplane for an inspection visit. He drove around in a command car, stopping here and there for a spot-check. He was particularly attentive to a company of the 22nd Infantry Regiment. He walked up to a private who stood in formation.

"What is your job?" he asked.

"I am a clerk in the orderly room, sir," replied the private unfazed by the three-starred power looming before him.

"Do you know why I ask you this?" continued the general.

"No Sir."

"Your face is white; you don't get any sun. Captain, see to it that this man goes out in the field a few days and gets some color in his face."

According to legend, General Lear is noted for snap judgment verdicts. He reputedly walked into a mess hall one day, noticed a spot of grease at the bottom of a cleaned pan and said to the mess sergeant, "You are now a private."

The anniversary had its benefit—after inspection the General declared a one day holiday. After he left he sent this telegram, "I am highly pleased at the results of the inspection. You have a splendid division. You are now ready for combat. I have a deep affection for you."

December 5.

"Did you hear?" said Jessie, "they're forming an Austrian infantry

battalion up in Indiana. Well, I'm going to try to get in; I have some
Austrian in me."

"What are you running away from? You know how sorry the fellows
are who struggled to transfer out of this outfit and succeeded."

"Yes, but this company I'm in is getting worse to live in. There is
a royal family running it; the First Sergeant is king. If you're not a
member, if you don't drink beer with the right people you are dirt
and can't get any consideration from the orderly room."

"That is true in every company, that's the Army."

"Yes, I guess so. Maybe we don't have it as bad as some companies.
But from now on I am going to fight for my rights even if I have to
run to the company commander and raise a stink twice a day."

"Now you're talking, but make sure you have a legitimate case."

December 6, 1942.

Case history of a suicide: last night he shot himself. He had somehow
gotten possession of a live round, and he leaned the butt of his
Springfield '03 rifle against the wall, the barrel pressing into his chest
as he pulled the trigger. The bullet went directly into his heart, killing
him instantly (another fellow once tried it—he thought the heart is
on the right side and only injured himself). He was a young boy,
twenty, who had enlisted at eighteen.

"He was high-strung, nervous and erratic," observed one who knew
him, "a good-looking kid from the hills of Tennessee. I'd bet a girl
had something to do with it."

His Army career had been marked with considerable company
punishment and one minor court-martial at which he drew eighteen
days in the guardhouse. The longer he remained stationed in garrison
the more restless and unstable he became. One can conclude that
given his age and temperament, he might better have survived on an
active fighting front where his self-destructive impulses would likely
become channeled against an enemy rather than against himself.

December 7, 1942.

All men on special duty—cooks, motor pool personnel, clerks—are
now receiving field instruction for an hour each day, from 4 to 5 P.M.

The reason, presumably, is that General Richardson, commander of the 7th Army Corps, returned from Australia with a recommendation from General Douglas MacArthur that every man should know how to handle every weapon in his own company. We are taking a refresher course in the M.T.P. (Mobilization Training Program) and have to absorb in one hour what the companies are getting all day. To assure a proper response, a regimental order provides that ordinary furloughs will be given only those passing a test. That we will see next week when some 14-day (!) Christmas furloughs are due to be handed out.

December 8, 1942.

For the first time at Camp Gordon, Georgia, I am participating in a regular field training schedule—even if it is for only an hour a day. But an hour can be a long time when it begins with the second lieutenant in command saying, "We haven't time for loosening up exercises," and we go right into deep knee-bending exercises and similar strenuous movements for fifteen minutes, followed by a period of close order drill: "Hup two three four Hup two three four To the rear-MARCH, Ca-dence, COUNT."

"From the looks of it," commented the lieutenant mechanically as though reciting from a textbook the prescribed speech for the occasion, "you need plenty of practice. Oil the bolts of your rifles so they won't stick tomorrow when you try to do Inspection Arms."

December 9.

"Everybody in the company is sore at each other," said Lanny, "half the men were restricted to the company area for three days because they took shortcuts on a six mile run and the other half didn't go on it. Several are restricted for being caught with their hands in their pockets; a good soldier never keeps his hands in his pockets, says the War Department."

"What are they kicking about," said Perry, "I got a letter from a fellow in Florida who was in basic training camp with me. Do you know what they are doing? They're jumping from a height of thirty feet into water wearing battle packs!"

The six-mile-an-hour run-walk course replaces the long hikes of last summer. Men in their thirties are making it, and one man who is forty. About eighty percent of a company is fully capable of keeping up consistently, but after the first few times many lack the incentive to maintain the pace. They feel justified in conserving their energy by lagging behind or trying to get out of making it at all.

December 10, 1942.

The windows were half-masted and the lights out as we got into bed. Said Sillene: "Play just one tune on your mouth organ, Carlos, and I'll go to sleep. Play me 'I'm Dreaming of a White Christmas.'"

"You can dream, Joe," responded Carlos in the darkness, "that's as close as you'll come to it."

"I hear civilians will not be allowed to travel over the holidays," said another.

"That's a lot of baloney; civilians have to travel as much as soldiers."

Spoke 'Chicken' Pyle from his corner, "Hey one time, when is this blink'n war going to be over? Don't they ever get sick of fighting over there?"

"What's the difference? So we'll have peace for twenty years and then go to war again. Why not just have war all the time?"

"That's not true; this time they'll fix things better."

"Well I disagree, I think they'll repeat, something like last time. Rothbart, you write in your journal that I said on this date in twenty years or so the same thing will happen and we'll find ourselves in war again."

Carlos played softly on his mouth organ the tune, "When The Lights Go On Again All Over The World."

December 11.

My editorial in the *Double Deucer*, titled: 20TH CENTURY INFANTRY:

David slew Goliath with a stone from a slingshot. He was an infantryman. So was Genghis Khan, who conquered more territory than any other ambitious warmonger to this day, including Napoleon. Napoleon was an infantryman, too. The point is that the backbone of our armed forces is still the infantry. No one doubts it is the infantry that will do our most important fighting, and the most dangerous, before the war is won. Airplanes, tanks and battleships can prostrate an enemy but it requires foot troops to put him out of action permanently and take possession of the area. Another thing about the infantry—it represents the American people in its diversity of population more truly than any other branch of the service. Our training to date in this regiment and division is a fine commentary on American methods. The soldier is given opportunities to advance as in few foreign armies. A few years ago Spain was in a situation somewhat similar to ours. Mussolini and Franco ganged up on it, and together with Hitler used it as a proving ground for Fascist weapons and tactics. The famous Fifth Column tactic was developed there. Just as the American Army today, the Loyalist Spaniards had to compose a citizen army in a hurry. One young American adventurer who went to fight with the Loyalists against the Fascists told how duties were distributed among the soldiers. They lined up, rifles were passed around, then machine guns, and whatever came to him determined a man's position in the squad. Likely as not the men were in battle a few hours after receiving the weapons. We know such conditions do not exist here. Our military leaders do not intend sending us into battle before training and weaponry is in our favor. We have cause for pride in the Army and the infantry.

December 12, 1942.

Like a busman on his day off, we strolled this Sunday on Sixth Avenue in camp. Sixth Avenue is fifteen blocks long. It begins at Tobacco Road, the original Tobacco Road made famous by the stage play of the same name, and extends to 33rd St. Cannon Company of the 22nd Infantry Regiment is located on the corner of Tobacco Road. Several members were playing touch football as we walked by. The sky was clear and the sun bright but it is definitely overcoat weather. We are after all only 700 odd miles south of New York and a similar distance north of Miami Beach. Personnel Headquarters at 21st St. was almost deserted though it is payroll-making time near the middle of the month. Regimental Headquarters on 25th St. marks the line separating the 22nd from the 12th Infantry Regiment. Here the street was active with jeeps. We saluted our first officer at the 12th's 1st Battalion

Headquarters building on 29th St. Further at the 8th Infantry Regiment we were mystified at seeing men outside in formation. At a signal, they hit the ground in unison with gusto. Perhaps they were putting on a special Sunday demonstration for visiting officers. At 32nd Street, Theater Number Two bustled at the ticket office for the 2:30 film showing of *Seven Days Leave* starring Victor Mature and Lucille Ball.

December 13.

An old aphorism advises "when in Rome do as the Romans do." To follow this advice I must now turn to thievery. I should sneak into a barracks at an unguarded moment or in dead of night and loot someone's footlocker for a pair of leather gloves. Next I'll have to remove a gas mask that hangs on a peg over somebody's bunk and hang it over mine. He needn't feel too badly though—he can duplicate my stunt. After that I should undo the straps of someone's haversack and snatch a raincoat, preferably size Medium. Then if all goes smoothly I have but to purloin one bath towel and swipe a cartridge of Schick injector razor blades for the score to be evened. These are the articles I have been involuntarily separated from in the last four months. The Statement of Charges I'll have to sign will come to $19.60 which, unless remedied in the manner herein specified, will be deducted from my Private's pittance.

December 14, 1942.

"What was President Wilson's first name?" asked the quizzer of me on a camp radio quiz program. Here I had an opportunity to make some money and my reputation for cleverness.

"Woodrow," I answered confidently.

"Wrong."

That's all. I was finished. No money, no cleverness, nothing. The correct answer is Thomas. Out of perhaps 497 persons I subsequently asked the question, at least 300 with a high school education or better, all answered Woodrow. I was the first on the program and the only one stymied. All other contestants won a few dollars by answering questions such as "Who wrote Beethoven's "Moonlight Sonata?" I am off any and all quiz programs for life (may it be a long one).

December 15, 1942.

Herb half-seriously considered placing a time bomb underneath the orderly room of his company. Rejecting that, he prospected his memory for the most incendiary curses he could heap on all concerned including the company commander. In salty terms he unburdened himself of bitterness toward the immediate scoundrels in the orderly room, the Army in general, the cursedness of fate, and the war. Finally he simmered down to: "What's the use, you can't fight city hall. You have to be a schemer in the Army or you'll always get screwed."

Herb had qualified for priority listing to receive a fourteen-day Christmas furlough. The orderly room capriciously changed him to the list receiving fourteen day New Year furloughs. The Christmas group left on schedule. Today the New Year furloughs were called off. Herb was left with nothing, unfairly short circuited by the orderly room which overlooked his priority qualification. I readily sympathize with him; I am exactly in the same boat.

December 16.

We crept and crawled in commando fashion, slithering like lizards through the white surface sand.

"Down, Down," prompted the young lieutenant, only he pronounced it "daown." "Keep those buttocks low or you'll by golly get them shot off.

"All right, enough of this. We'll now have thirty minutes of first aid. Don't confuse first aid with sanitation."

We were quite in the dark as to why he thought we would confuse the two.

"If you find a buddy who is wounded don't use YOUR first aid packet, use his. You might need yours later on for yourself."

His voice rose and fell in a choirboy crescendo. The Colonel came walking toward us, "AttenSHUN!" shouted the lieutenant as he wheeled around, sprinted swift as a jackrabbit toward the Colonel, halted six paces in front and saluted.

"These young lieuys," whispered a neighbor to my right, "I hear that all Boy Scouts over the age of fifteen are urged to accept an officer commission."

December 17, 1942.

Bzz-z-z—rumors in the wind—gathering evidence-bzz-z—substantiation—the crates that have been abuilding are soon to be distributed—bzz—clothing and equipment inspections—bz—SUPER clothing and equipment inspections—new life insurance—bring all service records up to date, the Colonel made a special visit to Personnel to advise clerks that the service records must be perfect and if they're not so when we reach the port of embarkation we will have to work day and night for perhaps two weeks up to the time the boat pushes off.

"This outfit will spearhead the Big Fight."

"I always said the Fourth will break the ice for the Real Battle when it comes."

"We will begin the Crushing Drive and that's why we've been held back so long."

Such are the comments on the present situation.

December 18.

"The platoon sergeant got himself all goofed off," commented Chuck, "he runs in, gets his men together and gives them a speech as if we are getting on the boat tomorrow. You should see how nice he talked to us. He's one of the noncoms everybody hates. All these guys are like that. They get meek as a lamb when it comes to a showdown. They try to get friendly with those they bullied for months."

"It really looks serious this time, doesn't it, Chuck."

"Kinda, though you can never figure the War Department. Funny how the mind works about things like going across. The boys want to go. They are tired of fighting the battle of Georgia."

There is frank fear yet a certain fascination at prospect of the ocean voyage and moving toward far-flung battle regions. Nobody seems able to picture himself in the thick of a fierce bloody battle. The mind refuses to believe he can in any way become a war casualty.

December 19, 1942

Former Bronx haberdasher Ben Peterson, in the Army one year, is a member of one of the new tank destroyer outfits.

"You've read about this secret weapon we used against Rommel in Africa," said Ben, "well, it's all that it's cracked up to be. I know—I operate one and have taken it apart and put it together."

According to newspaper reports it is a gun mounted on a full-track that operates by a revolutionary air pressure mechanism.

"We work with the infantry," continued Ben, "and when the Germans send tanks against you they won't know what hit them. We are everywhere once we spot tanks. We just returned from a 128-mile hike. It took us seven days, through cold, mud and rain. In our battalion we have to know something about everything. I've been taught to shoot cannons, antiaircraft guns, rifles, Tommy guns and heavy machine guns."

December 20.

Hail to the spirit of Christmas but when, oh, when will this holiday season end! There is a plague of packages from home, a kill-with-kindness inquisition of nutcake, fruitcake, sponge, layer cake, devil-food cake, angel cake, chocolates, mints. Each day the packages are set beneath the Christmas tree that Jack Zencheck had erected with elaborate trimmings in the Day Room (Zencheck Hall) between the magazine stand and ping-pong table. Jack passes out the packages at noon. They are opened one at a time, the contents passed around and consumed. The first, second, third and fourth helpings fill the void nicely, left by a skimpy lunch in the mess hall. After that—and you can't refuse—the stuff turns to acid resulting in heartburn and other acute gastronomical disturbances. This has been going on for two weeks. Praise the Lord and pass the baking soda.

December 21, 1942.

It was quieter than usual in the Day Room. The coal stove glowed red with heat. "Indian Joe" Dashner (he is one-fourth Indian) measured a combination on the billiard table and plunged forward his cue stick. The cue ball missed badly and jumped clear over the table.

"You couldn't hit a bull in the back with a banjo," commented Pete Loder wryly.

In turn he resined the tip of his stick and aimed carefully. The ball missed the pocket by a fraction and spent its force ricocheting several times from one side to another.

"How can I hit anything with that radio dial turning to a different station every second—hey Zeek, how about getting just one program on?"

Zeek settled on a hillbilly program.

"Come take my love, here is my heart—" yodeled a female voice.

"Ouch! 'Come take my love,'—they're all the same, these hillbilly songs," moaned Pete.

"You hain't got the sense to carry your guts to a hungry bear," retorted Zeek peevishly, ending the inter-cultural exchange.

The door opened and in walked a group returning from a beer session at the PX. The room began bustling with noise and activity, the radio now inaudible so the program immaterial. Pete and Indian Joe did not finish their game. The men surrounded both pool tables, and on each a half-dozen billiard balls bounced randomly off one another on the green velvet.

December 22, 1942.

Private Hedge was picked up as a deserter and remanded to the custody of camp authorities. He was tried and found guilty because there was no other choice. He could furnish no shred of evidence to back up his story that he had extended his weekend pass for the reason that he was hot on the trail of saboteurs. True, he had wired the Army for funds to finance the alleged pursuit and wonder of wonders the Army sent him fifteen dollars, presumably because he was known as a man who always tread the straight and narrow. Something in him must have snapped. Weeks passed and no sign of Private Hedge. His self-authorized leave ended in the maw of a barroom brawl, nailed by the ubiquitous Military Police. Since entering the stockade letters have been forwarded to him by his company. Each letter that arrived was addressed in a fine feminine handwriting and successively advanced his rank from private, pfc, corporal, sergeant. Today a letter arrived addressed to "Master Sergeant Hedge (congratulations)."

December 23, 1942.

The staff sergeant has attracted much attention since he joined the regiment a few weeks ago. He had been in the Japanese air raid of Pearl Harbor last December and had fired a fifty-caliber machine gun at the attacking Rising Sun airplanes.

"Did you hit anything?" was the first question asked.

"I don't know," he replied, "I don't think so. They came over mighty fast, bombing and strafing. You have to judge their speed and shoot far enough in front of them so your bullets hit the right spot at the same instant as the plane."

"What does it feel like being in combat?"

"I was scared some; I saw two of my friends killed nearby, and maybe that's why I want to be in more of it. This stuff around here isn't for me. I want to be where the action is."

Therefore he is applying for a transfer to Parachute School. He had come back to the States in the first place in order to attend Infantry Officer Candidate School.

"I had just ten days left before being commissioned an officer," he said regretfully, "but I went into town, drank a little too much and that finished me."

December 24.

One night several weeks ago I was stopped on the street near my barracks by a private who swayed dizzily under the influence of liquor. In his hands he held two gigantic sticks of what looked like dynamite.

"How do I get to the Hospital Road?" he inquired.

"What you got there?" I asked.

"Firecrackers."

I would have forgotten the incident though it seemed mighty strange that anyone would be playing with fireworks this time of year, especially in an army camp where any explosion is taken for the real thing, but since then every night has been like the Fourth of July.

One went off last night that whistled like an artillery shell then burst with a loud detonation into a blaze of light. What goes on here!

December 25, Christmas Day.

Today no one works except the mess hall crew and men on details. Jack Zencheck volunteered to be Charge of Quarters considering the holiday is less for him than for Christians. Last night, Christmas Eve, only Nat Davis hung up a stocking. On awaking this morning he looked in it and found an empty bottle of bourbon. Everybody slept late. All week we had been getting up two and a half hours early, at 5, because part of the company had to do so for their schedule at the rifle and machine gun range. The holiday noon meal measured up well to the Thanksgiving dinner, which was very good. Both times we had turkey, and together with the other courses our fare was every bit the equal of the officers'. "You'd better do a good job on it," I said to our mess sergeant, "I gave up a fourteen day furlough to eat this meal."

December 26, 1942.

No store in Augusta had the watch my friend and I were looking for except an obscure combination pawn and clothing shop in a honky-tonk section of Broad Street. It was a cheap round ("onion") pocket watch; it is not prudent to soldier with an expensive watch. In pre-war days it high-pressure sold for 95 cents. Now we had to pay $1.95 ("we was robbed"). The shop was antique in atmosphere if not in merchandise, which consisted mostly of bargain-basement type bric-a-brac. The proprietor reminisced to us of the time he left his native habitat to see the world—as much as could be seen mainly from the porthole of an ocean freighter. He hadn't talked long when he looked toward the door and saw, leaning on a counter and smiling, a stocky silver-haired sailor garbed in the uniform and gold insignia of a chief petty officer with many hash stripes on his sleeve. The two men looked at each other, then effusively greeted one another.

"Hey there you old salt," bubbled the pawnbroker, "how long is it now that you are in the Navy?"

"Twenty-eight years, and I've been recalled twice from retirement," chuckled the sailor. The two Augustans had many tales to exchange.

December 27, 1942.

The Second Army is divided into corps, each with about 120,000. We are in the 7th Corps, which is presently conducting a limited program of physical fitness tests that resemble intramural racing contests. A portion of the parade ground is set off for the purpose and arranged as a modified obstacle course. A number of men are drawn from different companies each day and put through the paces. A loudspeaker blares instructions and the results of every contest. "Corps" men stand by with whistles, notebooks and pencils. The tenor of popular opinion about it is mildly uncomplimentary: "What are they doing, trying to prove we have an athletic army?"

"I did this stuff twenty years ago."

"It is a foolish waste of time."

Here's hoping there is a valid purpose aside from trying to keep everybody busy.

December 28.

Soldiers must sing! Singing is the order of any day, a standard military function. At every plausible opportunity song sheets are passed out and singing commences. Not that the men mind, except for a few who superciliously look at it as a juvenile endeavor by boy-leaders to boost the morale of grown men by inducing them to give forth unspontaneously in song. As a means of enhancing their refinement, it is unnecessary. The average American soldier is the best mannered gentleman in the world. Last night's demonstration proved it. We were returning from Augusta. We got off at the camp station and boarded the huge shuttle trailer. As usual it filled slowly and we had to wait until it became packed. A drunken soldier came aboard. He was mean. He jostled several men, tried to fight with everyone trying to board, pushed three or four hard enough that they fell to the ground. Yet realizing his condition not one of the two dozen or more men he had given cause to do so struck back at him. It was a beautiful study in patience and tolerance for a fellow soldier who knew not what he was doing. In like spirit the soldiers humor the Army's order to sing.

December 29, 1942.

There is no doubt about it—whoever is in the infantry, hikes. I, a clerk, just returned from a marathon nine-mile hike carrying full field pack. We made in two and a half hours the distance usually covered in three and a half. I was winded at the end of the first mile but soon got my second wind, then third, then fourth, fifth, sixth, seventh. Before my seventh wind gave out we arrived back at home base. We had kept up a brisk walking pace and no double-time. We had no breaks. No one fell out—it was too cold, you either keep moving or freeze. "Pick 'em up and lay 'em down," chanted the veterans of many a hike. And so we did.

December 30.

The whole division went by truck to the Artillery Impact Area and assembled for an all day demonstration in elements of warfare we had not previously witnessed. We watched dive bombers in action, strafing and bombing. The Field Artillery showed what they do with 105-millimeter guns, and 155s. We sat atop a hill at a safe distance from "no man's land." The shells were fired over our heads; we heard them swish by as the artillery batteries fired, salvos and volleys. It was a great spectacle. There before us we saw an actual battlefield with acres and acres of ground under a concentrated barrage of deadly shrapnel. It seemed not an inch of ground was missed and every living creature must have perished. When such a barrage ceases the infantry advances and none is there to say him nay.

December 31.

Several officers had taken turns in speaking over the public address system at the demonstration. The General made a little speech too. He said this would be the last time the whole division will be together in an assembly in this country.

"You will soon be on boats," he announced, "and I want you to know what you are in for. Crowded shipping space will cause the trip to be very bad. It will be uncomfortable, filthy and smelly. You can expect the worst, and I think you all understand why this must be. The purpose of this demonstration is to show how the Infantry works as a team with the Artillery and Air Corps. Learn not to be afraid when your artillery batteries fire over your heads. And learn to recognize your own airplanes so you won't shoot at them when they try to help you."

He left hardly a trace of doubt that now the division will truly be going to a port of embarkation, and to war.

January 10, 1943.

Developments during the past ten days have been breathtaking. Insofar as our division is concerned this camp became a staging area where all final preparations are made for embarking overseas. We were inoculated with stimulating doses of antitoxins. We were ordered to begin using an APO (Army Post Office) numbered return address, to make our wills, assign a personal power of attorney and tidy up other personal affairs in anticipation of a long absence. Then packing—everybody packed something, guns in cosmoline (grease), machinery in crates. We got rid of superfluous items and requisitioned equipment we were short. Finally everyone had to sign an embarkation form. That cinched it, until the dramatic anticlimax two days ago when instead of being whisked aboard a ship waiting with full steam up as anticipated, suddenly all preparation froze in suspension. What subtle plan or maneuver had we here? This I suspect will forever remain a mystery. Today an order came down: the issuing of routine passes and furloughs may now be resumed.

January 11.

Things were quiet today as though nothing unusual had occurred. Still the atmosphere lay heavy with expectation; surely it hadn't all been just a game, spoke and thought everybody. No orders were given to unpack. The filled crates were temporarily stored wherever most convenient and out of the way. At the same time schedules were drawn to proceed with normal training programs. On the other hand word leaked out that certain authorities were mapping plans for another division to move in when ours moves out. During the period of intensive preparation the whole city of Augusta seemed to know everything that went on. As each phase of activity began any civilian could have explained in detail what was going on with the division, often before the soldiers knew themselves. Meanwhile I am a little feverish, and have been for a week, from three typhoid antitoxin injections administered at short intervals. To date the Army has pen-e-trated my epidermis with a total of thirteen inoculations. My left arm is like a pincushion.

January 12.

This time my furlough will be designated ordinary instead of emergency. I am allowed seven days starting Tuesday. Now comes the sweating-out period; seven days is very brief for a north-bound soldier having to travel on war-congested railroads. A little scheming might help; scheming for self-interest is informally regarded as a credit to a soldier, marking him as aggressive and resourceful if he comes up with a ploy that harms no one and also providing he gets away with it. I approached the First Sergeant.

"Requesting a favor," I said, "I'd like to be excused from reveille Monday morning." He knew exactly what I meant to do.

"Okay, if you can get off from work at the office," he granted. I assured him this would be no obstacle. Now I can extend my furlough to begin Saturday afternoon instead of Tuesday, at least theoretically. First I must overcome several other conditions and roadblocks before it will materialize, and I won't be sure until I'm on the way.

January 13, 1943.

Contrary to an impression one may have of army life, soldiers do not cringe before men of higher rank. The lowly private, seasoned and tempered by hard knocks, does not flinch before his platoon sergeant's reproofs and certainly not at his corporal's. Sam Bevins had been an early draftee. As a soldier he developed proficiency in using weapons, in field activities and squad tactics. He feared no man and asserting his independence in the manner he did assured him the permanent rank of private. He catered to no one. At a formation one day the first sergeant was giving a pep talk. When he finished a sound came from the lines known as a Bronx cheer—the mock quacking of a duck. He walked over and said in a mildly ruffled voice, "Bevins, was that you making that noise?"

"Yes," replied Sam without a quaver.

"What makes you do that, is it a nervous condition?"

"No, I like to do it."

The first sergeant walked away without further comment.

"It wasn't me," Sam remarked, "but if he wants to accuse me that's up to him; let him find out different for himself."

There were no repercussions; one fearless sharp-tongued soldier had had words with another, that was all.

January 26, 1943.

The train steamed out of Pittsburgh's Union Depot downtown, traveled through East Liberty, Edgewood, Greensburg, Altoona, Washington D.C., each scene slipping by like changing movie sets.

"How fast do you reckon we're going?" asked a talkative draft-exempted young man.

"Huh? Oh, it's nine o'clock," I responded tactfully in an effort to deter him from conversing further with me. My furlough was over and I was busy reflecting—had it been worthwhile? Hardly, I concluded. The war notwithstanding, the city struck me as so peaceful and genteel, a place of serenity to which I dream of returning after the war but now so unsettling while there is so much yet to be done.

January 27.

With all that has been written about the progress of the war, I never read anything that indicated the Allies would have an easy time of wresting control from the Nazis of all Africa. Yet that has practically been accomplished. The small portion of Tunisia still held by the Germans is in a similar isolated position that Singapore was in last year before she fell to the Japanese. In the last few days Roosevelt and Churchill have been meeting at a hotel in Casablanca, North Africa. The results of their conference will become known to the public by deeds accomplished rather than by verbal bombast. Accordingly, the future strategy of the Allies will probably be far afield from the predictions made by nonmilitary observers just as they were off about the conquest of Africa.

January 28, 1943.

If it seems futile to speculate about broad war strategy, it is equally so in local matters. Here is our division in near suspended animation, the usual channels of personnel turnover—such as Officer Candidate Schools—frozen. Are we about to go to war or aren't we? We have no basis for judging. To our knowledge no unit is ever handled in quite the same way as any other. Collaterally we rarely hear of divisions being dispatched to ports of embarkation and sent overseas as intact units. They are broken up, some fragments put aboard ship, others scattered to camps around the country.

February 14, 1943.

"Hey there, what'cha celebrating?" said Len Hunter (I was only drinking orange pop).

"One year in the Army, Len."

"Hm-m; next week will be the end of my second. I'm still here, waiting for action. What's the latest?"

"Beats me, what's your guess?"

"Well, there's talk of maneuvers in March or April, or May."

"Could be."

"The news on the radio is good. I just heard that the Russians recaptured Rostov and Voroshilovgrad. They'll soon be heading for Berlin."

"Not so fast, Len, and you know it."

"Yes, there will be terrible butchery before the Germans are licked. It will take hard fighting with hundreds of thousands of Americans battling on foreign soil. I am ready. I fervently hope I will be sent over, You can't leave the fighting to someone else if you want to have a say in how the peace is settled after it is over, and I want plenty to say about that."

"Okay, Len—Let's Go!"

"Well, gotta hit the hay. My company is firing on the range tomorrow and I'm on the target pit detail. See you later."

"Yeh, so long."

Portrait of Private David Rothbart taken while on his first furlough in Pittsburgh, August 24, 1942. This was the first time that his family saw him in uniform. Soldiers on their first furlough usually had their portraits taken dressed in OD's (Orderly Dress uniform which includes necktie). *Author's collection.*

Family portrait (left to right) Pearl, Jacob, and Sergeant David Rothbart, taken just before David embarked for England, January 10, 1944. *Author's collection.*

Basic Training, Camp Wheeler, Georgia, April 1942. A platoon of new recruits prepares to march with full field pack. *Author's collection.*

Pvt. David Rothbart posing with his Springfield '03 rifle at Camp Wheeler, Georgia, April 1942. Platoons were assembled for marching drill in combat uniform. The drill included the Manual of Arms, short order drill, and marching in formation. Note the use of puttees as part of the uniform. *Author's collection.*

Pvt. Rothbart sitting outside his barracks at Camp Wheeler, Macon, Georgia, April 1942. *Author's collection.*

Sergeant David Rothbart visiting Torquay, Devonshire, England, March 19, 1944. He was stationed in England for five months. David found Torquay, located near his base camp, to be an attractive resort town, one of many that overlooked the English Channel. Soldiers from the camp would visit Torquay when on weekend leave. *Author's collection.*

PERSONNEL SECTION, 22nd Infantry Regiment, Huberville, France, July 1944 From left to right:

First Row: Stephen Mamrosh, Roy Ippolito, Edward Ryan, Roland Rice, Generoso Senarchia, Paul Dellecese, David Jaffee, Jacob Epstein, James Cesaro, Leo Gorelick.

Second Row: John Gahl, Nicholas Boccalino, Clyde Phillips, Walter Humm, Sam Stringfellow, John Seabright, Pat Akins, Paul Limkemann, Frank Rule, William Bonebrake, Donald Fahy.

Third Row: William Hyde, John Lysiak, Carlos Rodriguez, Jackson Pastor, Arthur Stoots, Horace Stevens, Roy Cagle, Homer Bagley, Lt. Robert G. Hoehn, John Powers, John Cooper, Jack Magee, Capt. J. Herbert Brill, Leo Levine, Gerald Van Walbeck, Edward Rosenbaum, Howard Jameson, Henry Prytula, William Dyer, Phillip R. Henderson, Paul Bozyk, Harold R. Zolldan, Clayton White, Joseph Williamson, Sol Romaner, David Rothbart, Douglas Hamer. *Author's collection.*

with it. I approached the 1st sergeant. "Requesting a favor," I said, "I'd like to be excused from Reveille Monday morning." He knew what I meant. "Okay," he granted, "if you can get off from work at the office." I assured him that this was no obstacle. As it stands, then, I can theoretically now extend my furlough to start Saturday afternoon instead of Tuesday. There are several other conditions, ifs, ands and buts that have to be overcome before this materializes. The sweating out will be an intense nervous strain till the last moment, and possibly not worth-while.

Jan. 13. 1943

Contrary to a popular impression of army life, soldiers do not cringe before men of higher grade. The lowly Private, seasoned and tempered by hard knocks, does not flinch at his platoon sergeant's jibes, and certainly not at his corporal's. Sam Bevins was an early draftee. As a soldier, he developed proficiency in using weapons, in field duties and in squad tactics. He feared no man, and by asserting his spirit of independence, dealt to himself the rank of perennial Private. He catered to no-one. At a formation one day, his 1st sergeant was giving a pep-talk. When he was finished, a sound was heard from the lines like a Bronx cheer - a mock quacking of a duck. The sergeant walked over later and said in a slightly ruffled tone of voice, "Bevins, was that you making that noise before?" "Yes," replied Sam without a tremor. "What makes you do that - is it a nervous condition?" "No. I like to do it." The 1st sergeant walked away. "If wasn't me," Sam spoke, "but if he wants to accuse me, that's his business, and let him find out different for himself." There were no repercussions. One sharp, fearless soldier had had words with the other. That was all.

Jan. 26. 1943

The train steamed out of Union Depot, past down-town, East Liberty, Edgewood, Greensburg, Altoona, Washington, slipped

(158)

by like changing movie scenes. How fast do you reckon we're going?" asked a talkative young draft-exempt clod. "Huh? Oh, it's 9:00 o'clock." The furlough was over, and — was it worth-while? Hardly. War or no war, the city appeared extremely civilian and peaceful. It is hardly fair to shock a soldier thus, to dispell the serenity of his rationalizations toward his part in the war by placing him so that he directly faces the life to which he aspires and dreams of returning.

Jan. 27, 1943

With all the commentaries and predictions that are written as regards the progress of the war, I have never read anything that hinted at the possibility of an easy conquest by the Allies over all of Africa. Yet, that has practically been accomplished. The small portion of Tunisia that Germany still holds is in a similar position today that Singapore was in last year right before she fell to the Japs. In the past few days, Roosevelt and Churchill met in a hotel in Casablanca, north Africa. The results of that conference will be translated and become known to the public by deeds accomplished, rather than by reels of bombast. Accordingly, the future strategy of the Allies will probably be far off the path of predictions made hitherto, just as was the relatively easy invasion of Africa.

Jan. 28. 1943.

If it seems futile to speculate on broad war strategy, it is equally so with local affairs. Here is our division, in a state of near suspended animation. The usual channels of personnel turn-over, such as Officers Candidates Schools, have been frozen. Are we about to go to war or aren't we? There is no precedent by which to judge. No organization, to our available knowledge, has ever been handled in quite the same way as any other. On the other hand, we have rarely heard of any divisions

(159)

Two V-Mail letters written by David to his family in Pittsburgh. David would type his V-Mail letters whenever he had access to a typewriter. Most of his V-Mails, like those of other soldiers, were hand written. V-Mail letters were written on special sheets designed to be photographed and transferred to microfilm for bulk shipping. Note the censor's stamp in the upper left hand corner. *Author's collection.*

Paris, France, August 29, 1944, in front of Notre Dame Cathedral. Left to right: Captain Herbert Brill, Sgt. John Cooper, Corporal Bill Dyer, and Sgt David Rothbart. The entry for August 29, reads: "Captain Brill, John Cooper, Bill Dyer, and I got into a jeep and went to look for the Regimental Command Post in Paris. Someone happened to bring along a camera and we took some pictures. 'Paree' is very gay and the women ooh, la, la!!!"
Courtesy J. Herbert Brill

Spa, Belgium, October 1944. Five members of the 22ND Infantry Regiment
Personnel Section: David Rothbart on the left, John Seabright on right.
Author's collection.

Classification Staff, Personnel Department, 22nd Infantry, December 1944, Luxembourg. Left to right: Phil Henderson, assistant, David Rothbart, head of personnel section, John Gaul, assistant. Rothbart recalled, "Shortly after this picture was taken, shortages of personnel caused my two assistants to be sent as replacements to the regular combat companies and I remained the only classification specialist." *Author's collection.*

Sergeant David Rothbart in Mondorf, Luxembourg, December 1944. During the Battle of the Bulge, David's unit was forced to evacuate the town. The German army briefly occupied Mondorf, terrorizing the populace. When David's unit returned, the people of Mondorf were greatly relieved. Never a cigarette smoker, David developed a taste for cigars while in the army. Shortly after his discharge he quit after discovering it was the smell of cigars that he enjoyed and not the smoking experience itself. He briefly toyed with the idea of inventing a machine that would smoke the cigars for him. *Author's collection.*

Postcard of Stavelot, Belgium, sent at the height of the Battle of the Bulge. Stavelot was a strategic town in the Ardennes. David's letter reads: "Dear Everybody: You no doubt read of this town in Belgium (Stavelot). There was quite a battle and the Germans re-took it temporarily about 3 or 4 days after I left. I had gotten to know many of the townsfolks, some very well, well enough for the first time in this war (except for bombing in England), to be personally apprehensive concerning their welfare. Am well. Regards to all. Dave." *Author's collection.*

David Rothbart at the reunion of
the 22nd Infantry Regiment Society
in Cleveland, Ohio, October 2000.

PART TWO

Overseas

January 18, 1944, Tuesday.

At 3:30 A.M. we boarded the twenty-seven thousand ton British ship, "His Majesty's Transport" *CapetownCastle*. This converted luxury liner, built in 1938, used to run regularly between London and Capetown, South Africa. It was startling to find ourselves suddenly under the jurisdiction of British seamen, sailing under the Union Jack. But then everything else was startling, though we had known pretty well what to expect. We stepped off the Hoboken Ferry onto a pier near W. 14th Street, New York City. Each carrying a large green duffel bag and full field equipment, we were processed through the port in a few minutes including (just like in the movies) a quick serving of doughnuts and hot coffee by sentimental Red Cross women volunteer workers. I lugged my burden of pack and bag up a gangplank at midship, glancing left and right in appraisal of the ship that was to carry me to—Iceland? England? Asia? Its length and bulk were reassuring. I was directed to a compartment on "B" deck deep in the interior of the vessel, approximately amidship. Not until 11:30 A.M. were the ship's moorings cast off and we made out to sea. Through a porthole I could see the Statue of Liberty as we sailed past. After nearly two years of soldiering in anticipation of shipping overseas, it was difficult to realize that this was now taking place. It was a peculiar, if passive, emotional experience.

January 19.

A year ago the General told us about conditions to expect aboard ship. He spoke of crowding, discomfort and smelliness. He did not exaggerate in the least. Only a few of us are as yet affected by seasickness but most have felt a mild nausea which threatened to develop into that notorious malady.

"Keep the men busy and there will be less seasickness," said my company commander. "It is mainly a matter of the mind. Those who lay around and sleep all the time are the most likely to succumb."

I agree with him. The air below decks is usually foul. Three hundred and sixty-one men live in my small compartment which is at once a mess hall and sleeping quarters. Above the tables we hang up hammocks attached to ceiling hooks at night. They are close together, almost touching one another. To reach the tiny latrine one stoops low, but cannot avoid brushing against each hammock as he walks. Thus, a light sleeper may be aroused often during the night with varying degrees of pressure brushing against his bottom. We eat out of our mess kits. It takes us ten minutes to eat a meal and two hours to clean up afterward. Only two meals a day are served, but under the circumstances it is a relief it isn't three. Tempers all around are short, and supervision over the men is not easy to maintain. Our company has the detail of providing the guards in nearby corridors and outside decks of the ship. The best assignment I could achieve was that of latrine guard for a few hours to keep the long waiting line in order.

January 20, 1944.

The fire bell rang and we went out on deck for the "Abandon Ship" drill which we have every day about noon. At all times except sleeping we wear life jackets and have suitable clothing on hand so we are ready any time the fire bell may ring. Within ten minutes all United States troops were outside on one of the four decks. We stood there for two hours while ship and troop officers inspected our quarters below. The sea appeared restless and the waves quite high, but not unusually so, said a passing British sailor. The many other ships in the convoy were scattered around us in all directions as far as the eye can see. They are of many sizes and types. We seem to be well protected. I saw two aircraft carriers, a corvette, a destroyer and a battleship—or it may have been a cruiser. Everything—sky, ships, sea—looked the color of lead. Our ship rolled evenly for the most part but occasionally took a low dip just before an exceptionally high wave lifted the bow high and set her down again. Some of the other ships seemed to be rocking violently. The seagulls which followed us out to sea have long since left us and the pattern of scenery was broken only by the brief appearance of a school of black porpoises.

January 21.

Our crammed compartment in the stern of the ship is in marked contrast to the quarters occupied by our officers. They live in the luxurious first-class staterooms that civilian passengers had formerly occupied. There is little evidence that their part of the ship had been converted to war needs. They have a lavishly furnished lounge and smoking room, and their mess hall is grand in the most fashionable sense. In all fairness it must be added that Lt. Col. Williams gave us a talk as follows: "We are not going high-hat on you, men. This is a British ship and we have to go according to their ways." This apologetic attitude is not rare among the officers. In addition, they are detailed to have at least one of them in our compartment at all times to see that everything is clean and orderly, and otherwise to look out for the enlisted troops. Not all the enlisted men have conditions as bad as ours. One company has the swimming pool and gymnasium where tiers of bunks had been installed with an eye to comfort. They eat in a separate mess hall out of plates instead of mess kits. Some others were similarly fortunate, but the majority live like as. It is hard to find a place to sit. Men sleep on the floor of lobbies in the better part of the ship without permission, and unceremoniously flop anywhere else oblivious to noise, lights, dampness, or men walking over and around them. I was fortunate last night in taking possession of a couch to sleep on in the lobby adjoining the officers' mess, after I found there was a shortage of hammocks in my assigned quarters.

January 22, 1944.

The fifth day out and "all's well." The sea is fairly calm. An occasional bird is still seen though we are well out to sea. I saw a few flying fish gliding several feet above the water for about twenty yards. I got my "sea legs" and am hardly aware of the ship's rolling. Chow is fairly good, especially the afternoon meal. A commercial canteen supplies us with Coca-Colas, candy and cookies, still honoring American money as exchange. By now everyone has explored the ship and is pretty well acquainted with her from bow to stern. It is immense, reputedly the twelfth largest commercial passenger liner afloat. It is a "motor vessel" powered by a diesel engine.

We are kept abreast of world news by means of two radio broadcasts a day, one British in the morning and in the afternoon an American. At the latest, Russia has at last broken the long German siege of Leningrad and captured the rail junction at Novgorod which separates Germany from her ally Finland. Not much is heard of Russia's southern winter offensive which was recently reported as having cut off and surrounded huge German forces.

In Italy, Allied amphibious troops have landed thirty-eight miles from Rome, which is thirty miles north of the battle going on at Cassino. Great Allied air raids are constantly waged against Berlin and the French invasion coast opposite the English channel. And slow, steady progress is being made against Japanese forces in New Guinea.

January 23, 1944.

The ship's loud speaker announced, "All Company E man report to their compartment to receive shots." We reported and marched to the hospital on C deck for our third, final typhus inoculation in as many weeks, the previous two received at the overseas staging area, Camp Kilmer. These are among the most painful of shots, burning like anti-tetanus. They are not entirely unwelcome considering reports that a typhus epidemic has hit Italy but not affected the inoculated Allied troops fighting in the south.

Corporal "Goldy," Special Services entertainment director, has organized the ukelele, accordion, mouth-organ and violin players and send them troubadoring through the ship at scheduled times to help keep up morale. "But hell, they keep moving around, in and out, playing cards," vociferated Goldy, "so half the time we don't know if we are putting on a show or just making noise. Tonight we are playing at the hospital. They won't be moving around much there; at least we'll have one audience we're sure of!"

January 24.

Where the crest of the waves curls and dissolves into spraying whitecaps, and when the ship's motion sends an aggressive wave whirling backward into its own wash, the water often changes color from leaden to a whitish-blue hue. This, clarified one who knew something of the sea, is due to a phosphorous reaction of the brine to the stimulus of motion. It is especially colorful by moonlight. Each soldier gazes at the sea, at the other ships of the convoy, and perhaps wonders how he can go "over the hill" now. He ponders the vast expanse of water, the distance to the nearest shore, and even an habitual over-the-hiller must conclude that such an attempt would be unwise. He speculates on the depth of the ocean and of the species of marine life that may be found under the waves. Whatever the variety, he perceives that Neptune of Greek mythology fame has much to rule over in this great liquid domain. Then his reveries turn practical and he considers, for the hundredth time, whether he would have been better or worse off in the Navy or Merchant Marine. Brooding thus, he is touched on the arm by a fellow soldier and informed, "You are wanted below to do your turn at washing the pans."

January 25, 1944.

We don't know where we are going but we will all be very much astonished if we do not land in the British Isles. For one thing we have been issued booklets on how to get along with the British. In it we are forewarned of what will quickly offend the folks of Britain, and what is regarded as good, commonplace etiquette. One mention seems especially poignant, the fact that in World War I England lost one million men killed in combat compared with our sixty thousand. This to refute the often-heard canard that "the English will fight to the last American," expressed by a small element of Anglophobes among my fellow soldiers. Their criticism would be acceptable if confined to British foreign diplomacy or other aspects of honest controversy rather than snide prejudice. Maybe direct contact with the British people will change their tone.

January 26.

"You are a unique lot," quoth an English sailor in what my limited experience took to be a cockney accent. "You fellows are all cheerful and don't seem to give a damn."

"I guess that's because most of us have been in the Army long enough to develop a good thick crust," responded one of our group, and continued brightly, "When you know you are going into battle and may die or get crippled are you better off beforehand to be morbid or happy and pretend you are on a pleasure trip?"

The sailor smiled thinly and said, "You might like to know that one of our escort vessels picked up the trail of German U-boat submarines last night on radar. We had to change our course to try throwing them off." He casually studied our faces to see what effect his words would create.

If he expected consternation he was mistaken, for only a detached interest was shown and someone remarked, "I wouldn't mind seeing a little action. It's awfully boring here. I'd like to see them drop those 'ash-cans' in the water and throw around a few shells."

January 27, 1944.

Two points of land were barely visible off to starboard. That would be beyond a doubt the north coast of Ireland. Now we may consider ourselves as having arrived at the other side of "the pond." Distance, space is but an illusion for all we did was merely step onto a big boat, like stepping into a subway; we slept a little, read some and covered nearly four thousand miles with only an occasional awareness of balancing on a seesaw. The "dry canteen" is now closed as announced twenty-four hours in advance of docking. It is nearly sold out anyway. I bought one of the last boxes of chocolate bars, perhaps the last I will have for a long time if stories of rigid rationing in England are true and such luxuries as "sweets" particularly rare. Some men bought as many boxes of chocolates as they could carry for the sole purpose of endearing themselves to the townsfolk they meet.

January 28, 1944.

"Over there is Belfast," pointed a youth standing beside me on deck, "you can't quite see it but I recognize the landmarks."

"How do you know where we are? Those cliffs look pretty bare to me," I disputed.

"Oh I've been here before; it's unmistakable, look how green the water is," he joshed, "and the Irish potato shapes to our right."

Walking across ship to the port side, I made out the Scottish shoreline. It was clear on the map that we had passed the breach of Scotland where the Firth of Clyde cuts in and then caught up with it again. We are now coursing through the placid and indeed greenish waters of the narrow channel separating Ireland from Scotland and heading toward the Isle of Man and the Irish sea. At this rate we should reach the port of Liverpool in a few hours.

January 29.

We tied up to the dock about 3:00 P.M. after being piloted through a buoy-marked channel in the estuary and river leading to Liverpool. We were permitted to remain on deck during the complicated steering operation bringing us into the harbor. We looked with great interest at the scene spread before us of one of the world's great seaports. The city beyond the waterfront showed itself in distinct detail. It gave an impression of being large and metropolitan. An elevated train approached on tracks above the waterfront buildings. The passengers, mostly women, saw us and started waving their hands excitedly. A bobby in a blue uniform and tall helmet walked stolidly along the street fronting the water. Evidence of German bombing was not hard to find; in fact, the five-story building on our pier is minus a large portion of its top three stories. This occurred, said a sailor, when a German bomb fell right down the funnel of an ammunition ship that was being unloaded. The last air raid here was about eighteen months ago. We crowded the decks absorbed in the scene until nightfall.

Then a voice spoke over the ship's loud speaker: "You are now in a Theater of Operations. You are an hour's flying distance from German air bases and in the second most bombed city in England. It may be a day or two before you debark. When you start meeting the public, learn to be cordial according to their ways. And keep your trap shut about military affairs!"

January 30, 1944.

Several workers came aboard, and American MP's to guard the gangplanks. They were immediately surrounded by troops desiring to know the local situation concerning such matters as women, whiskey, and the translation of English currency into American money values. Of the latter, we were all struck by the flimsiness of the English pound note. It resembled a soap-advertising coupon.

"Aren't they easy to counterfeit?" we asked an MP.

He took a pound note and tore it a quarter of an inch, revealing a thin strand of silver. "That silver strand runs all the way around at the edge," he replied. "You can always tell by that if it's genuine or not—and you see that water mark when you hold it up to the light? It can't be duplicated. Now you know something most Englishmen do not know."

Another group plied a civilian worker with questions.

"Wales?" he was saying, "yes, it is around here. You can see it across the river on a clear day. I'm a Welshman. The name is Jones, shortened from Johnson long ago, and I guess Johnson came from the Norwegian 'Yonson.'"

January 31.

From the ship to the railroad station is a fifteen minute walk over old cobblestone streets through a penurious waterfront neighborhood. We trudged the distance with our heavy packs and a bevy of shabbily dressed children skipping along and venturing into our ranks asking for chewing gum. We entrained at 7 P.M. It was dark, and in that I felt cheated; we would be traveling twelve hours through some of the most interesting country in England and see very little at night! My disappointment was partly alleviated by the train conductor emulating a Cook's Tour guide, pointing out notable towns en route blacked out against air raids but illuminated by a bright moon, and landmarks such as the famous Manchester Ship Canal and Crews Engine Works. Our journey from America terminated in our arrival at a southwest

English town called Newton Abbot, in the shire (county) of Devon, exactly two weeks after embarking from New York. The journey took place without noteworthy incident, in a manner that has become routine, of millions of American troops pouring into the British Isles which English newspapers describe as "strap-hanging across the Atlantic." Except just as we entered Liverpool channel a private of our division in one of the other ships decided he would have none of it and leaped overboard, sinking like a rock. Perhaps it was a delayed reaction to "gangplank fever." At any rate it did not represent the general mood of the men.

February 1, 1944.

To begin with it appears that unlike in the "States," a division is not stationed entirely in one camp but is strung out by battalions for up to a hundred miles. And so with ours. I am located with Regimental Headquarters and the Second Battalion at a camp roughly thirty-five miles from the city of Exeter, forty miles from Plymouth and one hundred eighty miles from London. The camp is a neatly laid out little military community in a rolling hill region of variegated farmland and moors. It contains camouflage-painted single story barracks, two central mess halls which the companies take turns at operating, a theater, Post Exchange, and a "Church Canteen." The buildings are very close together and arranged so that the camp can quickly be converted into a hospital. Unlike some other camps near the southern coast that have been bombed severely, this one has had only one machine-gun strafing by a lone German raider plane. But in case the air raid siren should sound off tonight I have in mind a certain air raid shelter I spotted built sturdily into the side of a nearby hill.

February 2.

Perhaps it is the season to be constantly damp. When it isn't raining it drizzles, or at least the clouds are dark and menacing. Even the paved roads and sidewalks are muddy. It does not get extremely cold. We sleep on folding cots with mattresses consisting of mattress covers filled loosely with straw. We eat out of our metal mess kits. One might say our living conditions are on the whole satisfactory. It is strange using a latrine which a sign at the entrance introduces as "Ablutions and Water Closets." Strange also it is that many of my compatriots have taken to growing moustaches.

The facility most conspicuously lacking is the service club we were accustomed to at every camp in the States and which permitted us some independence about eating. If a G.I. meal in the mess hall did not appeal we could say the hell with it and go to the service club cafeteria. No longer, alas. We have to eat G.I. food exclusively and like it, or not eat at all except for flat-tasting buns with unsweet cocoa or tea that may be purchased at the Church Canteen, a civilian organization that tries its best but cannot begin to pacify the cravings of our pampered palates.

February 3.

The following barracks discussion took place in a mood of light-humored irony.

Said Joe, "This division will never go overseas. It is strictly a station-complement outfit."

"Yes," echoed Harry, "we're too old and broken down; they will have to weed out all of us over thirty before they can send us."

"Besides." resumed Joe, "they never send over a division intact. They break it up, replace officers and shuffle everybody around."

"Sure," pursued Harry, "we are an experimental outfit. Maybe they'll stick us out on some quiet island outpost somewhere for guard duty because that's all we're good for."

Joe laughed and said, this time seriously, "All these notions have certainly gone with the wind. Some fellows were laying odds of eight to five that we would never go overseas. Some diehards still don't think we are here for combat duty and at most we will follow after the invasion troops to police up the brass."

"They're hurtin'," summed up Harry, "I guess they won't believe we're in till they find hot slugs flying at them."

February 4, 1944.

Letter writing is not what it used to be. Now it goes through a censor who has authority to cut out with a razor blade anything indicating our location beyond "somewhere in England" and other information he thinks might compromise military security. In my company the censor is a lieutenant who received one hour's instruction in performing the job. He must disregard anything written in the letters not requiring deletion. If someone writes that he hates his guts he is supposed to ignore it and not let it influence him against the man. These conditions seem innocent enough, but when writing a letter expressing viewpoints one finds himself suddenly inhibited. How will an idea strike the censor? What is his intellectual capacity, how will the words read to him; will he be contemptuous of style or thought intended to be read by someone else? The letter writer begins censoring his own writing to protect his privacy.

February 5.

It is taking us longer to reorganize after our journey than it would ordinarily after moving from one camp to another. We are established in barracks and headquarter buildings but cannot start functioning normally until our equipment arrives from the hold of the ship.

We are under a new command, the First Army headed by General Dwight Eisenhower who is also in charge of the project to invade Germany's "West Wall." We have to learn and assimilate new "S.O.P.s" (Standard Operating Procedures) of that command, including prescribed uniforms for every purpose in the ETO (European Theater of Operations) and courses of training to take up, which appear to follow along accustomed lines but there are variations. Hiking is not one of them. There is plenty of it to limber up after several weeks of comparative inactivity. The land is not the easiest for walking. Most of it is up and down hills.

February 6, 1944.

The town of Newton Abbot was fixed for the night when I arrived for a visit, meaning lights were "blacked out," and in England that means very black. I met a civilian and asked what one does in this town which looked as though its entire population had gone to sleep as soon as the sun went down.

"Well," he enumerated, "there are three cinemas, there is a dance at Saint Mary's Church, and plenty of pubs."

"How big is the town?" I asked.

"Thirty-four pubs," he replied without hesitation.

It being unclear whether the town consisted mainly of pubs or their number indicated the size of the population, I pressed further and he reckoned there were about thirty thousand inhabitants.

"Most of your soldiers want to know how many pubs there are," he added.

It was hard to make out in the darkness what each building housed, whether shop, pub, theater...I stumbled into an entrance, pushed open the door and walked in boldly past a light-shielding curtain. I was in the tiny lobby of "The Commercial Hotel." There my sight-seeing tour began, inside this building fashioned more quaintly than ever I saw outside a museum. Into this setting trod the proprietor dressed fittingly in knee-pants and hunting shirt. He spoke, and his words were modern as could be but not enough to dispel the illusion of an atmosphere belonging to an older era.

February 7, 1944.

Regulations do not permit us to carry American money. Our finance department soon had all our money changed into British currency. The paper pound notes and ten-shilling notes are larger than dollar bills, necessitating the purchase of a new wallet. The coins are larger than ours too, and their usage is such that one carries around two or three times the number of coins needed in America, which causes an appreciable strain on pocket linings and explains the common use of change purses by the English. The new money put a crimp in dice and poker playing for a while. Complications would arise interrupting the excitement of the game:

"Now you owe me five sixpences."

"Yes, that's 'two and six'; here you are."

"What do you mean, two and six-two what and six what?"

"Oh, that's a florin and sixpence, or to make it simpler, two shillings and sixpence, or a half-crown, or—"

"Wait a minute—how much is that in English, I mean American?"

"Fifty cents."

"Why the hell didn't you say so; on with the game!"

February 8.

We stood in line or as they say around here, "in queue," in front of the Post Exchange, looked at our new ration cards and sighed.

Said Landau, "Seven packs of cigarettes a week or twenty-one cigars, or three packages of pipe tobacco. What will I do—I'm a cigar smoker at the rate of six a day; in between I smoke a pipe and cigarettes."

"I'll buy my full ration of smokes and sell it to you for your two bars of candy," someone offered.

Bartering went on up and down the line. Everything edible is rationed, and almost everything else. The new manager of the PX failed to study the money carefully enough and had trouble making change. We who troubled to figure out the "pences" found our change either short or long. No one complained except when shortchanged.

February 9, 1944.

The towns hereabouts are amazing; the village of Denbury, for example, which is just out of sight from camp behind a hill, is a storybook come to life. Chaucer, Bacon, Shakespeare may have passed through centuries ago and seen it almost the same as we see it today. I went into one of the two pubs. The owner, a middle-aged gentleman named Thomas Lark, was telling a pair of American soldiers of his talent as a horseshoer. He pointed to a large framed certificate on the wall certifying him as a Master Farrier by virtue of having won the annual Devonshire contest in 1922.

"It is my proudest possession," he said turning to me. "What will you have? But I'll tell you beforehand that we've used up our rations of ale, stout and Guinness. You can have sweet or rough cider, ginger beer or a swig of peppermint."

I tried the latter, a colorless liquid of six percent alcoholic strength. I marveled aloud about the antiquity of buildings and layout of the village set on an uneven slope, each building resting against another on both sides of very narrow, crooked, stone-paved streets.

"You will find much of the old world in this part of England," commented Mr. Lark. "I don't know how old these buildings are but they are constructed of materials and methods not used in over two hundred years. In those days they used mud, clay and straw. It is reinforced now to some extent but underneath the thin layer of modern plaster you can easily crumble the walls with your hand."

He stepped outside to point out a landmark in the center of the village in the light of a full moon.

"A nice night for Jerry bombers," said Mr. Lark looking up at the clear sky.

February 10.

A few British soldiers are billeted with us in camp. Conversing with them, we learned that on the average they have not been in uniform much longer than we. Some have seen action, mainly in the Dunkirk evacuation of France, and the rest have been in service within the country. Contrary to American journalistic reports imputing to them mystical calm and stoicism, they gripe as much as we. They have a gift for invective as colorful as ours though perhaps a shade less versatile. Their wages are low, their first lieutenants receiving about the same as our buck privates. Most of their pay goes into cigarettes costing in military canteens the same exorbitant price as for civilians, fifty cents a pack. They are granted more furloughs than we, ten days every three months.

Asked in the mess hall how he liked our American chow, one replied: "Better than ours. You get more meat and variety than we, and it is better prepared. By Jove, you blokes know how to cook spuds!"

February 11, 1944.

"Good evening," said Pfc. Harry Golinos to a girl standing forlornly on the sidelines at the first overseas dance put on by the battalion in the gymnasium; "will you dance with me?"

The place was crowded, almost as much with girls as soldiers. The girl perked up and responded keenly. She was attired in the dull unimaginative style prevalent among the English women, probably due to a shortage of good clothing designers.

"From Newton Abbot?" chatted Harry. "How are things with you?"

"Oh as good as can be expected; there is a war going on, you know."

"How is the rationing—do you get enough to eat?"

"Oh yes, Spam and bread, jam, tea..."

"Any meat?"

"Only a shilling's worth a week."

"Is that all? How can you stand it!"

"Well, it isn't good but there is a war going on, you know."

"War or no war, I couldn't do it," returned Harry, "I would have to get more meat and things."

"But how would you do it?"

"I'd get around it—I'd steal!" exclaimed Harry savagely.

The girl winced.

"Maybe not; I guess I'd live like everybody," Harry appeased.

A door opened at the far end of the gym, revealing a room where refreshments were being prepared.

Upon seeing it the girl said eagerly, "Are they going to serve? I'm starved!"

"I think so, after this number."

"What have they, sandwiches? Let's go over now, we can dance later. I'm starved!"

"Yes," accommodated Harry, following her, "I guess there is a war going on."

February 12, 1944.

Our driver kept the jeep hugging the left edge of the road from which a cliff-like embankment rose abruptly. Blindly and trustingly, he negotiated at full speed sharp turns and hills on the constantly twisting narrow highway. Phil Henderson and I held on tightly to the shallow rear seat. The captain sitting next to the driver huddled in his overcoat against the sharp breeze coming in at the unprotected sides. We were jeeping through the southwest English countryside to a headquarter unit forty miles away, over terrain which the Germans would find most disadvantageous were they to attempt an invasion of England.

The farms are divided into small fields, and around each field there is a high thick ivy-covered wall of rocks mortared with clay. The British passion for walls becomes annoying when one's view of beautiful landscape is obstructed by unnecessarily high walls or solid fences along the open highway.

The towns and villages we passed frequently were compact, with few houses strewn individually at their outskirts. There were no signs on the road giving directions or naming localities. We knew we had arrived in the city of Exeter only because it was large enough to be it. This is a war-time precaution, of course. More than once German saboteurs parachuted onto the land failed for want of signs to find their targets and gave themselves away in trying to get oriented.

February 13, 1944.

Being stationed ten miles from Torquay (pronounced Torkee) is like being near Atlantic City or a similar American sea resort. The English Channel serves as the equivalent of the French Riviera. Torquay has not been bombed much compared with other places. The war has somewhat tarnished its appearance, but essentially it remains the same attractive resort, the town built largely atop sheer palisades overlooking the water where the English Channel figuratively meets the Atlantic Ocean. Picturesqueness, however, is not enough, given that the keynote of a vacation resort is a leisurely ambience. Lacking in that, Torquay presents the aspect of any town where one stands in long "queues" waiting to get into a restaurant or theater.

Once seated in the restaurant, this American reads the menu, finds nothing that interests him and out of politeness orders a cup of tea which he gulps down hurriedly so he may go on elsewhere in quest of a substantial meal. After a few tries he may be fortunate in finding a place whose rationed allotment has not yet run out and can offer something other than powdered-egg omelets, baked beans and sausages.

Compared with England, American war-rationed food is a joke.

One institution vigorously maintained in Torquay is the thirty-four piece Municipal Symphony Orchestra. I went Sunday afternoon to The Pavilion and for a shilling and thru'pence (25 cents) heard pianist

Mark Hambourg with the orchestra render a creditable performance of the Brahms 2nd Piano Concerto.

February 14.

My associates are unimpressed with my announcement that today marks my second anniversary in the Army.

"Is that all?" say the men disdainfully who will this month start drawing an extra five percent for being in three years, "you are a rookie."

Like many of them, I have been in the same infantry division since emerging from Basic Training at Camp Wheeler, Georgia. Upon joining the Rolling Fourth—now the strolling Fourth—in its 22nd Infantry Regiment, I have since participated in its functions at various locations in a capacity titled "Classification Specialist" as authorized in Army Regulation number AR 615-26, SSN 275.

From Camp Gordon, Georgia, we transferred to Fort Dix, New Jersey, where we trained for five months. From there we went to Camp Gordon Johnston below Tallahassee, Florida, for two months of amphibious training in the use of Infantry Landing Craft in the Gulf of Mexico at Appilachicola. Then we went to Fort Jackson near Columbia, South Carolina, for a month before heading finally for the New York Port of Embarkation processing facility at Camp Kilmer.

Within two weeks, during which I visited New York City twice on twelve-hour passes and bid farewell to my parents who came from Pittsburgh for the purpose, we boarded a train late one night and without further ado were whisked speedily to the boat. In the United States we were a highly regarded division. Here our reputation as a combat unit must start from scratch.

February 16, 1944.

In England virtually every man, woman, and child is a potential conscript for war service whether such service is military or nonmilitary. The citizen in effect is an instrument of the government which is empowered to place him on any job anywhere, failure to obey subjecting him to drastic fine or imprisonment. American proponents of this plan consider it would be most constructive in both unifying the country and preventing labor strikes during wartime. Yet according to British newspapers there is no less strife in England between labor and industry than in America. Strikes appear to be as frequent, based on wide discrepancies in wage scales between diverse labor groups.

Comparisons between the two democracies are given considerable journalistic space. The English are prone to use the word decadent in assessing American internal politics. Americans sniff at the British preservation of nobility, consider it an anachronistic structure which helps perpetuate class distinction. Both nations are manifestly equal in their devotion to democracy.

February 17, 1944.

Last night in Newton Abbot whites and Negroes of the United States Army clashed with knives, blackjacks, bare fists, and any other weapon at hand. An investigation of cause and instigators will doubtless take into account that a Negro soldier had been severely beaten by white soldiers who ganged up on him the previous night and left him lying in a store entranceway. In turn, ten minutes before the dance ended in St. Mary's church last night the Negro soldiers left the hall and waited outside for the white soldiers to come out, then attacked. Something was bound to happen sooner or later.

The whites have been showing resentment toward the Negro troops in this war zone. They resent the English hospitality accorded equally, especially by the girls. When questioned the girls reply, "You sent them to us, didn't you? We didn't know they are fighting on Hitler's side."

Several days ago a Negro soldier walked into a restaurant accompanied by a good-looking English girl. A few white soldiers from the South seated at the next table made loud deprecatory remarks about the Negro. He motioned to leave rather than create a scene but the girl insisted on staying.

She walked over to the table of Negro-baiters and said calmly, "These dark-skinned, boys have at least good manners. I would sooner go out with them than with white trash like you."

The fact is, most English girls do not date Negroes, Sometimes

Negroes try passing themselves off as American Indians. Among many white soldiers from both North and South there is little less animosity toward Negroes than toward German Nazis or the Japanese.

February 21, 1944.

The day's work was ended and the blackout shutters put up. At the far end of the barracks a modest game of pinochle had begun, thru'pence ante. Nearer the entrance several of the platoon were sprawled leisurely on cots listening to Ben Stedder's monologue reviewing the day's activities and other matters.

Ben has a disease—talking, but he never lacks an audience, for he is entertaining as well as prolific. Tonight his anecdotes centered on a young fellow given to irreverence toward officers. Particularly he had become anathema to certain officers he disliked whom he had a knack for making to look foolish.

Like, said Ben, the day a lieutenant came into the barracks and tried to wake him. Pretending to be asleep, he finally responded drowsily.

"What the hell 'ya bothering me for?" he drawled.

"Hm-m, just call me Joe," said the lieutenant sarcastically.

"Okay, Joe," complied the kid genially, at which the lieutenant disgustedly walked away.

"I happened to be on guard duty with him today," narrated Ben. "He had the stationary post at the rear gate while I walked back and forth in front. He stood inside the guard shack when the captain came snooping. He looked in and told the kid the shack could use a cleaning. The kid stood with his rifle in a stiff military pose and said nothing.

"'Didn't you hear me? Get a bucket and clean up the trash,' said the captain.

"The kid suddenly shouted at top of his voice, 'Sergeant of the guard, Post Number Two!'

"The sergeant of the guard was there on the spot.

"'You'll have to get someone to relieve me from guard duty while I clean up here,' the kid told him.

"The captain stood with his mouth open at the kid's nerve but could do nothing; the technicalities were on the kid's side. The captain got into his jeep and drove off without saying another word."

February 22.

Air raid sirens sounded briefly and then the "all clear" signal but in the distance could still be heard a series of antiaircraft gun detonations while many searchlight beams crisscrossed in the sky against a high cloud ceiling. German raider planes had strayed farther west than usual these days but not quite near enough to let us see what "Jerry" looks like.

The war is gradually creeping in on us. We carry our unloaded rifles everywhere, to chow, the theater, even to the latrine a few yards from our cots. To leave camp on a pass for a few hours and return is almost as complicated as passing through foreign customs. We give the day's password, show passes and dog-tags and are searched for pocket knives or other small concealed weapons that could be used in a brawl.

We are no longer allowed in town every night, but must alternate with the Negro troops to avoid a new flare-up of violence. Casualties have already taken a toll in our ranks though not directly in battle. Eight men in our division's Engineer battalion were killed and eight wounded when a German "teller mine" exploded accidentally during a training demonstration. A Field Artillery lieutenant-colonel got out of the war when his small artillery-observation plane hit an air pocket and crashed to earth.

February 23, 1944.

In Georgia, the outstanding feature of a three-day problem in the woods during the cold month of February was the weather. This week the battalion went on such a problem and the important feature to the average soldier was still the bitter-frosty air, especially at night when the sun went down and the hours till daybreak seemed endless. The locale of the problem (or "scheme" as the British call it) was a mountain ten miles away which took fully half a day merely to ascend.

Next on the program was taking positions and practicing battle maneuvers. Infantry tactics have not basically changed in centuries.

Our practice maneuvers endeavor to develop proficiency in the science of infiltration, in defense as well as offense. The basic formation for these tactics is the squad of twelve men, which may act with other squads in the platoon or independently in reconnaissance missions. The squad creed is at all times "concealment and cover." However grand the design, action in battle comes down in final analysis to this elementary squad formation whose primary concern is to seek concealment and cover.

February 24.

At 5:45 A.M. the Charge of Quarters noisily opened the barracks door, switched on the lights and redundantly instructed our squad leader to "wake 'em up." That gentleman said "wake up" and resumed sleeping. In fifteen minutes he roused himself, then us.

"What time is it?" asked Harry Hochstein.

"6:30; we fall out for reveille in two minutes," replied the sergeant.

"My watch only says 6:00, what's the rush?" argued Harry.

"You heard me, dammit, I gave you the time and I don't want any arguments."

"I guess you have a direct line to Central," observed Harry tersely as he wearily got out of bed.

Across the aisle Ted Marks groaned. "Oh what a college life! Another day. I think I'll give up; the whole thing doesn't pay."

"Maybe if you'd stay in at night once in a while and get some sleep you wouldn't feel like that. By the way, you're married, aren't you? Are you two-timing your wife?"

"Not me—I use a prophylactic!"

The squad leader shouted, "All right, fall out for reveille. Let's go!"

"Oh what a college life," yelped Marks, "I thought they'd cut out all this G.I. runaround when we got over here but they're just like always, everyone bucking for more stripes or afraid to lose what they've got!"

February 25, 1944.

Corporal Seabright, nicknamed "Mister Seabright" for his civilian mien, laid down the newspaper *Stars and Stripes*. He relit his pipe contemplatively and said, "We're trying to make history here and I see they are making history back home, too. Now I don't care a rap about politics, I'm interested in finishing this business and getting home. I don't even give a damn about voting in this year's presidential election. Still, it is interesting to see the way the political situation is lining up. It looks like Franklin Roosevelt has been slapped hard by Senator Barkley's revolt over his veto of the tax bill."

"I'm not sure about that, Mister Seabright," responded Ned Robinson, "it might look that way at first, especially after Congress overruled Roosevelt's veto, but the people feel pretty strongly about this tax problem. They might not like the idea that Senator BarKlay fought vindictively against Roosevelt's veto because he resented the president calling it 'a tax relief bill providing relief not for the needy but for the greedy.'"

"It's pretty bad when even the staunchest New Deal Democrat becomes sensitive to Republican accusations that Roosevelt is trying to dictate to Congress and run the country by himself, but I wouldn't wonder if the public sticks by him on election day if he runs for a fourth term."

"I'd vote for him," declared Mister Seabright, "because I don't believe in changing horses in the middle of the stream. Ordinarily, though, I believe a change of politics occasionally is good for the country."

February 27, 1944.

I'll call him John Doe, for although the matter ended legally long ago he doesn't want to circulate the story of this extraordinary episode. I had to interview him on a minor point of his Classification Record, leading to this tale which he described humorously but in measured words:

"It wasn't always funny though I laugh about it now. I sweated for months. No one would have discovered it yet but for the fact that I wanted to get out when 28-year-old men were being discharged from the Army in 1941.

'You're not 28 yet,' they told me when I applied for the discharge.

"'You mean my brother isn't 28,' I said–'your records are of my brother, not of me; I changed places with him after he was inducted.'

"Naturally this blew up a storm. I was cross-examined twenty times and fingerprinted by the FBI. What happened was this—I had requested in the first place to be drafted instead of my brother but the draft board said it was too late to change. They sent my brother to an induction camp near New York. The night before he was to be sent down south I changed places with him, got into his uniform which was way too big on me and he went back home in my civvies.

"He and I have almost the same first and middle names but we don't look alike. Two bunkmates knew about the change but didn't say anything because they thought we couldn't possibly get away with it and would soon be discovered.

"An officer saw me in my brother's uniform and bawled out the supply sergeant for giving me such a bad fit. Months later when the 28-year-old business came up and I told my company commander about it he was going to court-martial me at first for fraudulent enlistment, but changed his mind. My brother is in the army now anyway, and overseas."

He went on in considerable detail but left much unanswered. It seems impossible to carry out such a fraud for an extended period of time. If he should some day reveal all the details of the episode it will probably rival anything a Hollywood script writer can think up.

February 28, 1944.

The "ETO" (European Theater of Operations) in England seems full of divisions and regiments that we knew in the States. The 2nd Armored Division, whose tanks used to team up with our infantry division on maneuvers in the Carolinas, has seen action in Tunisia and Sicily.

At the Red Cross Service Club in Torquay, I met a field artillery corporal of the 9th Infantry Division who had also been in those campaigns. His casual smiling demeanor suggested more a newly arrived innocent from the States than one who had been in the thick of battle. He said his outfit had more than once been in a position to catch "wholesale hell."

"I think those Germans use their artillery with greater effectiveness than we. They seem able to do more damage with less guns, though maybe it is because they were always on the defensive in prepared positions, besides being more experienced. Our infantry? They caught particular hell, but not as bad as the 1st Division whose infantry was almost wiped out when Rommel's tanks broke through in Tunisia."

He had recently come to England with his division. "This is the first decent living conditions we've had in many months. We are filled with replacements and are back to training again. You would think that after being in action we would be treated with less formality and boyscoutishness, but they are as GI as ever."

March 6.

Never has there been so much restlessness among the men as now when the time for invasion draws nearer. There is greater danger of getting hurt by our own troops than by the enemy. In one outfit a private managed get hold of a live round of ammunition. He loaded his rifle, went in to where his 1st sergeant was sleeping and shot him between the eyes. Then he walked outside and said to a group of buddies, "You don't have to worry any more about the first sergeant, fellows, he's dead." (When they start going after sergeant-technicians I'll hand in my dog-tags and resign.)

Conditions in town are worse than ever. It is hardly safe to walk on the streets at night even in the company of three or four others. Last night in Torquay a quartet of white soldiers was cornered by fifteen colored and beaten up in the dark. It happens that they indiscriminately picked on four of impeccable reputation who never get into trouble. While it is true that whites are generally the provokers, it is not doing the Negro cause any good when they jump whites at random. The matter has reached major proportions of national scandal which America may not live down for years.

March 25, 1944.

At 10:30 sharp each morning without fail, an elderly grey Englishman trudges in solemnly through the camp gate with a bundle of newspapers carried in a sack at his side. He peddles from hut to hut an assortment including the *Express, Herald, The People, Daily Sketch, News*

Chronicle, Reynold's News, and Mirror. Purchasing one from him is a highlight of the day; never has news been of more sustained interest, and the papers offer a microscopic examination of one of history's most spectacular episodes as it unfolds.

Participating as a soldier is not enough; one must also understand the war, see its social impact in which political play is nearly as significant as gun-play. Militarily, the stage seems set for the "Second Front."

For the American troops, failure in that second front when it occurs is unthinkable, for until it is successful and they can again become civilians they consider their time wasted. But these millions of soldiers also know the outcome of World War I with its inconclusive victory that led to the present war and are interested in everything that will go into the making of a long-term peace: postwar planning, democratic elections at home and abroad, labor strikes, economics, etc.

March 28, 1944.

Our division's present six-day problem is probably the last large scale "dry run" before entering actual combat. It is an amphibious assault maneuver incorporating all the tactics our troops have practiced since coming to England. By now each individual has a fairly clear understanding of the role he will play and what is expected of him in the coming action.

At this juncture I am still a member of the 22nd Infantry Regiment's Personnel unit as the noncommissioned officer in charge of Classification. As such I expect to be with rear echelon support troops, which presumably is a safer place to be than with front line troops. We anticipate following as close behind as prudent to prevent our records from falling into enemy hands.

Formerly our records were classified as confidential. Since arriving at this "theater" they became "Secret."

The prospect of being safer than our first-wave assault troops cannot sadden me; neither can it make me gloat or be apologetic, for I feel myself no less ready than they to face direct fire. I anticipate coming within range of artillery fire and to experience Luftwaffe air attacks designed to disrupt rear communications. More I cannot surmise, but as every other soldier in this dauntless army, I adamantly believe that the bullet capable of harming me has not yet been invented.

March 30, 1944.

The World War I song, *Mademoiselle From Armentiers*, exposes the lax morals that supposedly prevailed between American soldiers and French women. How this war will compare in that respect with the last might show up in statistics on social diseases. As a lay observer I judge that presently the situation is not too bad despite much loose talk.

Americans love to describe in lavish, lewd detail their conquests in fast love-making. There is much exaggeration and considerable truth, but not enough of the latter to support the notion that G.I.s let down all barriers upon touching foreign soil. Usually the real womanizers say little of their adventures. It appears, oddly, that the married men seek romance more than the single.

As for the English women, they seem much like the American in degree of submission to a war-time relaxation of the moral code. Recently one of the boys went into a pub, ordered a drink and sat down at a table partly occupied by a comely, mature young woman. He sociably invited her to join him in drinking a toast. They downed one, then another, and walked outside together. As they strolled down the street she saw him looking about intently as though seeking something.

"What are you looking for?" she asked.

Innocently he replied, "What do you usually do after you drink?"

"Oh I have to catch the last bus," she said, "I don't think we'll have enough time for that."

March 31.

Today's *Stars and Stripes* carries an article advising that diaries are now banned in the ETO. States the newspaper: "It has been found that men in combat have a habit of keeping diaries in their pockets where they are liable to capture by the enemy."

Webster defines the word diary as a register of daily events and

experiences. I do not regard this writing as a diary. It does not system-
atically record each day's happenings. I intend it to be a journalistic
scrapbook of broadly stated impressions while participating as a soldier
during one of the greatest crises ever to befall mankind. From the
standpoint of restricted military information, little more can be gleaned
from the manuscript than from general publications distributed among
civilians. Both typed and handwritten, it is always kept under lock
together with the other records of my department. In light of the new
order, I am aware more than ever that these pages must not risk
compromising military security.

April 5, 1944.

It was beginning to appear that I would be in England for months
and leave without ever seeing London. By a stroke of luck I received
a 48-hour pass and boarded a train for that metropolis. To see as
much of the city as possible in that short a time required careful
planning which I undertook without benefit (or hindrance) of a tour
guide. I saw almost everything of historic interest that tourists usually
cover: Westminster Abbey, Parliament, Buckingham Palace, London
Bridge, Hyde Park, Piccadilly Circus.

I climbed the winding staircase to the top of St. Paul's Cathedral
for a bird's eye view of the city. I visited the outside of Scotland Yard,
walked in the Soho district, strode through Regent Street to Oxford
Circus, and took a bus east to Clapton Pond.

In some parts of the city bomb damage looked severe and in others
not very noticeable. Wartime London shows a certain shabbiness
aside from bombing but at times a pre-war luster shows through.
"Underground" trains for example are more luxurious than New York
subway trains. I find a cosmopolitan resemblance between London
and New York.

I was able to get some good meals and, for the first time, real lager
beer, both probably products of the "black market" that flourishes as
in America. I entered a restaurant on a side street and came upon a
waiter whispering to the proprietor just inside. A soldier wearing a
British uniform with POLAND imprinted on his shoulder patch stood
uneasily to the side.

"All right, we'll take up a collection," said the proprietor.

Later the waiter explained to me in a confidential tone that the Polish soldier was one among a number of Jews who ran away from the western-sponsored Polish Army in England because of anti-semitic persecution. He was trying to transfer to the British Army, and meanwhile had gone into hiding since conditions became intolerable in the Polish "Government-in-Exile" Army.

April 10, 1944.

Non-commissioned officers always work under threat of being broken to private in case they fail to perform effectively. This is not so with commissioned officers. Presently in preparing for the Second Front a new note is sounded. Strong pressure is being applied to commissioned officers displaying poor leadership. In some outfits it is common knowledge that battalion commanders, even regimental commanders, lieutenant-colonels and colonels, have been relieved of their commands after poor showings in field problems. Rarely does a superior know an officer's abilities as well as the enlisted men working under him. In one instance, a battalion commander was relieved of his command by an observing three-star general who told him he wouldn't make a good sergeant. His lack of competence had long been known to enlisted men who watched him get promotion after promotion until he reached the highly responsible position where he would have led one thousand men in battle; men who knew he couldn't properly read a field map. He was well-liked for his congenial personality—they referred to him as "Colonel Morale"—but the men were not taken in. They prefer placing their lives in the hands of a first-rate leader and tactician, even a strict disciplinarian "West Pointer." Lower-rank officers are regarded more critically now, the men less inclined than formerly to "go to hell" for lieutenants and captains who please them personally.

April 14, 1944.

Periodically we are visited by military leaders of highest rank. Among those allotting their valuable time to observe our regiment were General "Ike" Eisenhower and Lieutenant General Omar Bradley, the commander of all ETO ground forces. Today our tiny camp nestled in the rolling Devonshire farmlands made ready to again receive "a high dignitary." Component companies of our regiment scattered over twenty miles arrived in a stream by truck and afoot to gather for review. Into this setting drove a long black sedan with a British flag attached to the hood, and out of it emerged General Sir Bernard Montgomery, the man credited with sweeping German General Rommel's "Afrika Korps" from the desert during a critical phase of the war. He walked through our ranks looking us over. We stood informally and looked him over. Next to our troops he appeared short and slim, his face lean and furrowed, eyes open wide and registering no expression.

To address us he stepped onto the engine hood of a jeep and bade us break ranks and gather round. He spoke crisply in a logical, reasoning manner, his tone conveying more humility than bravado.

"The newspapers and radio," he began, "have been doing a great deal of talking about a 'Second Front.' Maybe it will be a second front but if so, I wonder what the numbers were of the other fronts I have been fighting on!

"In the coming business," he concluded, "you and I, Americans and British, will be fighting side by side. I want us to know each other, to have confidence in each other. The German soldiers are still tough and stubbornly determined to stand by Hitler to the end. But the German high command is weak in strategic options, much weaker than when they started the war and qualitatively inferior to the Allied high command."

April 30, 1944.

Only a skeleton crew remained behind when the regiment went out a week ago. The weather all week had been warm and sunny. Those of us remaining in camp spent one of the easiest weeks since I entered the army. We took sunbaths, read back issues of newspapers and magazines from the states and waited for news from the regiment. Each day friendly planes roared overhead to and from the English Channel. Also some enemy planes came over, mainly at night. We blissfully ignored them and remained asleep, bombs or "ack-ack" (antiaircraft) fire notwithstanding. They have never bombed close enough to throw a scare into us.

Today the regiment is back. The men reported they were loaded into invasion craft and carried out thirty miles across the Channel accompanied by a huge naval fleet and air escort. They were loaded down with ammunition, each carrying about eighty rounds. Enemy reconnaissance planes prodded feverishly at the armada of our escort planes in an effort to take photos. A few were shot down.

Our fleet returned at the end of three days and the men made a mock invasion of the English coast. After a high pitch of expectancy the exercise turned out to be just another dry run.

May 3, 1944.

"I give up trying to outguess Eisenhower," said "Mister" Seabright tersely. "Who would have thought that by now, in May, we would still be here waiting for things to start humming!"

The war of nerves doubtless works both ways, affecting ourselves as well as the enemy, albeit differently. With us it is sweating out something to relieve the boredom, like an expected furlough, while the Germans have at stake their status as supermen and are sweating out demotion to ordinary mortals.

There is little outward concern among us about personal hazard upon invading the mainland of Europe. Rather, concern is centered on how long it will take to get the job over, and after will we be stuck long as an army of occupation or worse, be rerouted to the Pacific for a second gauntlet of danger in finishing off Japan, assuming we survive the first?

This is also a presidential election year and opinion runs from idealistic to cynical, the latter expressed with offhanded indifference such as: "My vote goes to the one who offers the biggest postwar soldier-veteran bonus."

Also said cynically is that "presidential politics will decide the date of the invasion." But for the most there is approval in the expectation that Roosevelt will be retained as president to end the war and estab-lish the peace. Meanwhile, relief from tension and boredom is sought

in the usual way by going whenever possible on "white" nights to
Newton Abbot to drink whatever spirits are available.

May 5.

Humor helps fight this war, and not especially professional humor.
Leo Gorelick (pronounced Go-rel-ick), for instance, only recently developed a reputation as a comedian. After working in our midst for
nearly two years this trait surfaced one day while he appeared en-
grossed in his work. Suddenly he stopped and exclaimed, "What do
I know about all this? Give me a white apron and I'll know what I'm
doing!"

Since making this remark Leo, an ex-restaurateur from Brooklyn,
cultivated a fabulous monologue based on the exalted delights of his
civilian profession.

"I am a pfc," he would say, "so I do a pfc's work for pfc pay. A
thirty-one year old man and I have to stand here cleaning a silly piece
of iron. I should be making pastrami sandwiches with pickle.

"When I came into the army I had an old sergeant who spoke an
English that only an old army man could understand. I got in wrong
with him right away when he told me to go down and 'bunk' the fire.
I didn't know what he meant.

"'Bunk the fire, bunk the fire, dumbbell' he yelled, getting madder
and madder every minute. I finally made out that he meant I should
bank the fire in the boiler room.

"He used to tell us, 'If you want to be a good soldier you have to
foist loin to s'ine you' s'oes.'"

One day Leo conversed with himself aloud as follows, "Well, Leo,
how is Gorelick? Gorelick isn't feeling so well; he had a fight with
Leo. They don't get along well..."

With such whimsy and an infallible sense of getting it across, this
pfc does more than a pfc's job in contributing to morale.

May 14, 1944.

Two bandoliers of live ammunition—eighty rounds—now repose in
my duffel bag. My overcoat, dress blouse, and other extraneous items

have been taken away from me. I am now, in short, streamlined for action. If ever a time is ripe, it is now.

Life in England until now has been quite pleasant, a vast improvement over at least one of our stations in the States—Camp Gordon Johnson, Florida, the isolated camp at the Gulf of Mexico that journalist Walter Winchell once called "the Alcatraz of the Army." Here we are far from isolated. In the past few weeks there have been frequent dances in camp with girls from surrounding towns; gaudy, unchaperoned affairs, almost debauched with hard cider and beer flowing freely and nearly as many couples outside the hall in the dark as inside.

For three and a half months we have been settled in a garrison affording us as many advantages as one could reasonably expect in wartime overseas. Chow is good (SPAM served only once to my knowledge). The powdered eggs are palatable; I prefer omelets made from them, steamed, over the fried fresh eggs the army has a nasty habit of serving drenched in slimy oil. The powdered milk is also palatable, almost indistinguishable from fresh milk except when the cooks fail to mix the powder thoroughly and pour milk on our porridge containing lumps of undissolved powder.

During this time we have seen many planes fly towards the Channel to soften up the enemy. We have even been entertained by German propaganda radio broadcasts, with reception often better than from local stations and superior programming including symphonic and chamber music. These tolerable conditions did not, however, deter our ambition to get the campaign going.

May 29, 1944

In new pre-invasion terminology, our personnel section is in the "Residue" segment of the invasion task force, as are kitchen staffs and company mail orderlies. We parted from our companies two weeks ago; we left Denbury, moved to "Camp Bypass" at Exeter where we stayed for a week, then came to the city of Bournemouth where we are now functioning in evacuated mansions near the English Channel in a section known as Millionaire's Row, Dorsetshire, 90 miles from London. The elegance of our surroundings is compromised only by our having to continue sleeping on straw-filled mattress covers on the floor and standing in the omnipresent chow line with our tin mess kits.

Our companies left Denbury about the same time and are now in a secret marshalling area, one of many called "Sausage Links" along the Channel coast. Presently they are in a Top Secret category and practically incommunicado from us. The men have been briefed on their coming mission. They live in camouflaged tents and are not permitted to walk around in the open more than necessary to avoid detection of their concentrated numbers by enemy scout planes. There is a general feeling as never before that everything is worked out in minutest detail and is being executed with a secrecy that baffles even the participants.

June 5, 1944.

According to nonmilitary predictions Rome should have fallen to the Allies last December. That it has just fallen today bespeaks a wide gap between amateur expectation and professional. Similarly, it is almost a shock to all but top brass that today is June 5 and we have still not landed across the Channel. We see convincing evidence of our readiness. The waters off Bournemouth are jammed with ships that come in close during the day and disperse at night. The peacetime vacation resort is crowded with soldiers but few civilians. Theaters and restaurants are plentiful and the "Pavilion" is in the style of Torquay's, with a symphony orchestra, concerts and plays. On a cliff overlooking the Channel is the renowned Russel-Cotes art gallery and museum, still open to visitors.

We are little troubled by enemy air raids, though occasionally reminded of proximity to danger by incidents such as last week's bombing of Torquay. Forty were killed Sunday night by a direct hit on Queens Hotel where we often went Sunday evening for a glass of ale. We hear little from our forward echelon in the marshalling area but it has trickled through that the men are aboard ships, each provided with 200 French francs ($4) in invasion money. An announcement of having invaded would not come as a surprise.

June 6.

Our triumph in Rome is quickly overshadowed by today's electric "Communique Number 1" from Eisenhower's headquarters. This is the day we have been waiting for since 1933, the year Hitler came into power in Germany and the world felt an unarticulated foreboding of the monstrous events that have since taken place. The drone of our planes heading toward the Channel last night was heavier and longer than ever before but we could no more guess that this is The Day than on many other seemingly significant days in recent weeks, except this time we knew that our outfit was aboard ships.

Here at "Residue" we were much surprised at not being alerted. We were permitted to go out on pass in the evening as usual. There were many fewer soldiers in Bournemouth than before, but still a considerable number. Many ships were still lying in near shore. Farther out I could make out seven large ships resembling ocean passenger liners plying toward the Isle of Wight five miles to the left. We conjectured that they were hospital ships carrying back the first assault force casualties.

June 13, 1944.

It was the Germans who first announced that the 4th Infantry Division was in the initial D-Day assault on the beaches of Normandy. SHAEF Headquarters confirmed this publicly today and disclosed that our division, which would "never go overseas," which is "too old for combat," is spearheading the drive to secure the Cherbourg peninsula. So far we haven't received precise reports of our tactics except we know the division had been assigned the mission of assaulting on the extreme right flank of the invasion.

Our 3rd Battalion, attached to the 8th Infantry Regiment, was the first of our troops to land in France. Our other units continued to land through the day and some not until the next day. We just received casualty reports of the first three days in action. It came as a great surprise that we had far fewer casualties the first day than the second and third. Revealed in these early reports is that the death ratio among the casualties was one in eight. Of these wounded, more are listed as "Seriously Wounded in Action" than "Lightly Wounded in Action."

Now I can see why Washington insists on having a big army, Even with moderate casualties it would not take long to realize a 100% turnover of personnel in a combat infantry unit.

June 19.

Right from the start providence is very much with me, for my escape from injury today was nothing less than miraculous. Our section had boarded ship about noon. An hour later, while sitting around the deck, a 40-millimeter shell was discharged accidentally from a ship next to ours and hit a beam twenty feet above me. Shrapnel sprayed over and around me and others, inflicting numerous jagged holes in the deck armor and bulkheads but neither I nor they were hit.

The ship we are on is called an LST, for "Landing Ship Tank." It has been through four invasions, in Sicily, Salerno, Anzio and Normandy, and this is the worst hit it ever received. We left Bournemouth two days ago, went to a marshalling area near Dorchester, and boarded ship at Weymouth.

June 20.

We went to France last night but right now are sitting in the harbor at Portsmouth, England. It had been a rough trip and very few of us landlubbers avoided "feeding the fish." It was discouraging then that this morning we suddenly turned around and headed back just when we reached sight of the Normandy beachhead. A ship's crewman explained the sea was too stormy along the beach to make a landing.

June 21, 1944.

We are still "hove to" though the weather now seems fair enough. Hundreds of ships are around us in the harbor, all loaded with troops and materiel. "Scuttlebut" has it that the beachhead is supplied five days ahead of schedule. The sailors uniformly advance an opinion that another invasion landing will be made around Dieppe. Our LST, Number 351, is one of the oldest in service. It has a flat bottom and displaces 5,500 tons. The crew is composed of young veterans of numerous air raids, shellings, and escapes from enemy submarines and mine fields.

One, a pharmacist mate, described carrying in 4th Division assault troops on D-Day, "We had been briefed to expect fantastic defenses but it was a bluff. The worst damage to our ships was from mines. In the worst air raid, three bombs were dropped and they were far off the mark. Anzio and Salerno were much worse. We learned at Salerno that just the day before, the Germans had practiced landing on the very beaches we landed on to figure out the best defense. Every night there were air raids of a hundred to a hundred and fifty bombers. We were constantly amazed at how little the Germans hit with so many bombs dropped. Their aim was terrible."

Life on this small ship is quite different than on the *Capetown Castle*. Only 250 men are aboard including the crew. Discipline is lax, we eat three meals a day instead of two, and hot coffee is available at all times. The news about the Cherbourg peninsula is good and we expect at any hour to hear that the port city of Cherbourg is in our hands. Our delay aboard ship is putting us far behind in our work on battle casualty reports. We are sweating out learning how bad casualties are since the last report. We know now that from a strategic standpoint our division is fighting in probably the most important mission to date of this war.

June 22, 1944.

We finally made it across the English Channel, on a smooth sea and clear day. We cruised in toward Omaha Beach then turned right to follow the shoreline five or six miles to Utah Beach where mine sweepers were still cutting in and out among the many ships standing offshore. Twice I heard a loud explosion signifying that mines had been found and neutralized. Several of our ships lay half sunk in the water, mute testimony to the effectiveness of mines. Far inland I watched an airplane fall toward earth till out of sight it crashed loudly, sending up a column of dense black smoke against the skyline.

There is a continual rumble of artillery fire from the direction of Cherbourg where the Germans are still resisting. A few minutes ago a flight of our Flying Fortresses flew over us and now we hear their bombs detonate in even tempo as each row of planes drops its load.

June 23, 1944.

We disembarked on the beach at low tide, hiked through partially cleared wreckage, past battered German pillbox fortifications of their Atlantic Wall then inland seven miles where we picked up the rest of our division's Residue units including kitchen trucks. Our regimental sergeant-major met us and we heard for the first time a direct account of happenings in the organization since D-Day:

"The 4th Division is doing the bulk of the fighting on the Cherbourg peninsula and the 22nd Infantry Regiment is doing most of it. At one time the Germans thought the 22nd was a whole division in itself and so reported on their radio. Our boys are fighting mad."

Our truck convoy assembled and we took off toward Cherbourg on the main highway which was crowded with American trucks. We drove through Monteburg, Valognes, and it was hard to decide which was ruined the most.

It seemed unreal—the sight of Frenchmen dragging a few belongings from crumbled buildings; the picture of utter destruction was something that could happen only in newsreels. Yet the few remaining civilians smiled at us as we rode by and often appeared more interested in looking at us than in browsing among the ruins.

Three miles before the city of Cherbourg we turned into a field area occupied by our regimental rear command post. From there we could almost see the Cherbourg battle line where the fighting raged intensely. We heard we are in possession of all the high ground and our regiment reached the outer streets of Cherbourg where they are now held up to await the 12th Infantry Regiment catching up on their sector.

Our casualties are very heavy. Some companies have already had 3 or 4 different first sergeants and company commanders. Names of rifle company personnel have changed almost beyond recognition. In just one day we have become oriented; even we now appear grimy and unshaven, though clean compared with those who landed over two weeks ago and now carry German pistols, pocket knives, watches and other souvenirs taken from German soldiers, either dead or live prisoners. Some ride on captured motorcycles, have a ready stash of cognac or cider, and are considerably different than as we knew them before.

June 24, 1944.

Our section is set up in an orchard five miles from Cherbourg. The Germans who left a few days ago did not police the area well. A scrap of their newspaper had an article criticizing President Roosevelt for dictatorial behavior toward the head of Montgomery Ward Company.

Heavily bearded First Sergeant LeFlore of Regimental Headquarters Company visited us and observed, "The Heinies are no chumps; their eighty-eights are sweet weapons. But separate the Germans from their eighty-eights and they lose their courage. Their screaming meemies are awful; the concussion lifts a man two feet into the air though it has no shrapnel. We are stringing wire for communications but the eighty-eights knock it out almost as fast as we string it. The battalion and company commanders are all right up front and performing brilliantly."

The French, especially children, have plenty of cider to sell in return for cigarettes and candy. They are short of bread and like our K-ration biscuits. They have been of some help against the enemy by giving information, but many soldiers do not trust them and believe some are aiding the Germans.

Enemy snipers are causing trouble. Today the Germans are counter-attacking with heavy mortar barrages and machine gun fire. Our side doesn't give an inch.

Already we've had one general court-martial, against a soldier who shot a French girl, the verdict not announced. Each regiment thinks it is doing all the fighting. I suppose that can be judged by comparing casualty reports.

The General has promised that after we take Cherbourg he has a pleasant surprise in store for us. There is much speculation on what it will be. Cherbourg should fall soon; right now the Germans are being shelled and bombed from all sides.

Our personnel records have not yet caught up with us and administrative conditions are chaotic. Casualty reports will be considerably delayed while we unravel the tangle. Had our personnel section arrived ten days earlier we would all have been used on line as riflemen, as every available man was badly needed. There is still sniper fire even in captured parts of Normandy. We are very careful in our vicinity to carry our loaded guns everywhere, never walk alone but in pairs, post double guard at night and not permit smoke from our fires to give away our position during the day. Water is not scarce but we use it sparingly in order to save transportation for other purposes.

June 25, 1944.

Last night a few "Jerry" planes flew over looking for our artillery. They dropped a few bombs in the vicinity but were driven off quickly by heavy ack-ack fire. Every time our artillery let one go the blast is followed by a loud wail from a bray ass pastured nearby. Bursts of small arms fire go off occasionally, at whom or what God only knows.

The fields in this region are all small and hemmed in by thick, high hedgerows growing atop mounded earth. The Germans cut an opening in each hedgerow to enable them to make a fast getaway. They retreated rapidly in this section, one day moving eleven miles without our infantry firing a shot.

Though all is supposedly "fair in love and war" our troops are hot about German foul play, like cutting up our disabled wounded soldiers instead of taking them prisoner. In retaliation many "Huns" are treated in kind.

In one instance, a paratrooper offered to relieve an MP of thirty prisoners. He marched them to a field hidden from observers, lined them up, opened fire with his Tommy gun and annihilated them to a man. But even before there was a feeling of retaliation for German atrocities, our troops landed in France with the intention to take no prisoners for at least the first few days.

The briefing preceding D-Day Normandy made clear that we would be at a disadvantage to encumber ourselves with prisoners while trying to secure a beachhead. About the second day, however, an order was issued rescinding this understanding.

Our artillery is highly praised by every infantryman on line, especially after a German counterattack was repulsed on the second day of fighting which would have driven us into the sea had it succeeded.

This afternoon I went with Captain Herbert Brill by jeep to a forward position for the purpose of assigning new replacements to the line companies.

In the midst of our work with the several hundred men in an open field, suddenly the enemy zeroed in on us with several 88-millimeter shells. We hit the ground instantly.

Finding no foxhole handy, I hugged a hedgerow embankment on the side opposite the direction of incoming fire. Each shell whistled ominously near as I waited tensely to hear where it would land. The nearest fell about fifty yards from me. Soon the firing stopped. We found three of our new men were hit, before we had a chance to assign them. Having thus been "baptized" briefly by enemy shellfire, I can now appreciate what the boys on line have endured for the last 19 days. Only men with nerves of steel can survive the ordeal of continuous shellfire without becoming victims of shellshock.

June 26, 1944.

Today is wet. There is little artillery fire. Cherbourg fell to us last night. Only some pockets of resistance remain to mop up. So many German prisoners are streaming in that it is hard to find room for them in the forward stockades. It is easy now to take prisoners. One of our men walked into the woods to relieve himself and returned with a dozen prisoners.

The French "underground" has been somewhat helpful around Cherbourg. There seems to be much competition and jealousy among our forces, each division and even regiment insisting the boundaries marking its progress not be trespassed by a neighboring outfit. Each is frankly out for glory.

A little while ago I met an elderly Frenchman walking on the road carrying a pair of wooden shoes in his hands while he strode barefoot. He hailed me apparently for a chat and counted in English from one to twenty to display his linguistic versatility, which included a few additional English words. He sang 'It's a Long Way to Tipperary' and knew the words better than I. The Americans are wonderful soldiers, he said; the English—he smiled—not bad. He bummed some cigarettes and ceremoniously went on his way.

June 27, 1944.

The capture of Cherbourg doesn't mean a damn thing to the 22nd Infantry in light of having a bad day yesterday in casualties. Our regiment had the job of mopping up the beaches that had been bypassed along a sizable portion of the peninsula. Yesterday's operation was a broad frontal attack that ended leaving a thousand yard gap it was hoped the enemy would not discover. Unfortunately they did. Last night a fierce artillery duel took place with our 105's and 155's against their 88's and 12-inch shore batteries that they had turned inland and were firing at us without trying to aim at specific targets. Several of the large shells narrowly missed our personnel section.

During the night Captain Brill and I went for more replacements. We loaded two truckloads of men into open trucks and drove ten miles to our regimental command post. It was a bad ride; very dark, the rain driven by a cold wind swept us in our open jeep as we sped through a hail of shell fire that seemed to keep apace with us all the way. We rode without lights—even blackout lights—as the tiniest glimmer of light became a glare that could be seen at a distance.

Upon reaching our destination the captain said to the new men, "You'll have to spend the night in this field. Suit yourself about setting up a pup tent or digging a foxhole. I'm sorry we can't offer you better accommodations."

We also experienced an uncomfortably close air raid during the night.

Today there was to have been a victory parade in the city of Cherbourg but it was called off because of still hot pockets of resistance. A French priest dressed in black cape and tunic came to our headquarters to give the location of an 88 field gun that the Germans had infiltrated inside our lines and with it have been shelling our rear positions every night.

I spoke to "Goldy," our Special Service entertainment director presently assisting at an ammunition dump. He told me of a captured young German who lay dying and called for a chaplain. He appeared to be a Nazi "jugend" fanatically indoctrinated since childhood.

Chaplain Frank went to him and said, "I am the only chaplain here but I am a Jewish chaplain."

Replied the young Nazi: "I don't care, just so you are a chaplain; I'm dying."

June 28, 1944.

Like all men who have been in battle since D-Day the staff sergeant spoke slowly, enunciating clearly, careful not to spill the heavy burden of words that his great weariness managed to support. He told his story in a manner suggesting that the most important thing in his life at this moment was to convey what was on his mind to anyone who would listen and understand:

"When we landed on the beach D-Day, it was fairly quiet. We landed at noon and the beach had already been cleared. My company started inland; we walked half a mile before they opened up at us from a pillbox. The pillbox was a tremendous thing, most of it underground. We pounded it with everything we had, including a flame-thrower.

"We made our first mistake when two or three of them came out to surrender. Some of our trigger-happy boys shot them down. That made them close up again for three hours more, till finally they could stand it no longer. One hundred eighty-four of them came out of that one pillbox.

"We had slow going like that all the way. It took us eight days to take an objective that was supposed to be taken in one day.

"Once we took a pillbox and then went outside to bivouac for the night. I suggested we blow up the heavy guns in the pillbox so it would be useless if retaken. That is a job for the engineers, said my C.O., and we left it alone, During the night some Jerries managed to get back in and open fire on us. We had to take it all over again.

"Another pillbox was such a tough nut to crack that we called for tank support, but it was useless and succeeded only in drawing artillery fire. We had no bazookas or flamethrowers with us and had to send for some. Meanwhile my lieutenant suddenly ordered us to go right up to the pillbox. I thought what the hell good would that do, but I went with my squad thinking the lieutenant was coming, too. He didn't.

"We ran through a murderous stream of machine gun fire which lost us two men, but we got up to the pillbox. Now what? There was nothing we could do against six feet of concrete. We had to go back, and we ran through the machine gun fire again.

"I said: 'Lieutenant, why did you send us up there?'

"He mumbled something.

"I said: 'Next time you send me on a fool mission like that you are going to go right in front of me instead of sitting here on your behind.'

"He didn't say a word."

"I was sent on one other suicide mission. The lieutenant had been hanging around the captain's CP, than he told me to take my squad up the hill where snipers had been shooting at us, walk up and down the hedgerows and clean them out. We didn't know what was on that hill. My squad objected to going where a tank could handle it with much less risk.

"'That was the order I got,' insisted the lieutenant.

"'If you wouldn't hang around the CP you would not get such missions,' I told him.

"We started to go up, 'till suddenly they opened up at us with a heavy machine gun. That really saved us, and the plan of attack had to be changed. If we had advanced on that mission and the enemy had held their fire a little longer, we all would have been wiped out.;

"The worst weapons of all that we had to face were their screaming meemies. They are rockets filled with oil and phosphorous, I think. I got so I could tell where they would hit, and let me tell you I hugged that ground hard. They can shoot it about a mile. I have seen its concussion lift a man clean out of a foxhole. Fortunately the Germans have few of them, and little ammunition. I never heard them fire more than twice in one day, at least fifteen minutes apart. I think if the Germans had enough of them they could almost stop us cold.

"We never operated the way we were taught, with reserve companies and a reserve battalion. Every company and battalion has fought abreast all the way. Half the time the companies would be mixed with men from other companies. The only bit of relief we had has been from the wine we got from the Frenchies. Sometimes we went into battle half drunk."

After hearing experiences like these I am repeatedly amazed that any men so exposed for three weeks could have come through unharmed; and the ones who did are in the minority.

Today Captain Brill went to see some "brass" at the regimental CP. When he returned we asked, "What's the news Captain?"

"All fighting on the Cherbourg peninsula has officially ceased."

Then he added as an afterthought, "All that's going on now is some shooting."

From this I gather there are still a few Germans left who do not know that their side has surrendered in this sector.

June 29, 1944.

Our section moved forward to join the regiment near the Cherbourg airfield and met many men of the line companies we had not seen in over a month. They are getting their first rest since D-Day. Now we hear the painful details of how our comrades whose names appeared on the casualty reports met their personal Waterloos. It was shocking to hear about certain friends, but it is impossible to function as a soldier and brood over these tragedies. A soldier describing the death or maiming of his best friend relates the details with no display of emotion, almost as though speaking of a baseball game which his side lost. At the same time he has come to hate the enemy and has lost all inhibitions about killing humans who wear Nazi swastikas. Today we ate our first hot meal from a mobile kitchen. We also ate captured German bread and canned sardines with a Portuguese label and found them a welcome change from canned C-rations.

June 30.

No sooner have we our work tent set up and are busy trying to straighten our administrative tangle, an order comes to move again. We moved by truck down the peninsula to a field near the village of St. Mere Eglise, still with the regiment. We traveled on the road adjacent to the sea, and through every hamlet were greeted warmly by the French whose sincerity could possibly be gauged by the fact that throughout the German occupation they had saved their French flags and now had them waving proudly from their homes.

With one hand the people wave at us and with the other motion for cigarettes; nevertheless their friendliness seems genuine. The children shout "Bonbons" (candy) and "Cigarettes pour papa!" The older folks are more restrained and a little embarrassed at asking for things but are encouraged by the Americans' willingness to share with them in their obvious need.

The terrain is lower here than at Cherbourg, and swampy. We see many gliders that apparently crashed violently, possibly accounting for more losses than this invasion technique warrants though the airborne corps so transported have been cited for accomplishing their mission. So far our only source of news is the *Stars and Stripes* that reaches us sporadically and at best contains officially-sanctioned news with little of commentaries or analysis that makes good civilian newspapers popular and often great. Yet the experience of participation is even greater and more educational.

I do not regret being here, in danger of bombers who harass us nightly, or the occasional shellings, and exposure to snipers who are an ever-present menace. At the same time I am thankful for assignment to an important job that is performed somewhat removed from the front battle lines where the chances of coming through without being killed or badly wounded are minute.

A little while ago a new replacement said to me, "I hear casualties are worse in rifle companies than in others, aren't they?"

I tried to avoid giving a straight answer but he knew as well as I that it was so. The turnover of personnel in the rifle companies since D-Day is over one hundred percent.

July 1, 1944.

Joe and Fred are to all appearances average, good-natured GI's performing routinely with the rest. But they are unusual specialists, members of a small team of interrogators whose task is extracting information from the Prisoners of War. At that they are expert and have gained a fine reputation. They try to stick to the rules as near as possible. That outlaws using force, yet they succeed in drawing out information even from the most obstinate Nazis.

It is easy to get the Poles, Russians, Czechs and others who had been impressed into the German Army to talk. They rarely know anything of value anyway; they were simply put into the front line and told to shoot, with the Germans watching and ready to shoot them at any sign of betrayal, regarding then more like prisoners than as soldiers of the Reich. Before the fighting started they were kept in stockades and fed less than the Germans.

The deeply indoctrinated Nazis are the ones who have to be bluffed and bulldozed for information. They are deathly afraid of cold steel; the mere sight of a trench knife is enough to make them open up. Joe and Fred are experts at map reading. They interrogate prisoners separately, then compare notes to verify truthful information before turning in their reports to G2 (Intelligence). Almost without fail, their information about enemy gun positions, pillboxes and other strong positions has proven correct.

It takes much more than the ability to speak German to be a good interrogator. Many of them are like Joe and Fred who came to America as refugees from Nazi Germany, joined the Army and were sent to Intelligence schools. They have a personal score to settle with the Nazis. Like many special groups operating in a support capacity to the line troops, this team had wondered in advance just how much of an asset they would be in combat. Now they know, and are satisfied.

July 2, 1944.

The rest area is eight miles from the front facing south. We were told not to expect a long rest, which psychologically may be best; there is hardly a soldier who doesn't dread going back again to be in the hell at the front, but an extended rest would probably exacerbate their dread. We have now caught up in record keeping to the extent of knowing the names still in the regiment and new replacements.

The nightly shelling and bombing have not let up, but even worse are the mosquitoes in this marshy region. We are beginning to wonder, too, if there isn't more rain in Normandy than in England. The axiom that there are no atheists in foxholes holds true in this battle zone; religious services today were attended better than ever before, including men never seen at services.

As always, many rumors are afloat concerning the near future. The most persistent has it that General "Blood and Guts" Patton (commonly interpreted as your blood and his guts) is in France with several armored tank divisions and has boasted that we would take Paris in the next sixteen days. But whatever the plans for a coming offensive, everyone hopes the casualty rate will decrease. Several of the thirty survivors in a company that started with two hundred stated they had been subjected to more risks than air force flyers who are relieved of hazardous duty after fifty missions. It is probably impossible to find an infantry action equivalent for fifty air combat missions, but in the name of fairness some such provision should be made for infantrymen whose chances in the lottery of war are the poorest.

July 3, 1944.

Captains, lieutenants and even first sergeants have been as hard hit in action as privates and squad leaders. The tales of valor I hear are far more numerous than the number who were awarded decorations. One captain gained the admiration and wonder of his troops by performing his duties without flinching while under the most devastating enemy fire. With men falling all around him, he remained unfazed. His runner told me the man couldn't possibly be so brazen were he not doped up on cognac, which he had been drinking continuously since capturing the first case of the French beverage early in the campaign.

His most spectacular feat was in capturing a high-rank German general in a strongly fortified dugout near Cherbourg. The captain marched a captured German major to the pillbox and threatened to shoot him if he failed to talk the German occupants into surrendering. The major applied himself to that end and succeeded. Later the captain asked the general why he didn't surrender sooner rather than sacrifice his men in a hopeless endeavor.

The general replied, "What do I care? Just so it slows you up a little."

Most of the men I spoke to marveled that the Cherbourg peninsula fell as fast as it did, though longer than officially anticipated. The tiny fields in this country, each surrounded by a hedgerow of shrubs and trees densely growing atop a four-foot high earth embankment, render every field a veritable fortress. A few were booby-trapped.

The men took souvenirs, mostly from dead German soldiers, including valuable wrist watches, pistols and field glasses. In the next action, however, everyone expects many more booby traps and will be more careful in seeking trophies. Near the end when the Germans were low on 88-mm ammunition, they very effectively lowered the trajectory of their antiaircraft guns and used them as artillery.

July 4, 1944.

There is no visible celebration hereabouts this Fourth of July. Even the serious fireworks are light. To supplement the packaged food our field kitchens have been dishing out, some of the boys went gunning for cows. It is illegal, and one company paid a forty-dollar fine when caught with one, but the company considered it well worthwhile and had themselves some fine steaks.

A couple of men from a different company shot one and were about to heave it onto their truck when a farmer drove up in a horse-drawn wagon and, thinking the cow had been killed by shellfire, requested they help load the cow onto his wagon and thanked them warmly when they complied.

Among the many distasteful occurrences in combat is a category known as "self-inflicted wounds," usually gunshot wounds of the feet. Hereafter anyone legitimately struck in the foot by an enemy bullet may have to bear the suspicion of his fellow-soldiers that he did it himself. Several such cases came under suspicion but court-martial charges were not pressed as they would be difficult to prove. A man could also claim his gun discharged accidentally.

One first sergeant, notorious for staying in his foxhole more than necessary, announced one day suddenly and uncharacteristically that he was going into a woods to shoot a sniper he claimed was in the vicinity. He took along another man, a private also known for his timidity. They went a few yards till out of sight, then two shots rang out in the section that had until then been quiet. Soon they returned, both limping, each with a bullet in his foot. Similarly, a lieutenant received a gunshot wound in his right foot before he quite reached the front line.

July 5.

It cannot be stated as a rule, but clearly the loudest braggarts in garrison made poor showings in combat. Some did make good, but not in proportion to the quiet boys whose service records are marred with courtmartials, mostly for going AWOL during garrison life in the States. Many older men "blew up" mentally or fell out from physical exhaustion. A doctor in a forward aid station gave way mentally; in the midst of working he suddenly reeled and moaned, "All these men, butchered, butchered."

Captain Raynes, a dentist, grabbed him by the shoulders, shook him and said, "Take it easy, take it easy."

The doctor was evacuated.

One of the medical noncoms, Jake Brill, is a German refugee and has it in for all Nazis. He delights in administering blood plasma to wounded German prisoners and telling them, "This is Jewish blood from New York, do you mind it mixing with your blood?"

They say they don't mind.

One rapidly becomes conditioned to discussing the dead and wounded. Men who have been through the worst are able to smile and laugh shortly after. There is little morbidity after a battle; the atmosphere smelling of blood and gore dissipates rapidly from the fields. Towns almost completely razed by bombs and shells have little of a tragic aura about them. The townsfolk show little emotion as they search through the ruins. The sinister, tragic aspects of the war impact later.

July 6, 1944.

Our section together with other rear echelon components moved back to Huberville, near Valognes. Here the thunder of artillery is still loud though we are farther removed from the front. We are now practically caught up with our battle casualty reports. So far we've had only one instance of a man reported to Washington as "Killed in Action" then changing the report to "Wounded in Action." We are sweating out our companies going back into action.

Yesterday evening I rode a captured German bicycle on a personal reconnaissance of the countryside. Near Valognes an elderly Frenchman offered me a glass of cognac from his nearly depleted wine cellar. In appreciation I gave him cigarettes and matches, which he took as if they were gold.

The town of Valognes is Off Limits to military personnel so the civilians may salvage whatever they can without our interference. I spoke to some civilians outside town limits. They begged for shoes and soap. Few could speak any English and we labored to communicate through my one-year high school French. It is amazing how much I can convey with just a few key words. I made a deal with a gentleman to give him a pair of worn GI shoes in exchange for a liter (less than a quart) of cognac.

I gave away some K-ration chocolates, a confection designed to hold up in adverse conditions and disliked by Americans but received by the civilians as manna from heaven. They had not tasted chocolate in four years.

I asked a man if he had heard any free world news during the German occupation. He said he is a radio technician and after his radio was taken from him he built a galena set with earphones that enabled him to listen secretly to broadcasts from England.

A girl whose husband is a "Vichy Government" naval engineer in Paris said she visited him a few months ago in Paris and found conditions so bad that she subsisted mainly on the food she had brought with her from Normandy.

Some I spoke to claim they worked in ammunition factories for the Germans and assisted the French underground by sabotaging artillery shells, producing many duds. I heard an instance from our troops of a shell that landed, fell apart without exploding and a note fell out reading, "We did our part, now you do yours." None of the shells that came in my direction failed to explode, but one soldier said he owes his life to three 88-mm duds that fell near him.

July 7, 1944.

Until we entered combat new men coming into the regiment were assigned pretty well according to their civilian or military skills. Contrary to a widespread impression, "Classification" functioned quite effectively. In combat, men coming into the regiment have been

thrown indiscriminately into battle as riflemen; men trained as cannoneers, cooks, radio operators, clerks were shoved *en masse* into
rifle companies at the front, including some who never had a close
look at an Ml rifle. The non-rifle companies which could have used
their skills sustained relatively few casualties, hence required few replacements.

Recent recruits with specialized skills stand a poorer chance of being
assigned for utilization of their skills than those who have been in
the army longer. Now there is an almost indiscriminate need for
"cannon fodder;" the battlefield is grotesque and soulless as a Sal-
vador Dali painting and the infantry a sausage machine consuming
human beings without limit.

The average man in battle has mixed emotions of fear and gallantry,
with fear predominant when shells come at him, at which time his
total concentration is on estimating the shells' destination, hugging
the earth, cringing with every muscle. He neither prays nor weeps.
That comes later. Any exhilaration one may feel on the battlefield is
a surrealistic dance with death.

The casualty reports are dispassionate and generally accurate. Observed one company clerk: "When I go home I'll be able to talk shop
with my undertaker friend. I'll say to him, 'I've handled the death reports of more men than you'll bury the rest of your life.'"

July 8, 1944.

Our division is in action again. It seems the 4th is called on to spearhead where others fail. One division, the 83rd, is said to have been a
flop in action and all the top officers had to be tossed out. The present
front is on flooded land where the water at some points comes up to
the chest. German defenses are tight, but a map captured from a
German colonel reportedly indicates that in a few miles their pillboxes
and solid emplacements end and the terrain changes, becoming suitable for deploying our armored divisions.

Germany appears to have enough petroleum for its mechanized
land equipment but not for airplanes, judging by the decreased
activity of their Luftwaffe.

The French attitude toward their German-dominated Vichy Govern-

ment may be about as one Frenchman summed up for me: "Field
Marshal Petain? I don't know, I really have little opinion on the
matter. You see, when France fell to the Germans England was alone
and English propaganda broadcasts to France spoke of England's
ability to resist a German invasion but held out only vague promises
for the French, and America was very, very far away. Petain seemed
able at least to keep the Germans from drafting French labor to work
in Germany."

He was surprised to hear that I have been in the Army two and a
half years, in England five months and that I liked the English people.

"But aren't they cold?" he asked.

I did not find them so, I replied. He told me the French have been
sabotaging railroads and were not deterred even when French civilians
were forced to ride on German troop trains. He said that aside from
shoes and soap, the nonedible commodity the French need most is
toilet paper, though they haven't been asking us for it.

July 9, 1944.

Today is bleak, cold, windy and my regiment is having a hell of a
time on line against the troops and tanks of a German panzer (armored) division. Chaplain Boice came back to our area to write letters
to the families of men who had been hit. He is being recommended
for a Silver Star citation for heroism. He is highly thought of by the
men in the regiment, though he started with two strikes against him
for appearing frail, almost effeminate. He is also an interesting, albeit
rambling, talker: "The paratroopers were the bravest soldiers as a class
that I met. They searched out the enemy, asked which unit was suffering the most casualties and they would then attach themselves to that
regular infantry unit. Our average infantryman acted reluctant to
press into action until forced by circumstances. We've had two regimental commanders so far. Both were relieved of their command allegedly for not being aggressive enough, but I think they were simply
trying to accomplish their missions with conservative methods that
would have caused us fewer losses."

Our division commander General Barton, said Chaplain Boice, is a
good strategist but loses too many men in forced assaults, though he

admits in the long run it may be the most economical (in terms of casualties) way to do battle.

He is bitter at the failure of high officers to come down personally to see the men they were sending back into combat and convey their sympathy and encouragement. The commanding General's promise of a pleasant surprise after Cherbourg fell never materialized.

Said Chaplain Boice, "Tanks are at a premium; men are easier to obtain and therefore more readily sent into combat. Tanks rarely advance in front of the foot soldiers and when they do, at the first sign of 88 fire they scoot for cover. One tank commander, more courageous than the others we have seen, brought up his tanks to where an infantry battalion had been pinned down for hours by antiaircraft fired at point-blank range. He ascertained their positions, then rolled right over the guns with his tanks, machinegunned the gunners and released our pinned down troops.

"Often the tanks wait for the infantry to go forward and the infantry waits for the tanks, till finally someone phones down to find out what is holding up the action. They work well together once they get moving."

One of Chaplain Boice's major gripes is the way psychoneurotic cases are handled. The medics theorize that an effective cure is for a psychiatrist to speak soothingly to them and talk away their fears. This supposedly cures nine out of ten, and in two or three days they are again sent into action. Being well disciplined soldiers, they obey. Then when the first shots are fired they become raving, sometimes hopeless lunatics. Chaplain Boice has often gone to foxholes where men half-crazed with fear refused to come out when the action was over.

He would say to them, "Don't you know me?"

"Yes, you are the chaplain."

"You trust me, don't you?"

And so he convinced them to come out and be sent back for treatment.

July 10, 1944.

The opposition put up now by the Germans is fiercer than ever. Their artillery continues to take a large toll of our troops, though at no time does theirs match our artillery in either numbers or effectiveness. The Germans seem to lose out by their specious tactic of sending shells at us in all directions and just when they succeed in boxing us in they stop firing. They can be counted on to send over a barrage during breakfast, lunch, dinner, at 11 P.M. and 2 A.M. Apparently they choose these times for their nuisance value.

Our tactics are generally different; we pinpoint our objectives and at least once a day "serenade" the enemy. This is done by selecting a single area, then firing every artillery piece we have for miles around in one salvo timed exactly for each to hit the target area at the same instant. A captured German officer said he had fought on the Russian front and experienced the famous Russian artillery fire, and that ours was much worse.

In yesterday's fighting our troops again took punishment from our own planes. This happens accidentally now and then; this time it was ordered on purpose by a general who said it has to be done, against a hill overlooking the marshland where the Germans were dug in. Every time our troops attacked through the marshes the Germans held their fire until we were well exposed, then opened fire with every-thing they had. Some of our troops got through and were fighting on the hill when our airplanes came over to "assist."

Our new replacements are not really hit more than veterans, though the veterans think they are. Once in the midst of an enemy artillery barrage a platoon sergeant saw a new man stick his head out of his foxhole. The sergeant threw a stone at him to get it down. When the barrage ended he asked the man why he had his head up and received the reply that he "wanted to see what was going on." Some veterans think if a man survives his first action he has a good chance of coming through the next one or two by simply sticking to his foxhole and holding back a little when told to advance.

We had a little trouble in our vicinity by what we thought was a sniper taking pot-shots at us. We hunted for him without success, and decided the shooting may have come from a trio of Negro soldiers nearby who have been forcing their way into farmhouses, demanding wine and terrorizing the inhabitants by shooting off their guns. Last night a woman came to our field in terror and asked for protection from a colored American soldier who tried to attack her. We escorted her home. He had already left. Perhaps some Negroes are reacting in this fashion as a result of the repression they experienced in England.

July 11, 1944.

An infantry regiment contains twenty companies, all dangerous to be in during combat but the nine rifle companies far worse than the others, suffering 72 percent of the casualties. The three heavy weapons companies account for 12 percent and the balance of 16 percent occurs among the remaining eight companies. It is common for a rifle company to start fighting with a strength of 170 men and the next day go into battle with 70, while in that same day turning over three or four company commanders. The new replacements seem to understand this, either from sensing or hearing tales. They know that the type of company they are assigned to may make the difference between their living or dying. I have the job of doing the assigning, which at this time does not require a great deal of judgment as the rifle companies need most of them.

Yesterday when I went to a forward position to assign replacements one asked me, "Are we going right into combat?" Yes, I replied, and knew that like as not he would by tomorrow be some sort of casualty. Another man asked with tears in his eyes to give him a break on grounds that he was 37 years of age, had a wife and child, and at previous garrison stations had been given light physical duties because he couldn't hike. He asked me where I'm from. Pittsburgh, I replied.

"Well, we're neighbors," he said, "I'm from Pennsylvania too."

It was pitiful; I could do nothing for him. The infantry is loaded with men similarly handicapped. A new second lieutenant asked me "the score." I suggested he remove his insignia of rank to prevent singling out of an officer by the enemy. Noncoms also remove their stripes in battle. In addition I advised him to trade his light carbine for a soldier-size Ml rifle which most officers at the front prefer to carry. At this point a few enemy shells whizzed by and everyone ducked for nearest cover.

July 12.

Our section moved closer to the front for better liaison. It is warmer here, in a manner of speaking. Our troops are not doing very well in this sector. We advanced two miles in five days, with heavy losses. One of our companies was badly shot up by mortar shells from the 83rd Infantry Division that was supposed to be helping us. The enemy took heavy losses too, but we only give a damn for our own.

Now we are fighting the real Nazis instead of Poles and Russians, and are taking few prisoners. All our field kitchens are now in operation. As soon as our forward troops are relieved they come back for hot meals, one battalion at a time. Their "rest area" is back only a couple of hundred yards from the front.

We are almost clear of the marshes and a few of our tanks have been in action, but we don't expect any major armored action until we secure St. LÔ and Coutances.

We were saddened to hear that General Teddy Roosevelt (Jr.) died today of a heart attack. He had been our assistant division commander since shortly before we left England. An amiable man, he was highly regarded by all and has been recommended to be awarded the Congressional Medal of Honor for his part in leading the 4th Infantry Division task force that first hit the Normandy beach. He kept "hitting the bottle" pretty hard also, which apparently did not do his heart much good.

July 13, 1944.

Our artillery is so close to the regimental command post that for the short time I was there every time one of our guns fired my knees buckled from the blast. The enemy shelled the CP heavily last night, and we had a couple of casualties. A sergeant came back from the front line a mile away and observed that the recent bunch of new men was good except they didn't know anything.

"Then what do you do with them?" I asked.

"Teach them how to load their Ml rifles," he replied. "I like to advance, never stop; seems like the worst casualties we get are when we stop and the jerries have a chance to zero in on us."

He was bitter about our tanks. "We infantrymen offered to take over the tanks ourselves, but they wouldn't let us. Hell, they run away when just a machine gun opens up at them."

Many of our casualties now are "Combat Fatigue" cases, men who came through all right from the start and are beginning to break down physically and emotionally. They need a rest badly; a real rest—the short one after Cherbourg fell was entirely inadequate and during it they were even ordered, of all things, to march in close-order drill for the benefit of the new men.

We are now getting replacements who were still in the States on D-Day. In the last two groups one man in each shot himself before getting to the front line, ostensibly by accident. One hit himself in the left hand, the other in the arm.

I visited Service Company today when a Frenchman came and tried to tell the first sergeant something, without success. I went over and was able to grasp that down the road an American soldier had threatened a 14-year-old girl with his gun and was terrorizing several other civilians. We walked down to the crossroad and met the fellow. He was from our regiment and possibly AWOL from his company on line. He appeared to me fatigued, nervous, fit more for psychiatric treatment than disciplinary action. We delivered him to some passing MPs.

July 14, 1944.

Today is the French holiday, Bastille Day. In battered Carentan there is a festive spirit. Every building strong enough to support them is decorated with French, American and British flags. The public still congregates at the side of the road to gawk and wave at each vehicle in the endless military stream on the main highway through town. Some women bring out pots and pans to clean while they look. Judging by the reconstruction going on, the American army is not anticipating setbacks. Our Engineer Corps is repairing roads, telephone wires and railroads (already back in operation) right up to the edge of the front. There are signs the French underground is mobilizing in the open; some wearing armbands in lieu of uniforms are carrying rifles and pistols. So far we have little contact with the French other

than negotiating occasionally for cider, cognac or "des oeufs," eggs.
An American M.P. directs traffic at every crossroad.

Normandy is now a vast Allied arsenal; it would hardly be possible
for Germany to bomb any field on the Cherbourg peninsula without
causing military damage. Fortunately they don't or can't very much.
Our mine detector teams go over every field carefully as we advance.
Land mines have knocked out quite a number of our jeeps and tanks,
visibly strewn at the side of the roads. One of the latest heroes turning
up in our outfit is a private who knocked out three enemy tanks with
a bazooka. He was to have been decorated by the division general
this afternoon, but somebody failed to bring him back early this
morning and just before he got around to it the private was killed.

July 15, 1944.

I recall the first time I ever stood guard duty, in 1942 at Camp
Wheeler, Georgia. It was night and the darkness cast a sinister spell.
Here the darkness is thrice sinister. When I walk guard at night I hold
my rifle in my hands instead of resting against my shoulder, my finger
ready at the trigger.

In forward outposts at the front men on guard seldom shoot when
they hear a sound ahead of them; they toss a hand grenade. Tonight
felt peaceful when I went on guard at dusk. A herd of cows and a
mare with her colt grazed sublimely on the far end of the field. Across
the road a new cemetery, almost completely full with row on row of
white wooden burial stakes, was abandoned for the night by a crew
of German-prisoner gravediggers and their M.P. escorts. Soon it became very dark and occasionally a pistol or rifle shot nearby broke
the quiet with startling effect. Who shot it and for what reason, I have
no idea.

Suddenly a very loud explosion shook the ground. In about six
seconds a tremendous burst of antiaircraft fire went up at all sides.
Many bright tracer shells streaked into the sky and powerful searchlight beams tried to spotlight the enemy planes.

Something landed near us with a dull thud and the two of us
walking guard hit the ground for protection. Most of the boys sprang
out of their pup tents and into foxholes they had dug. We decided

that the thud came from a falling piece of antiaircraft flak. The airplane that dropped the bomb scampered with throttle wide open as soon as our guns started firing. It quieted down for the rest of our guard shift, except for sporadic artillery detonations.

July 16, 1944.

The whole regiment is back in reserve. During this campaign segment two battalions fought until a few days ago when they were relieved by the third that had been in reserve and now also pulled off the line. The few men remaining who have never been hit are wearier than ever. They are not far enough back to sleep undisturbed, and there is little rest in their sleep. Two men who fought since D-Day and are considered excellent soldiers approached their company commander.

"Sir," said one, "I am not going on line any more. I've had enough and I'm not going to torture myself any more. You can do what you want—take out your pistol and shoot me if you wish; I won't go up there any more."

The other said, "That goes for me too."

They were evacuated and tagged "Exhaustion."

Our replacements are now better classified; they have at least seen an Ml rifle before. They haven't had nearly the extent of training the original men had going into combat, yet the division's capability is better than ever. It is becoming apparent that what makes this a good division is the little turnover of personnel in artillery, communications, heavy weapons teams and other supporting units; also, there are always just enough experienced men in the rifle companies to enable them to function effectively, and perhaps most important of all is the able leadership from battalion commanders on up. I think it is now proven that mixed personnel, older men with young, works satisfactorily in action and well that it is so, otherwise the younger would be discriminated against by doing all the worst sort of fighting.

Unlike another division fighting with us in the region, our flanks are seldom open and units exposed without support. In one operation, that division left enough equipment and ammunition lying around when they withdrew to supply us for days.

German anti-personnel land mines, one called a "castrator" model, have been giving us trouble. One engineer operating a mine detector stepped on something he immediately realized was a mine and kept his weight on it, knowing it would explode the instant he stepped off. He shouted for everybody to move out of the way, then threw himself backward to avoid as much of the blast as possible. It caught him in the shoulder, injuring him less than it would have otherwise.

July 17, 1944.

For no particular reason, it happens that Company F is made up of a large proportion of men whose names end in "ski" or "wicz," as Polish as Paderewski. These men feel their teamwork is distinctive, and it is indeed beyond reproach. Seventeen men are left who started on D-Day, among them a few who returned from the hospital for a second chance at the enemy and at death. Some are still stiff from their wounds and nearly all have shrapnel in their flesh which can be removed some day if they wish, they were told, at a veterans hospital. Since they must return to combat, they are pleased it is to the same company.

While the situation regarding new replacements has improved somewhat, our regiment has worked out an impromptu classification of its own that is proving admirably effective.

The other day the regimental adjutant told me: "Assign eight men to Cannon Company."

"But we weren't sent cannoneers, Sir," I advised."

"Just get me eight husky men," he said, "we'll make cannoneers out of them."

Right now the new men we assigned in the last few days to bring the regiment up to strength are practice-firing on a makeshift rifle, machine gun and mortar range so near the front it is often hard to decide which is the practice and which the enemy shooting for keeps.

July 18, 1944.

For our section the state of combat has settled down to a methodical pace. It is not slow, but we carry on mechanistically, anticipating daily to hear we advanced so far, and from medical reports learn that so many men became casualties yesterday. We can now take a shower in the field; from a crudely rigged apparatus but nonetheless a shower. A bugler sounds reveille in the morning from some distant field, and taps at night. We no longer have to struggle building a fire for every meal to heat our canned rations. Now we line up before a field kitchen in civilized army style. We have more cigarettes than we need to supply both ourselves (I don't use them) and civilians. We live spartanly, working every day including Sunday and almost every evening until dark. We spend practically no money; our trading with civilians is on a barter basis. Conditions are reminiscent of our 1942 summer maneuvers in the Carolinas, with mosquitoes, pup tents and dusty back roads; less of course going into town for a Saturday night break. That Carolina episode ended abruptly, returning us to the comparative comfort of barracks and service club at Camp Gordon, Georgia. Oh that this would end as abruptly and in like manner!

July 19.

We had our first Personnel Section casualty today. One of our company clerks visited his company to find out how many men wanted a partial pay, the balance of their pay left to accumulate. No one wanted more money now. They had plenty and nothing to do with it. The clerk chatted with a man cleaning a captured German pistol. The gun went off, catching him in the foot. We are experiencing many such accidental casualties from "empty" guns. The incident illustrates the fickleness of fate: a wound occurring out of action while a few men in action at the front all along scarcely received a scratch.

The companies are now "reorganized" and partially rested. Promotions have been handed out generously, with little adherence to the number of ratings authorized in the Table of Organization. Sometimes a field clerk working directly under the company commander would send in an order promoting himself to sergeant when the company commander had been evacuated and a new one not yet assigned.

One new captain discovered the fraud and said to the clerk, formerly a pfc, "Now you can write up an order reducing yourself in rank from sergeant to private."

Given the turnover as it is, he will probably soon make himself a sergeant again.

Tonight the regiment will move out to a new area. Our divsion's commanding general spoke to the regiment yesterday, told us if we do half as well as before—he won't promise, but it may be our last campaign. We can expect to fight a different style of battle than heretofore, to a certain extent motorized. Meantime we have drawn a special assignment in which we may be cut off behind enemy lines for a few days but will wind up all right. The men anticipate a fierce onslaught, probably assisting a tank division in a power drive through the center of the enemy line.

Both officers and enlisted men on line consider it a miracle they have come through so far and wonder how long it will take for the law of averages to catch up with them. Now they do hate the enemy, unlike before D-Day when they merely felt they have a job to do. They feel they have taken enough risks in this war and it is time others share by taking their places in front line battle.

July 21, 1944.

Rainy weather is holding up the war. We would like the weather to break because we somehow see the future prospects bright and Germany's end tantalizingly near. In a captured letter from a girl in Germany to her soldier boy friend, she pleads with him not to try being a hero. She concludes, though, with "Hell Hitler." Tonight we took time out for an old-fashioned discussion.

"How long can Germany go on like this?" said Henry. "Why don't the people revolt?"

"Nope," replied Joe spoiling for a good argument, "we've seen how one machine gun can hold up a whole infantry battalion. What the hell can unarmed civilians do against armed Nazi stormtroopers."

"Well, I guess so; it looks like we'll have Russia to thank for finishing the war fast."

"Why? What is the matter with how we are doing?"

"Oh, we're doing great but how can you compare it with Russia's big battles? The Cherbourg peninsula campaign was about the size of the Russian battle for Sevastopol on the Crimean peninsula."

"You know even Stalin admits our invasion was the biggest of its kind ever attempted in warfare."

"Sure, but it is eclipsed by the Russian front against the Germans. You underrate Russia's great accomplishments and idealism."

"And you underrate America's. Russia is fighting on her own soil. We gave them arms, diverted Japan from her rear, and started a second front in Europe. Talk about idealism—what other country would cross an ocean and fight two wars for democracy? We didn't have to come to Europe, and a lot of American soldiers would be alive today if we didn't. We could have stayed home and kept Germany or anyone else from invading us for centuries. We are economically self-sufficient. But we hate militarism so much that we just didn't want to remain armed and neutral while watching other countries being enslaved. Would you call Russia's idealism greater than that?"

July 22, 1944.

As the general told us, in the campaign to date our regiment has fought longer than any other. Going into battle has become as routine as our old training schedules in garrison with hikes, lectures and night problems. At the same time our division became one of the worst abattoirs in the Unites States Army it also developed into a well-oiled war machine. Our heroes are more for extended bravery in action than for sporadic flash-in-pan heroics rewarded with high posthumous decorations. One company commander said he was going to ask that the Bronze Star Medal be awarded everyone who hit the beach on D-Day and fought hard since then.

When the company commanders wish to recommend awards for bravery, they often cannot be more specific in their citations than to say, "Fought well" or, "Was an inspiration to the troops." Captain Raynes, a dentist, was cited for doing a physician's job when none was available for days. He has been around so long that he picked up enough surgical knowledge to act in emergencies, and in addition maintained a cheerful disposition that was at times as therapeutic as medicine.

Lieutenant Zuckerman of Riverside Drive in New York was recommended for the Silver Star for volunteering to expose himself to rifle fire from a sniper who was holding up an important operation and thus reveal the sniper's location. Division Headquarters sent back the recommendation with a request that it be resubmitted for the higher Distinguished Service Cross.

One of the most chronic AWOL offenders in garrison days, with so many courtmartials scribbled on his service record there wasn't room for more, volunteered for 23 patrol missions and brought in more enemy snipers than any other individual. He can't understand how he came through alive.

July 23, 1944.

Passing scenes:

(1) A new crop of war prisoners was brought in and turned over to the team of interrogators. An interrogator costumed for the encounter with a pup tent shelter half-draped importantly around him walked over to the group slowly, gave each prisoner a lingering, terror-inspiring gaze, then with a dramatic flourish selected one and sent him to another interrogator wearing a Russian gold star general's insignia. He began testily to question the prisoner, quit abruptly in a few moments and haughtily turned him over to a third interrogator. This one took a milder tone, drawing out the prisoner conversationally.

A lieutenant emerged from the headquarters tent and said loudly in German, "Everybody from the 5th Company step out."

Two prisoners began moving, caught themselves but it was too late; they had given themselves away and identified their unit. Finally the prisoners were segregated into two groups, one with those who would talk and the other who wouldn't.

"This group goes to America," said the lieutenant, then pointed to the nontalkers, "and this group goes to Russia."

Instantly the nontalkers outshouted each other saying, "I'll talk, I'll talk!"

(2) The next day after bringing troops back a little way for a much needed rest a battalion commander sent down an order to company officers that they are to stand a drill formation with their troops. The officers excitedly got together and agreed not to comply with the order. A second order came down calling the officers to the command post. They went in a body and one spokesman said to the battalion commander: "Sir, I don't know what you are going to do with

us—possibly court-martial the lot of us for mutiny. We just came out of a long stretch in combat; we need whatever rest we can get and are not going to ask our men to stand a drill formation." The lieutenant-colonel looked at each of them sternly, then his face relaxed and he said, "All right, that's all, boys."

(3) At one bad spot a battalion commander ordered a brief withdrawal. In the operation, two men were cut off and isolated. A lieutenant started forward to help them. The battalion commanding officer spotted him and ordered him back. The lieutenant started forward in mute refusal, determined to try rescuing the two men. The CO, himself known for reckless courage and ruthlessness, drew his pistol and said, "Come back or I'll shoot you."

The lieutenant hesitated a moment, then obeyed. Later someone asked the CO, "Would you really have shot him?"

"Yes," he replied, then added, "God I wish I had a dozen lieutenants like him!"

(4) One of the chaplains preaches his sermons in "holy roller" style. He devotes a portion of his sermon to calling on the Almighty for help and itemizes each request in detail. In one service he beseeched, "Lord, please make our artillery be of good aim. And Lord, do make it easier for the infantry. Another thing, Lord, please—please let us have some sunshine so our military plans may proceed successfully."

Just then the solid overcast of clouds that had caused rain for a week thinned at one spot for a brief moment and let through a hazy ray of sunshine.

The chaplain looked up ecstatically and said in a profound, humble voice, "Thank you, Lord."

(5) Two men walked back to the battalion aid station, one supporting the other who had been lightly hit. They paused for a smoke. The unhurt man took out two cigarettes and put both between his lips as he had once seen Bob Hope do in a movie. Just as he started to light them a stray 88 shell moaned by and fell twenty yards away. They sprawled on the ground, neither of them hit but the two cigarettes still between the well man's lips had blossomed into shreds. The injured man looked at him and laughed hysterically.

"What's so damn funny?" commented the other. They walked on

and came upon a cow wailing in agony with one foot blown clean away.

"I'll shoot her," said the well man. He brought up his rifle, aimed, then lowered it.

"I can't do it," he said. "If it were a German I'd kill him, but I can't shoot that cow."

The injured man took the gun and put the cow out of her misery.

July 24, 1944.

John Sarrens returned from England looking pretty good, the scar on his scalp where a bullet had skimmed it not too ugly. He was eager to talk.

"It happened two days after D-Day," he said about his wound. "Do you know what saved us in the invasion? It was the intelligence reports, especially the movies taken by hedge-hopping planes which showed every feature of the terrain. We saw two main roads off the beach and it was pointed out to us that one was busy with traffic and the other had no traffic on it at all. When we landed we avoided the one with no traffic. Later our sappers went over it and took out hundreds of land mines.

"The hospitals did a wonderful job in England, but as soon as you leave them it is bad. I was sent to Feese's Farm for recuperation. There we had to do more KP and guard duty than anywhere in the army. One of the boys refused to pull KP. He was ordered to see the commanding officer, a major.

"'Tell the major to come see me,' he answered back. The major came and the fellow told him, 'I've been wounded in battle and I'm here to recuperate. I'm not going to do any work.'

"The major answered, 'Being wounded doesn't mean you should have servants waiting on you here. You are still in the Army. You'll go back to France in a few days. Now I order you to go on KP.'

"'You can go to hell, Major,' the fellow said, 'and I wish you'd court-martial me and lock me up for six months or a year—I'll live that much longer.'

"The major walked away without saying another word. They really overdid their rehabilitation program; they had us on the go day and night with lectures, hikes, inspections and details. I think those replacement centers try to make it so miserable the boys would be glad to go back to the front.

"One day we had three full-field inspections, then they woke us three in the morning for another one. The payoff was an S.O.S (Services of Supplies) captain lecturing us on hedgerow fighting."

"'Were you in Normandy, Captain?' somebody asked. He ignored the question. Then they started moving us from one replacement pool to another. I went through a dozen in two days and had a clothing check at every one to make sure I had all the things I knew I'd throw away as soon as I hit France.

"Say, when is this outfit going to rest?"

"We've been out of action and are now going back in," I replied.

His face fell. I've rarely heard of anyone anxious to go back to the front. Since they must go back they want to be with the 4th Infantry Division again and are pleased the general demands they be returned to his division instead of sending them to another. Some of the returning men appear broken and nervous, their hearts and souls devoid of any feeling except panic at the mere mention of combat.

Chaplain Frank approached the general and proposed, "These men have served the division well; can't something be done for them—give them duty behind the lines?"

The general liked the idea and several have been assigned such duties after consultation with the division psychiatrist.

July 26, 1944.

With the conquest of most of Normandy, our high command apparently considers the first phase of the invasion accomplished. At the same time we have built up enough power to launch a drive aimed at conquering the rest of the German-dominated continent. This being done in the space of a month and a half seems a prodigious achievement, regardless of original expectations.

The second phase of the invasion began yesterday morning, July 25. Three thousand Allied aircraft flew over in concentration to soften up Germany's front line at a point so narrow it can be defended by a relatively small force, an advantage Germany is never again likely to possess. For nearly two hours our heavy bombers flew over us in flight formations that extended solidly from one horizon to the other. Compared with the swift fighter planes we usually see, they seemed to drift by slowly. As they released their bombloads not far away the earth trembled under us like an exaggerated vibrating of a ship's motors.

We watched from a hill and could see a few planes hit with anti-aircraft flack explode and spiral downwards. At the front our lines were marked with large white and orange covers to show where our lines end and the enemy's begin. Even so a few of the bombs fell inside our territory with some resulting damage.

When the bombing ended the 4th Division, minus our regiment, spearheaded an infantry assault. They found many Germans dead or stunned, they captured many, yet there remained quite stiff resistance and uncannily here and there an 88 would start shelling though the Germans were now hopelessly surrounded and disorganized.

This morning our regiment went into action as support troops for the 2nd Armored Division with whom we had once maneuvered in the Carolinas. Our infantrymen rode the tanks Russian style, some following on half-tracks and trucks. This team spearheaded the attempt to break through the enemy line near St. Lô and enter the open "tank country." If successful the operation will establish a corridor through which we can pour our mass of waiting troops and armor out of Normandy and into the French heartland toward Paris; but if we fail to secure the corridor the spearhead could be cut off deep behind enemy lines. Our troops have taken along supplies to last four days.

July 27, 1944.

Chuck Canter wanted very much to be a good soldier. He was young, small and the goat of his platoon. One night he volunteered to man an outpost with another man; an unusually dangerous outpost, almost as exposed to our own artillery as the enemys'. The two men crawled out and laid low. Soon they discerned four soldiers coming toward them, apparently Germans out on patrol.

Chuck called out, "Halt."

They stopped and threw up their hands. Chuck was at a loss; he didn't know how to converse with them. They all stood still a full ten minutes glaring mutely at each other, then Chuck told his companion to guard them while he ran back to consult his platoon sergeant.

"I've got four prisoners," he said excitedly, "what should I do with them?"

"Bring them in," replied the sergeant.

Chuck went back to bring them in; they were fierce-looking young Nazis armed to the teeth with machine pistols and concussion grenades but did not try to resist. The next day Chuck beamed with happiness as the men in his platoon patted him on the back for his feat of capturing four Germans; he was making good and showing he had "guts." Later that day the platoon got into difficulty, especially Chuck's squad which took cover in a shallow ravine from mortar fire. The lieutenant ordered the squad to withdraw. They all crawled out carefully except Chuck who for some reason stood up and was hit instantly. He fell lifeless.

The platoon sergeant saw him go down and commented to the lieutenant, "Chuck was a good soldier."

"Yes," agreed the lieutenant.

And the other men echoed, "Poor Chuck, always blundering but he turned out to be a damn good soldier."

July 28.

There is no such thing as an easy battle. Wherever the enemy is capable of shooting even one man he is dangerous, for no one would care to be that man. But there are varying degrees of intensity, and the men of Company I would not care to repeat one experience they had during the Cherbourg campaign.

The Germans had a large pillbox concealed innocently in the side of a hill, but it was unlike any other pillbox. The Germans had built it so an attacking force could reach it only from one narrow direction, and they had six machine guns fixed in a wide semicircle above the pillbox trained in that direction.

Company I approached and the German machine gunners held their fire till the right moment, then opened fire. The men ran for cover to a shallow gully twenty yards from the pillbox, a highly dubious refuge but they couldn't retreat. They were trapped. The enemy exploited their plight to the limit, throwing everything they had into the gully.

For seven hours Company I lay there under the continuous hail of bullets and shrapnel. Many men were hit. Anyone sticking his head up a little to appraise the situation was apt to have it shot off, so no one tried. They underwent a process of slow annihilation.

After seven hours another company managed from a distance to harass the enemy machine gunners enough to divert their aim. That was all Company I needed; one man got up with a flame thrower, fumbled with the lighting mechanism, couldn't get it to work and had to dig into his pocket for a match while bullets rained about him. Finally he got it lit and shot the flames at the pillbox, forcing those inside to immediately shut every opening.

Then another man ran up to the pillbox and set a 20 pound charge of TNT. He got barely ten yards away when it went off, and he was injured. But it turned the trick, and by now the machine guns above the pillbox were out of action. The pillbox entrance opened and 169 Germans came out with their hands up. The TNT had not dented the 12-foot thick wall but the concussion had been too much for them. Inside the immense pillbox Company I found that the Germans had enough ammunition and wine to hold out for six months.

July 29, 1944.

Before battling for Monteburg our 2nd Battalion had a terrible day at Azeville, but in the course of the day an incident occurred that provided sardonic merriment for the unhurt survivors.

Company E pushed out in advance that day after they received a heavy shelling. While waiting in a ravine for the rest of the battalion to come up on either flank, the company commander went up to the crest of the ravine to observe. He saw a body of men coming toward him. He could not ascertain their indentity but was positive it was a company of the battalion coming to position themselves alongside his.

"Don't shoot, don't shoot—friendly troops" he yelled to his men and waved an orange flag.

The approaching troops stopped and gaped in open-mouthed amazement.

Suddenly the captain stopped waving and said to the sergeant at his side, "Give me those field glasses."

He grabbed the glasses from the sergeant's hands, failing to consider that they were hung by a strap from the sergeant's neck which consequently remained sore for days from the captain's quick pull.

"They're Germans," screamed the captain, "get me a rifle grenade."

He forgot he had only one rifle grenadier left and he had gone for ammunition after leaving his rifle with the captain.

Frantically the captain hollered down the ravine, "Bring me rifle grenades, quick!" A private came walking slowly, cautiously up the hill toward the captain carrying clumsily one small grenade in both hands.

"Is this what you wanted, Sir?" he said meekly.

By now the Germans had turned and fled. The captain looked disgustedly at the private, then bowed from the waist, tenderly took the grenade from him and quietly said, "Thank you," following which he abruptly changed his tone.

"What the hell am I going to do with one measly grenade?" he shouted.

The private, too scared to notice the captain's wrathful sarcasm, replied, "Shoot it, Sir."

The captain resignedly fixed the grenade to rifle and fired at the Germans now far out of range.

July 31, 1944.

In the wake of our drive south of St. Lô and Coutances our section moved to Marigny, midway between the two towns. We rode through the area that had been saturation-bombed and saw that such was indeed the case. Craters were everywhere, seldom farther apart than 20 yards. There were many dead cows, disabled tanks and other vehicles, and a few dead Germans still unburied. If the rest of France must be "liberated" in this manner the natives may not be exactly ecstatic. So far they are sad at the destruction, yet gratified with the broad aspects of liberation.

Our advance is making good headway. The weather is favorable, with only brief interludes of rain during which our tanks are held up, less because of mud than for poor visibility through the periscope. The coordination of tanks with infantry is interesting; the tanks must know where to go and how to get there, but infantry commanders take over and direct the tanks when opposition is encountered.

The first day of the push our regiment traveled 15 miles before meeting substantial enemy resistance. One infantryman riding on a tank said he preferred it to riding on half-tracks or trucks as it is easier to leap off the sides when shells come over.

The Luftwaffe has become a little bolder in the past week. Last night a plane dropped flares directly above us. The brilliant magnesium lights parachuted down slowly, illuminating the area to daylight brightness. I ran almost nude from my pup tent to my foxhole, and though the night was cold I perspired freely knowing the flares will likely be followed by bombs; not necessarily large bombs—often small antipersonnel one-pounders that pepper down in the hundreds, most detonating when they hit the ground, others set to explode only when touched.

Apparently the Luftwaffe considered us a poor target; they dropped nothing but the flares. Still, they are apt to take pictures one night and return the next with evil intent. Night photos often reveal more than day photos.

August 1, 1944.

The town of Marigny, near St. Lô, is badly beat up as are most of the towns we have taken. When battle appears imminent the civilian population disappears into the fields together with as many valued belongings as possible. It is a wonder they are safe in the back woods, yet they always reappear after the battle and if anything at all is left of their homes they move back in.

The houses of Normandy are nearly all ancient, with few modern appurtenances such as flush commodes or indoor plumbing. Two or three huge wooden cider barrels are usually about the premises. Every home also has antiquated heirlooms that antique collectors would probably consider valuable.

In the wreckage at Marigny one sees evidence of some collaboration with the Germans. One cafe had its walls painted with large Teutonic cartoons and caption rhymes written in German. German troops often moved into French homes and had considerable voluntary collaboration from the French women. Besides many German graves, the Germans also left behind printed matter. One document I found strewn on the ground was a printed form signed by an enlisted man attesting his Aryan purity, absolutely free of Jewish or Russian blood. An article in the Dec. 1, 1943 issue of a pictorial magazine warned that Germany was in her last hour; the people must produce to the hilt or face disaster. The article was titled "Der Letste Stunde"–The Last Hour.

August 3.

Our regiment retired to an assembly area for a one day break from fighting below Percy. As usual, enemy shellfire found its way to the assembly area and did little damage except to prevent any real rest the men badly needed. Our current offensive has been spectacularly successful. Our armor penetrated deep into the Brittany peninsula and captured its capital, Rennes. But the fiercest battle raged less spectacularly, practically unnoticed, at Percy where the Germans tried to repair its crumbling Normandy line of defense. And as in all campaigns to date, our division is still where the fighting is the most intense. Statistics might show our division's overall rate of casualties since D-Day to be moderate, but several rifle companies have had a 200 percent turnover in personnel and the others are not far behind.

I recently spoke with one of the rare men who return from a hospital and are eager to return to the front. He was not a member of a rifle company. Despite our large turnover in personnel our regiment seems to have gained rather than lost effectiveness. It has been said by war correspondents at the front, among them Ernest Hemingway and Ernie Pyle, the latter having written a series of columns about the 4th Infantry Division's role in the breakthrough at St. Lô, that the 22nd Infantry Regiment is the "hottest" regiment in action and the 4th Division is by far the best infantry division in the United States Army. This may be pure fantasy, but our assignments tend to substantiate the characterization and it is reported that public praise of the division is held back for strategic purposes.

August 4, 1944.

Popular opinion in this outfit always held that Negro troops are not brave enough for combat and therefore are assigned mainly to rear supply units. The boys would say, "Well, I reckon it's safe now, the Negroes are here." This tune has changed; the vehicles in which our troops are advancing are driven by Negro soldiers whose comportment in the face of danger is conceded to be admirable even by the most persistent Negro-baiters. The road was under heavy shellfire at one point. An officer went up to a colored driver.

"Are you ready to go through?" he asked brusquely.

"Yes-Suh," replied the driver confidently, "just say the word, Suh, ah'm ready!"

Another Negro volunteered to go out on patrol with the infantry at every stop. He proved very handy with a rifle. Speaking of dauntlessness in action, this story was told during the last rest period: One night the troops had undergone bombing and at daybreak they were groggy from lack of sleep. Morale was low and went even lower when 88 shells started coming over before breakfast. The men scrambled to their foxholes, all except Sam Goldman from the Bronx. He stood upright with hands belligerently on hips and asked loudly, "Do you know what day this is?"

"No, what?" responded someone from his foxhole.

A shell tore the earth into a crater in the next field.

"Today is payday," growled Sam, "why aren't we getting paid?"

Everybody laughed hysterically, the gloom dispelled and Sam rushed to his foxhole.

August 5.

The unstable weather of Normandy has favored us during the past 12 days since our push began. While we are exploiting it to the fullest, the Luftwaffe does also, every night. As soon as it becomes dark we hear the low drone of aircraft, then a furious burst of ack-ack fire and an occasional loud bomb explosion. So far the Luftwaffe's best efforts have had a nuisance effect on us. Our division's quartermaster company had 18 trucks hit one night. By the next day twelve were repaired and back in operation, and nearly all the others took a day longer.

Last night, just on the verge of falling asleep I was suddenly shaken by several bomb explosions seemingly in our field. This is "It," I thought and decided there was no time to jump into my foxhole. Instead I crawled under my straw-filled mattress cover; the straw would not stop shrapnel, I calculated, but it might slow it a little. In seconds the barrage stopped as abruptly as it began and I looked out to see if there was any damage or anyone hurt. Only a few pieces of shrapnel had penetrated one of the pup tents. Nobody was injured. We found that a high hedgerow—one of the hedgerows that we much malign for inhibiting our progress—had stood between us and disaster.

August 6, 1944.

Passing scenes:

(1) At the supply depot serving three divisions and assorted smaller units Negro soldiers were loading five of one division's trucks. Several 4th Division trucks pulled up to await their turn. Seeing them, a colored clerk said to the drivers of the five trucks being loaded, "Get these trucks out of the way; here is the 4th Division, we load them first."

"But we are almost loaded," protested the leader of the 5-truck convoy, "and we were here first."

"Get them out of the way, we got to load the 4th Division. The 4th, they never stop moving. Other divisions—they stop; the 4th keeps on going. When the 4th Division comes here we drops everything else!"

"We can't do anything with these boys," explained a sergeant in charge who was white, "they are sold on the 4th; it is 'their' division."

(2) The troops had been on line incessantly for many days, a good number were dropping out from exhaustion, others from being hit; it was just a matter of time for either to happen. Morale—there wasn't any. One of the men shooting from behind a hedgerow suddenly stopped, wiped his brow and a wild look came into his eyes. He lay down on the ground, stuck one foot high enough to be exposed above

the hedgerow and shouted, "Shoot the sonofabitch, shoot the sonofabitch!"

(3) It appears that French mores provide an acceptance of the crudities of nature different from ours. In one typical instance, two French gendarmes were conversing on the highway with a lady pedestrian when one felt the call of nature. He walked casually a few feet off the road but not out of sight, relieved himself and returned to the conversation with no hint of embarrassment.

(4) Dumb beasts of the region have become uncommonly docile. Rabbits, dogs, horses, goats come up to us to be petted and reassured about the bombings and shellings. One night while preparing to retire I crawled into my pup tent, groped in the dark and touched a soft hairy creature. I lit a match; it was a dog, lying with his head low, a pleading look in his eyes. I had to push him out. He shivered, paralyzed with fear. But it was either "him or me," so I continued pushing him till he was all the way out, for he was incapable of locomotion of his own accord. I fully agreed with him that it was a wretched act on my part.

August 8, 1944.

Our entire division came back in reserve where preparations were in progress for everybody to get new clothing and equipment, take showers and relax. Before this took place the Germans broke through another division's lines and captured our intended shower and bivouac area. A quick change of plans soon had our troops recommitted to battle. Now the troops are being pushed hard to exploit both the situation and the good weather.

Our outfit is functioning smoothly, the operations and map men experienced to cope with almost any emergency and company commanders generally battle-wise. Once almost our whole regiment found itself suddenly pinned down by enemy artillery and machine gunners who had infiltrated our outposts and occupied a strategic position. One of our company commanders assessed the situation, then led his company around to the other side of the pinned-down troops and from this unlikely disadvantaged flank sent out a mortar barrage that wiped out the German position. His total casualties in the action consisted of one man's shoulder being lightly grazed by a bullet, putting him out of action for fifteen minutes.

August 9, 1944.

Our section moved to the village of La Trinité, below Villedeau. There we are not far from the regimental CP which is set up 500 hundred yards from the front and protected inside a large fortress-like chateau atop a high hill overlooking the battlefield in the broad valley below. The view from there at dusk on the second day of the enemy's thwarted counterattack showed the continuous action in stark detail. We were pounding the enemy with bombs and artillery. Every few minutes one landed on a tank, building, or supply dump and blasted it high in a brilliant flash of flame. Our foot troops crept and crawled on the ground in a steady advance to capture the terrain as the German grip loosened.

The Germans tried to shell our regimental CP exposed more like a forward artillery observation post than a command headquarters, but have not yet hit the building. The chateau inside is furnished ornately with elaborate, up-to-date curios. One of the men could not resist the temptation to sleep in one of the regal beds with thick innerspring mattress though he had previously refused to sleep in houses far less an enemy target.

In this sector, near Mortain, we knocked out more than 135 German tanks in one day. This number compares interestingly with the 87 that Russia proudly announced knocking out in a heavy battle at East Prussia. There is nothing small about this front.

August 10.

The CP chateau was still not directly hit when I went up to it today, but three mortar shells landed in the yard last night and caused the worst casualties yet suffered by Regimental Headquarters personnel. Several important members were struck with shrapnel; two were killed, several wounded. Most were inside the chateau when the first shell landed, then these experienced men, in combat since D-Day, decided they had to "see what was happening" and like rookies went outside. The next two shells got them.

One other man had taken cover in a foxhole when the shelling began. He was settled deep into the best constructed foxhole in the area when hit in the thigh and foot. That was "Goldie;" thus we lost our entertainment director and *Double Deucer* editor, more recently employed in assisting at an ammunition dump. When a medical aid-man ran over and dragged him out of the foxhole Goldie joked, "Will this stop me from jitterbugging?"

The incident illustrated the folly of setting up a command post so vulnerable to enemy attack. The regiment paid dearly for this blunder. Today I met Jack Zencheck of Company E. His hair had grown gray and his sprightly humor was subdued.

"I'm glad I still have a head to grow gray hair on," he responded acidly to my observation.

"How are you getting along?" I asked.

"I'm always scared and always tired," he replied.

August 11, 1944.

There is a science of war dealing with the handling of divisions that is understandably in the exclusive province of the higher commands. Which division is assigned to any given action is a matter the average soldier doesn't know except from hearsay, and he may deduce the reasoning that goes into such decisions. My impression derived of hearsay and circumstantial evidence goes about like this: the "Corps" commanding general assembles the several division generals under his command and describes to them the operations he is assigned by "Army" to undertake. He inquires of each division commander as to his readiness to perform the hardest mission, then assigns that mission to the division he thinks can handle it.

There are only two or three infantry divisions he entrusts with crucial spearheading tasks. No two divisions operate exactly alike. The commanders who fought in Africa and Sicily are inclined to be more conservative than others. Such a commander may stipulate when taking on a mission that he will need at least six hours to scout enemy positions before attacking, while others may be satisfied to plunge in within an hour or two after receiving their orders. He would rather fight shorthanded than throw in replacements in the middle of combat. After two weeks in action he starts calling for relief, and if granted takes his division pretty far back for a week's rest. Only then does he ask for replacements, his rationale being that the squad leaders should know at least the names of new men before going into action with them.

It seems that a division's need for a rest is pretty much left to the discretion of each division commander. Inconsistencies in policy are common and often create drastic differences in the treatment of troops from one division to another. Through all echelons of command there runs a political current that quests for glory and publicity. None of these factors taken separately determines the worth of a division; each division is as individualistic as different business concerns selling the same merchandise.

August 12, 1944.

When Lin Streeter was brought back recently to draw the cartoons for *The Ivy Leaf* weekly, things were not set up yet and in the interim he performed as "dog robber" for the journalists frequenting Division Headquarters.

"Some of them were pretty arrogant," observed Lin. "Ernest Hemingway and Ernie Pyle were among the unassuming. Pyle was sort of bashful. He would sit at the feet of other journalists and listen to them talk as though he were a student listening to professors. He always jumped when our artillery went off. Hemingway was very funny—a big portly man. He talked a lot while the others banged away at their typewriters. He would take out a little notebook about once a day, write three or four words and consider it a day's work. He got along very well with the general. They both come from Florida. I asked him what part. Key West, he said.

"'What the hell is down there?' I asked. Fish. He went in for big game fishing. The general and he usually drank some cognac together in the evening.

"'Should I escort you home?' he would say and the general smiled and answered, 'I guess I can find my way back myself.'

"Hemingway asked a lot of questions; peculiar ones. He seemed particularly interested in the hillbilly-type G.I. He asked me how the men felt about going back into action. I told him that not many would balk at an assignment but very few would volunteer for a dangerous mission until they realized it had to be done and then if one volunteered others would join him. He asked about battle fatigue and things like that. There was one newspaperman who acted like a big shot.

"Once he said to me, 'Boy, bring me a pillow.'

"He was kind of shocked when I replied, 'Corporal boy, Sir.'

"I liked the correspondent for The *New York Times*—I forgot his name, a slight, gray-headed chap. He would look at his typewriter, then at a bottle of cognac; he'd hesitate, then take the bottle, drain out half and go to work. The *Life* magazine photographer was funny. He spoke little English; I'm not sure what extraction he was, probably Russian. He would have his equipment ready to put in a jeep, then told he can't go and his expression was like a disappointed child. Sometimes he came to the table late and the others were spread out leaving no room for him on the bench. Instead of asking someone to move over he would back into a corner and brood until someone noticed and invited him to sit at the table."

August 13, 1944

Today is Sunday and the twentieth day of clear sunny weather. The French country folk are out in their Sunday finery, the children dressed in clean blue or white frocks, their elders wearing real leather shoes instead of wooden sabots. They greet us with a pleasant "Bonjour, M'sieur" as they stroll leisurely through their abundant apple orchards towards the church. They pause to look up at the groups of silvery heavy bombers swarming gracefully eastward. They are, peasantlike, almost inscrutable in their simplicity. "Le Boche," they like to say, "—kaput."

We wonder just how they acted with the Germans. We feel they sincerely welcome us and are glad to be free of the German yoke, but were they really cold toward them? They exhibit a disdainful regard for danger in carrying on their farm work within shelling distance of the enemy.

One asked a G-5 Civil Affairs soldier, "Can I go back to my farm now?"

"Where is it?" asked the soldier. The Frenchman pointed toward enemy held territory.

"Three miles that way," he replied, "my cows have to be milked."

The soldier advised him not to go unless he valued his cows more than his neck. For several days our regiment stood on one hill and exchanged shellfire with the Germans on the next hill. Then one night we quietly pulled out, moved around to the rear of the Germans and waited patly for the Germans to realize they were isolated in a pocket. With such strategy the German 7th Army, representing the bulk of German power in France, is now being liquidated. While waiting for the order to resume offensive action, our troops are resting the best they can, eating hot meals, taking showers and writing letters.

August 14, 1944.

Passing scenes:

(1) There are several ways in which men at the front can accumulate riches. About the only legal way is to find money lying loosely in pillboxes or on the ground. Some men employ other means, like taking money from prisoners while frisking them for weapons, or raiding evacuated banks. A provost-marshal who had formerly been on the Chicago police force walked into a bank in a liberated town and looked at the safe that had been blown open. He studied it a moment then said, "The Germans didn't do that. The job looks familiar to me."

(2) It is a toss-up whether the wine absorbed at the front is of greater or lesser value to our assault troops. There is evidence for either contention—that with wine men grow careless and needlessly expose themselves, or conversely that it provides "liquid guts" which allay fear and enable the men to carry out the necessary quasi-suicidal infantry attacks. Whatever the merit the fact is that much wine is consumed, and some men hold their liquor better than others.

There is a tale of one man who made himself a party with a bottle of Calvados, which is a regional brew the Americans call White Lightning. Calvados is manufactured, reportedly, by freezing hard cider until all except the alcohol is frozen solid. The alcohol is then drained off and labeled "Calvados." It goes down like firewater, with a throat-burning sensation. This chap drained the whole bottle, then happening to be near a medical first aid station lay down on a stretcher and fell asleep. A doctor on his rounds examined him, found no wounds and pinned a tag on him reading "Evacuate—battle fatigue."

(3) The men lined up before an American Red Cross "Clubmobile" for coffee and doughnuts handed out by two quite pretty uniformed Red Cross girls. A sergeant walked over and announced, "Are there any replacements here for the 22nd Infantry Regiment?"

Nobody answered.

"How about these girls, will they do?" suggested a boy in the line.

"Oh we wouldn't do any good there," responded the girls in chorus.

"That's what you think," countered the wit.

August 16, 1944.

In our country's general mobilization for war the drafting of men for the armed forces is often considered a muddled affair, especially in the lack of standardized policies among local draft boards. Some are quick to draft married men with families and older men that others put off for last. Yet it is debatable that the younger single men should carry the majority burden of mortal combat.

To the Army, these questions are almost immaterial. Men coming in daily to our outfit are nearly forty years of age, some with sons in the Marines. Since most replacements are needed in rifle companies, that is where they go alongside the younger men and apparently are accepted as equally effective soldiers.

In its hunger for riflemen the Army is sending us also men who worked in other non-infantry services for two or three years as mechanics, truck drivers, armorers, graduates of ASTP, the "Army Specialized Training program." Most were given two weeks of rifle training in France and sent to us classified as "Rifleman." All consider themselves "shanghaied." The Army cannot be blamed for such real or fancied inequities; it has its job to do.

Now however, two conditions have arisen that I consider serious injustices. First, many of the previous evacuees are returning to our division with records marked "Fit for LIMITED ASSIGNMENT duties only." Often their disabilities are not readily visible, such as weak joints or bad eyes. One man returned with his right hand fingers twisted and partly amputated would have been rejected at an Army induction station. There is little need for limited assignment men here and we have no choice but to send them to the front again to do the best they can with their handicaps.

Second are the men returned for combat duty who had been evacuated for "battle fatigue" or "psychoneurosis." They are obviously unfit for combat. Some go berserk upon hearing the first shell come over. One boy had been at the front sixteen days, then was wounded, captured and spent five days as a German prisoner before being freed when we took Cherbourg. Evacuated to England, his wound healed sufficiently to be sent back to us but mentally he was in sad shape. He literally shook, and in a nervous stutter repeated over and over that he was as good as dead if he went back into action. He went back, the Army either unable to put him in rear service duty or indifferent to his condition and fate.

August 17, 1944.

In our new location ten miles southeast of Mortain we in the rear echelon are actually deeper into France than our forward echelon, this due to the disintegration of the German line. In fact, we do not really know where the Germans are in this sector and where they aren't. A rear echelon lieutenant spotted three of them this morning. On the way here we passed through Mortain. It is the most beat-up town I have yet seen. Previously I had thought Monteburg and Valognes were in ruins; by comparison with Mortain they stood up straight.

The "tank country" we envisioned to exist beyond St. Lô is still not in evidence. St. Lô is eighty miles behind us and we still see hills and hedgerowed fields. The farmers do not appear to have been stripped by the German of their chickens, livestock or crops as our pre-invasion information indicated.

For the first time, however, I am hearing directly about atrocities committed by the Germans. I spoke to a middle-aged Frenchman who had been coerced into working for the German Army. He was transported to the Russian front and put to work digging holes sometimes as near as 200 yards from the front. They beat him often across the back and kept him in near-starvation. When the Normandy invasion began he was returned to France where he continued slave-laboring until freed by American action.

I spoke also to a woman with a leg still bandaged where she had been shot by Nazi SS troops who broke in seeking information. In addition they kicked and terrorized her five young children.

August 18, 1944.

The farmers pointed at a short shabby fellow and said, "Russky, Russky." My pup tent-mate Leo Gorelick addressed him in Russian, hearing which the fellow in an outburst of emotion embraced Leo and wept. Then he told his story: He was a native of Baku, in the Caucasus. In 1941 he left his wife and child to enter the Russian Army. Two years later he was captured by the Germans, and after a few months in Poland was examined to determine his fitness to either fight with the Germans or serve as a laborer. They chose him to work as a stable boy with the German cavalry on the French border of Spain.

A couple of weeks ago he escaped with eight others and split up to try reaching the American lines in Normandy. He walked all the way, once going four straight days without eating. Somewhere on the way a French Maquis underground member gave him a "To whom it may concern" note requesting he be given enough work en-route so he wouldn't go hungry and be forced to steal.

When he reached this sector the Germans had already left and he tried getting the Americans to take charge of him. His efforts at making himself understood with several G.I.'s were futile; they merely shrugged uncomprehendingly, except one who did understand but had his own troubles and didn't want to bother with him.

A farmer took pity on him, put him to work and was reluctant to lose the hard-working Russian mujik when we took him to turn him over to the appropriate authority. He had no "dog tags" or documents, and had forgotten his Russian Army serial number. He had deep marks on his back that appeared to have been inflicted by a lash, but he denied having been whipped. He said he was anxious to go back and fight with the Russian Army.

August 19, 1944.

We have had few casualties recently, primarily because the division is in reserve. This is cause for celebration, so last night we celebrated, with red wine, raw carrots, cheese, raw onions and captured German sardines. There is a plentiful supply of red wine in this section. It is dry, tasty and unexpectedly potent; we did not retire even when "bedcheck Charlie" came droning on schedule at dusk, which the Luftwaffe plane does every night without fail.

We purchased the wine for 40 francs (80 cents) from the owner of a large modern winery that had escaped damage. Our method of buying is an inconsistent hodgepodge of overpaying, underpaying, and barter. The French have apparently not lost their conviction that every American is a millionaire and the streets of America are paved with gold. For fresh eggs some farmers want money, others soap, or cigarettes. If they ask five francs we give them ten plus soap and cigarettes, reinforcing their millionaire image of us. But we aren't entirely dupes; we are a poor market for items offered in shops at inflated prices.

A merchant offered a plain ladies handbag for forty dollars. "It's good leather," she urged in broken English.

The people here appear well-fed, prosperous though poorly clothed, and pious Catholics. The women seem to work harder than the men. At present they are pitching hay and hauling manure. Families like working together as a group and few projects are started until the whole family gathers, even in details such as minor repairs of a fence. At frequent intervals they stop and take a swig from their bottomless bottle of cider or Calvados.

August 21, 1944.

We are now moving at the rate of about 40 miles per week. This pace would get us to Berlin in something like 18 weeks. Our division's code identification in combat is "Cactus." The division rear echelon is designated "Cactus Rear." It is composed of: the Adjutant General personnel, Inspector General, Judge Advocate, Finance, the personnel sections of the three regiments and Artillery, Engineers, Signal Company, Quartermaster and Medical Company; two field kitchens and a "Casual Company" which handles some of the men returning to duty from hospitals and a few of the new replacements.

In addition there is a full military band of some 50 men whose function other than keeping in practice by serenading the open fields is not apparent to me. It was once thought that bandsmen in combat would act as road guides and command post guards. In all, the rear echelon relieves the forward troops of all but the barest minimum of administrative processes.

We follow within practical liaison range, exceedingly mobile despite our impedimenta of field desks, typewriters, record cases; we can pull up stakes and move on very short notice. We haven't so far set up shop inside a town, but often found a schoolhouse or chateau to work in supplemented with a few pyramid tents we put up outside. We never sleep inside buildings, only in the surrounding fields where we set up our two-man pup tents, dig foxholes and take turns on guard shifts.

Recently we have been lax in digging foxholes; with the next scare we will again be digging them fast and deep. We rarely have the good fortune to bivouac in fields with foxholes already dug by our forward troops or Germans. It is easy to tell the difference between a German and American foxhole. The German is very deep, well concealed, straight and trim as though dug by a machine.

The American is dug according to the fancy of the digger, who is rarely concerned with its looks. We are presently near Alençon, in a large chateau said to be a hunting lodge for wealthy Parisians who formerly came on weekends to hunt and make love. Ten days ago it was a German headquarters. The woods roundabout have been used as hideouts in recent months by French Maquis and others trying to avoid the German labor draft.

August 23, 1944.

Our advance in France has been so swift and successful that news of a second landing in southern France came as a surprise, seeming unnecessary and anticlimactic. Published reports are that casualties were very small, hardly more than the accrued number of casualties in one of our average rifle companies. At this time, two and a half months after D-Day, our 3,000 man regiment has sustained almost a 100 percent turnover in personnel. This is the undiscriminating overall figure; in actuality the rate is well over 200 percent among the troops directly in combat. An analysis of the enlisted men's casualties shows 22 percent dead—about one in five. Among officer casualties 30 percent died, almost one in three.

"What Price Glory?" will some day again be asked, to no good answer except that in this war the infantryman's task is still indispensable.

August 25.

We moved 84 miles to a chateau near Dreux, forty miles from Paris. The chateau is huge, built and occupied by the Duke of Orleans during the reign of Louis XVI. Since then it has been remodeled several times, with many full-length mirrors installed, gaudy chandeliers and the nearest I have seen in France to a modern plumbing system. The Germans vacated it hurriedly, leaving food and other effects that reveals quite accurately the life they were leading here. They combined business with pleasure.

In one chamber we found a replica map of Normandy modeled on a table with contoured sand duplicating the terrain, tree-shaped twigs and toy-size buildings. In another chamber the walls are covered with lewd pencil sketches and lying about are articles of feminine wearing apparel.

Paris was reported liberated by our forward troops yesterday, but it is another case of being "all over except the fighting." Apparently the Germans evacuated the city to escape encirclement, discovered they were surrounded anyway and reentered the city to fight it out. Meanwhile the French announced "their victory" and when they discovered the Germans coming back delayed reporting it until they could determine whether they could handle them themselves, or would need the aid of Americans who would not hesitate to pour heavy artillery into the city if necessary in its customary policy of destroying property in preference to lives.

Late in the day our 4th Infantry Division went into action in the city, part of it coordinated with the French 2nd Armored Division tanks. The 22nd Infantry Regiment attempted a crossing of the Seine River in boats and withdrew under fire. Another attempt is scheduled for tonight.

August 26, 1944.

Leo Gorelick and I stopped in at a farmhouse to negotiate a deal for a few fresh eggs. The thought occurred to me upon seeing plenty of chickens running around that the woman could doubtless use some extra francs, and I asked if she would like to cook us a chicken dinner for the next evening. She agreed, and the next evening we came bearing gifts of coffee, biscuits, chocolate and soap. Her husband recently returned from a prison camp in Germany brought out a bottle of cider.

"Vive la France!" Leo and I toasted.

"Vive l'Amerique!" he returned.

We sat on one side of the round table, he with his two blond youngsters on the other side and they commenced eating bread spread with butter. His wife brought out a large roasted chicken, a platter of boiled small new potatoes and set them before Leo and me with two plates.

"Aren't you eating?" I asked.

"No, we eat at nine o'clock," replied the husband.

We felt embarrassed, and guessed they would eat what we left. The chicken was delicious, and Leo and I ravenous; we started on the drumsticks, after that couldn't resist the thighs, then still hungry we ravished the white meat of the breast. With each bite we were conscious there would be that much less left for the family and tried to appease guilt by mentally increasing the number of francs we will pay. At last not a shred of meat was left on that chicken. Before that the husband had excused himself and gone back to work.

He came in again when we had finished eating and were each contentedly smoking an exotic clear Havana cigar. We gave him one, at which he reacted as if it were a priceless diamond, which indeed it was. We had spent an hour and a half at the table; now it was time to leave. When we took out money to pay the woman she would not hear of it.

"Madame," I said in my best available French. "We have; and we want that you should have."

Tears rolled down her cheeks as she accepted the money, her gratitude as genuine as the rich gravy of her tender chicken.

August 27, 1944.

The closer we come to Paris, the more details I hear about the German occupation. A school teacher I met had just returned from Germany as a repatriated French prisoner of war. Reduced in weight from 220 pounds to 130, the Germans released him when he was no longer serviceable to work. He said the Germans from the northeast, the so-called High Dutch Germans, mistreated prisoners more than the Low Dutch of southwest Germany.

We are now in the great Paris basin, a flat fertile region that provides Paris with a large part of its food. Under current conditions the region is still productive except for livestock that has been reduced, and for the first time there is not an abundance of cider.

Seeing a farm tractor in operation was surprising after the near-primitive farm equipment we saw until now. At last we are well out of the hedgerow country. There are many woods. The roads we travel are lined all the way with the French who wave, cheer and occasionally play the "Star-Spangled Banner" on a banjo.

In return we throw into their outstretched hands a multitude of leftovers from our "K" and "10 in 1" rations. Sometimes one yields to a fleeting suspicion their cheers are for what it can bring them, and quickly recants upon seeing some simple, spontaneous gesture as when one little gray-haired old woman walking by waved, clapped her hands and smiled. Her greeting was unmistakably genuine.

August 28, 1944.

We are now at Villiers sur Orge on the outskirts of Paris. The scene here is quite urban. The people are better-dressed; wooden sabots are hardly seen even in the fields. It is a commuter's suburb, just far enough out so that the people have access to more food than those in the city. At least they have plenty of vegetables, though very short on nearly all other foods. They have not had real coffee in four years. The wines in the cafes are unappetising, perfumed and sweetened with saccharine.

If sometimes we felt uneasy about the patriotism of the French in Normandy, we have no such qualms here. Almost every able-bodied man wears a "Fifi" armband (for French Forces of the Interior), and they mean business. They have fought individually or in organized groups, and as impromptu troops operating with American and British Army units. Several have become attached to each company in our regiment. They wear our division insignia and are armed with our weapons. They say they have a grudge against the people of Normandy; they believe that fifty percent are guilty of unnecessarily close cooperation with the Germans.

The fighting in Paris goes on mainly on the other side of the Seine River where the 22nd Infantry Regiment established a bridgehead. Our regiment went into attack last night, two battalions abreast and one in reserve. Our casualties so far are slight.

The French show little regard for danger; they do not take seriously the blackout regulations at night. Last night lights were on after dark all over town and when a gendarme went around asking that lights be shielded to at least not shine directly into the sky, the residents cut them down to a mere ten times brighter than anywhere in England except Liverpool, which recently changed from "blackout" to "dimout."

August 29, 1944.

Captain Brill, John Cooper, Howard Jameson, Bill Dyer and I got into a jeep and went to look for the regimental command post in Paris. We looked high and low for the CP: at Champs Elysees, the Latin quarter, around the Eiffel Tower, Arc de Triomphe, Université de Paris, National Academy of Music, Chamber of Deputies, The Bastille, Notre Dame Cathedral, La Rue de St. Michel, Rivoli, Comic Opera and other places that one might visit if he happened to be on a sightseeing tour which of course we were not, though someone happened to bring along a camera and we took some pictures.

Paris is truly attractive and intriguing, a city to be visited at leisure in some distant civilian future. The populace is celebrating in an extended holiday, their appreciation deep at being liberated and their admiration for American soldiers translates into sheer love and hero worship.

Said one woman, "You cannot imagine how we feel; we breathe free air for the first time in four years."

The Messiah riding through the streets could not have been greeted warmer than we; now I know how President Roosevelt feels when he appears in public.

A few scattered snipers remain in the city. We accidentally rode through a couple of blocks roped off to civilians by gendarmes and luckily weren't sniped at, possibly because we rode through at top speed when we discovered our error.

Damage to the city is small, just enough to give the people a taste of battle, most of it confined to government buildings pockmarked by bullets which chipped out small chunks of cement. Pedestrians on the boulevards do not look underfed. We did not see much of poor districts where likely shortages are felt most. People with money could obtain plenty to eat through a vast black market which functioned almost openly.

The streets are filled with bicycle riders, as are the famous sidewalk cafes with well-dressed patrons holding glasses of beer, wine and absinthe.

Yes, "Paree" is verily gay and the women—oo la la!

At last we located our primary objective, the regimental CP, in a suburb three miles north of the city. Our heavy artillery is in action again, but Paris has been saved from the fate of Valognes and Mortain. Paris is not a good place for our army to be in, with its justly famed "les belles femmes" distracting to men trying to do a job. Some men out on reconnaissance have been known to detour into apartments with women and champagne, and the hell with the Germans!

August 30, 1944.

Our officers looked the other way, and emulating many other adventurous spirits in our unit Leo Gorelick and I took French leave to visit Paris for a few unauthorized hours. This time we walked instead of rode once we reached the city. At this time, an American soldier strolling in Paris among the milling sidewalk crowds is more conspicuous than Dorothy Lamour promenading on Broadway in a sarong. We went into a restaurant for champagne and food.

"Where are your tickets de ration?" asked the waiter.

He promptly dropped that stipulation in consideration for cigarettes, over which everybody we met in Paris goes hog-wild. He served us roast beef, dried lima beans, tomatoes, soup and bread. The place was obviously fashionable, yet I could see no other customers receiving that large a variety of courses.

A man at the next table had a glass of watery beer, a plate of dry beans and one small slice of bread for which he had to give a ration ticket. Leo and I received the bountiful sum of six bread slices, one of which we gave to the long-bearded gentleman sipping the watery beer. Then we went out looking for souvenirs.

The French shopkeepers were not afflicted with hero worship to the extent that it interfered with their business. I watched an American soldier buy a trinket tagged at 5 francs, then when he left the proprietor hastily changed the price tag to one reading 25 francs.

In the evening we went into a cafe named Sphinx, which had splendidly furnished appointments including bare-breasted young waitresses. Three fashionably attired gentlemen asked us to join them at their table for champagne. One was an architect, the other two oil-paint artists. The architect invited us to spend the night in his apartment located in the Latin quarter. His combined studio and bachelor apartment would do well as a setting for a glamorous movie. He stood in well with black-marketers, too; he served fried eggs and bacon at midnight. When we got up at 5 A.M. it was pitch-black outside. We would not know our way even in broad daylight, but miraculously we found our way back to our unit in time for work.

September 1, 1944.

Conditions under the German occupation interest me, especially the stories of atrocities committed by Germans that have circulated in America; therefore in a second opportunity to visit Paris, Leo and I sought out people just emerged from hiding, political refugees and Jews still occupying hideous quarters with secret chambers in dilapidated tenements in slums and back alleys of the city.

On the basis of talking with these people, I am convinced the atrocity tales are not exaggerated. No torment of another human was too base for Germans to inflict; it was their everyday enterprise to create maximum misery for men, women and children identified as Jew, Russian, Pole, Slovak.

The tales we heard related to us in Yiddish by Jews were monotonously repetitious, beginning with having all their worldly possessions taken from them and requiring Jews to wear a yellow patch with "Juif" prominently inscribed on it. Their men were taken to labor until they died of hunger or hard work, their young women sent to brothels, old people and children to be mass-executed in death camps; horrors too inconceivable for the imagination and future generations will consequently not fully believe.

There was one question that I asked everybody: have you known or heard of any German in uniform who privately expressed regret to Jew or Frenchman for barbaric behavior committed in the name of Germans? The answer was always an emphatic "no."

Then I asked, "What do you think should be done with Germany when the war is over?"

Their common reply: first, let Russians and Poles loose in Germany to do some cleaning up, then divide Germany into several small states, each self-governed and not permitted ever to ally with any of the others.

September 3, 1944.

Our regiment again mounted tanks and trucks and traveled clear to the border of Belgium. Our section, far behind, moved to Nanteuil, 30 miles northeast of Paris, a region flat as a table. The people of this town seem poorer than any we have seen to date. Their reception is less demonstrative toward us than were even the Normandy inhabitants.

A French civilian told me today that several women who had collaborated with the Germans were shorn of their hair by vengeful townsfolk, and doesn't that make me happy. I replied that if that is how they want it, good, and if not, also good; that we Americans are interested in finishing off Germany, return to America, and if the French want revenge against their collaborators it is their business.

He seemed satisfied with my answer. He said most Paris women had not made themselves attractive for the Germans, and when the Americans arrived they put on their pre-war finery in the hope of snagging an American who would take them to the United States.

I am not sure that Ernie Pyle's report of the Parisians being well-fed during the German occupation is quite accurate. They generally look well-fed, but many subsisted on little more than bread and potatoes, resulting in bad teeth and other less noticeable ailments caused by malnutrition.

Last night we had our first experience with the German Vl "flying bomb." In the middle of the night I was awakened by a noise which sounded like that made by a large truck straining up a hill with a heavy load and a bad muffler. I thought it might be an airplane in distress. I looked out of my pup tent and saw high in the air a ball of flame moving slowly westward, then it changed in appearance to a flame shooting out the rear of an exhaust pipe. Shortly after it passed out of sight I heard a distant thud of an explosion. Later it was announced on the radio that "buzz bombs" were falling in the Paris area.

September 6, 1944.

It took just three months after D-Day to liberate all of France, except for some mopping up. We are about ready to begin the Battle of Germany. The 4th Infantry Division swung to the right upon crossing the Belgian border and is converging on a point in the lower part of Belgium, toward Luxembourg. Our casualties recently have been almost negligible. In one drive our regiment had only three casualties.

The Free French (Fifi's) are doing a good job of harassing the Germans before we arrive and mopping up snipers after we leave. A formal French Army is mobilizing rapidly under a new government, but American "lendlease" is slow in organizing and often they are not getting food rations let alone guns and ammunition. In Nanteuil they have a hard time scraping together food for their one or two hundred new enlistees.

A Fifi gendarme told me the Germans customarily took anything they wanted, including breaking into private homes when nobody was home. Unlike Americans they never shared their cigarettes and "bonbons" with civilians. I asked him if the French would have thought any better of them had they so shared. Never, he asserted vigorously.

September 8.

Our section traveled 103 miles to catch up with the division and we are now eight miles from Belgium, in the village of Rimogne. It is a site where much action took place in World War I, and is marked with old military cemeteries and brush-covered trenches. Our route from Nanteuil revealed evidence that the German Wehrmacht retreat from Paris all the way to Germany had been not a planned withdrawal but a rout. Most convincing of this was at the town of Soisson, which lies in a fairly deep valley running north and south.

On the far hill overlooking the valley the Germans had a series of formidable obtacles against tanks, and fortifications tunneled deep into the hills with large artillery guns emplaced at the crest in dugouts hewn out of rock. There are no signs that they made a stand.

Most of the towns we passed were not in bad shape until Leon and Montcornet, where the Germans had attacked civilians in reprisal for Fifi guerilla activity. All across France we were surprised to see large factories intact. Other bomber objectives were pulverized, particularly railroads and airports. Even so, railroads were back in operation one day after the Germans left.

We passed many truckloads of German prisoners being transported westward. They were unkempt, bare-headed or wearing grey wool caps, some bandaged, and all with a stone-face expression. One of our boys yelled "Heil Hitler" as we rode past one truckload. A few prisoners cracked a grim half-smile, the rest showed no emotion.

September 10, 1944.

Three of us went by jeep to try to find the regimental CP. We found it in the village of Smuid, on the far side of the Belgian province of Luxembourg. Our regiment is in an assembly area awaiting the call to engage in the 3rd, and presumably final D-day, the plunge into Germany. After D-Day Normandy on June 6, we regard the breakthrough at St. Lô as a second D-Day.

In the past couple of weeks our regiment took fifteen hundred German war prisoners without trying very hard. There has been no real front, only scattered pockets in France and Belgium where the by-passed Germans half fought, half awaited capture. Our aircraft has done a thorough job of knocking out German armored tanks and other vehicles.

This part of Belgium differs little from northeastern France except where a stretch of mountains range briefly before the Belgian border. At the bottom of a deep ravine in those mountains flows the Meuse River, which we crossed at the coal-mining town of Fumay. The blown-out bridge spanning the narrow river proved no obstacle; next to it our Engineer Corps quickly put up a pontoon bridge which can apparently carry heavy tanks.

The countryside is largely wooded, part of the vast Ardennes forest. The German radio propaganda line presently explains that "we have gained time by fighting on territory that was not ours and that we did not want." But there is little doubt about Germany's intentions toward France.

Before Germany invaded France the wording on French coins read "French Republic" on one side and on the other, "Liberty, Equality, Fraternity." After, French coins were milled reading "French State" and "Work, Family, Patriotism." An old man in Rimogne told me the Germans had first urged, then compelled young Frenchmen to join an army fighting against Russia.

September 13, 1944.

By way of the city of Sedan and the picturesque castle town of Bouillon, we moved from Rimogne to the Belgian town of St. Hubert and set up shop next to the Church of St. Hubert which was built in 1568 and is a shrine to which Catholics from all over the world have made pilgrimages. This vicinity is "hot" with isolated bands of German soldiers who lurk in the woods, waylay lone vehicles and at night raid outlying farmhouses for food.

A civilian informed a couple of our boys that several Germans were at his place. They accompanied him home in the dark. The Germans fired a few shots and surrendered when the two Americans fired their carbines so rapidly the Germans thought they were automatic weapons. Fourteen were taken prisoner.

The Belgian people seem overwhelmingly pro-Allies. Many men were active in the underground during the four years of German occupation. Occasionally, though, something occurs that arouses suspicion that not all our welcome is sincere. One of our drivers passed two girls who waved enthusiastically at him; then glancing through his rear-view mirror he caught one of the girls spitting meanly toward him.

I accidentally discovered that several civilians can speak German fluently but deny it. By and large, though, one cannot believe that both the French and Belgians are less than ecstatic to be free of the Germans. Any doubt to the contrary can be attributed to subtle propaganda the Germans spread for four years, some absorbed at least subconsciously by many.

September 15, 1944.

The local headquarters of the Belgian Maquis is a small hotel that they had taken over for their exclusive use. A Maquis sergeant invited me to dine with the group, and I was duly seated at an extended home-size table in a small tastefully furnished dining room. At the head sat a lieutenant, the commander of the newly emerged from the underground garrison. At the foot of the table sat the adjutant, a rank comparable to our warrant officer. At the sides were seated the first sergeant and four lower-rank sergeants. All expressed thanks to the

American Army for liberating them from the confines of the surrounding forests. They still use the small radio receiving set that had been parachuted to them in the woods.

The cook brought out veal roast, pumpernickel bread and bock beer. I set out a couple of cigarette packs and we commenced to eat, at the same time carrying on a discussion with me employing basic French supplemented with verbal cross-breed improvisation which I devise as I go along and has proven marvelously coherent (I am a total convert to Churchill's "basic English" theory).

What did I do before I entered the army? asked the commandant. Business, I replied. They discussed this briefly among themselves, saying, I gathered, that I was a capitalist.

"Oui, a capitalist," I said, to their surprise for they did not know it is also an English word, "but now I am not a capitalist, just a solider fighting to free workers."

My explanation seemed to amuse and satisfy them. One picked up a package of cigarettes and offered it around, including to me.

"Thanks," I declined, at which they laughed uproariously, apparently for thanking them for my own cigarettes.

They showed me photos of Belgian girls with German officers, evidence they were going to use for punishing the girls. The adjutant insisted on showing me an account of their garrison's living expenses which amounted to 750 Belgian francs per day, about 30 American dollars, that they will pay out when they receive Belgian Army funds. They asked me to demonstrate the workings of my carbine.

A sergeant passing around cigarettes again observed that they were "gangstering" my cigarettes. Then we are even, I replied, for I have "gangstered" their meal.

September 17.

While radio and newspapers blare loudly that the war is all but over, the 22nd Infantry Regiment is spearheading the 4th Division in attacking the "Siegfried line."

Some commentators even speculate that Germany is giving us the green light to take over Germany before the Russians can get in. The fact is we are meeting lots of resistance and greater artillery opposition than ever before. There is a resemblance to the Cherbourg campaign in that we are again encountering pillbox fortifications and our casualties are heavy. The first few days of the attack have been costly, but it is too early to judge if it will develop into a Normandy-class meat-grinder. Our experience against pillboxes in Normandy is paying off.

The 22nd Infantry is deeper into the line than any other outfit. But nobody is backing up the regiment; after cleaning out an area and advancing, there is danger the Germans will infiltrate behind us. Shelling of rear positions is severe, and snipers the Germans left behind are a hazard. Coming up from the rear to contact Regimental CP, assistant personnel officer Lieutenant Hoehn narrowly missed being hit far behind the so-called front.

September 19, 1944.

It has rained almost continuously since the battle of the Siegfried Line began. This has cut heavily into our air support. Our casualties continue to be heavy and replacements are slow in reaching us. Of those that do, some men returning from hospitals have been wounded and evacuated three times. We have one man who is either missing in action or AWOL, it is not yet determined which. He is a first sergeant, and one of the few men in the regiment who came through front-line action since D-Day untouched. He had three times scampered into foxholes atop another occupant and each time the man underneath had been killed by shrapnel while he remained uninjured, only his clothing penetrated. He asked several times to be reduced in rank.

"I want to resign from this first sergeant job," he said to his company commander. "I can't take it any more, I just want to be a private and be able to go off in a corner once in a while by myself. I resign."

The company commander ignored his request and he continued on the job. The other day he again jumped into a foxhole when shelling began and landed on top another man. A shell landed nearby. The first sergeant looked at the man under him and saw his leg had clean blown off.

He again went to the company commander and said, "That's the last straw; I resign, transfer me to Headquarters Company as private, my nerves are shot."

Again the company commander ignored his request. The next day he was missing.

The *Stars and Stripes* newspaper is not very reliable in its news since it established a Paris edition. Two days ago it reported in a big headline: "SIEGFRIED LINE IS BURST." The body of the story told of an infantry company that went through the Siegfried Line with not a single casualty. Today our division is not through that line, nor is the situation encouraging either tactically or in terms of losses.

The pillboxes are not as bad as the German artillery which is mobile, well-handled, and on this terrain has us at a disadvantage. The Germans are now using "Screaming Meemies" that contain shrapnel; in Normandy they were bad enough with just concussion.

September 20, 1944.

The town of St. Hubert shows little outward disturbance. The shops still operate, though with little merchandise to sell. One can find a few fine knit cloths, doilies and scarves. Food is plentiful. The internal scene, however, is unsettled. The gendarmerie uses its power to jail Belgians who were informers for the German Gestapo. The local detention home for wayward boys is preparing to release several Jewish boys whom they had hidden from the Germans. Trivial problems arise daily for the local government that are momentarily big problems.

One night they were stuck without means of travel when they hadn't enough gas for even one of their few vehicles. In urgent need to communicate with their army headquarters in the next town, they begged American Army truck drivers for a little gas. The Americans had to refuse, lacking the authority to offer them even one gallon.

A Maquis representative went looking for the nearest American Civil Affairs Officer to request the return of a large meat cache that the Americans captured from the Germans. The Germans had taken the meat from them, say the Belgians, and therefore should be returned to Belgium for their army and civilian use. I don't know how he made out, but suddenly we were served a couple of meals with fresh meat for the first time in weeks.

The Belgians are greatly disturbed over their national political situation, even more than the French with theirs. Some are loyal to King Leopold who is presently a prisoner of the Germans, while others are dead set against him on grounds that he illegally married a commoner who happened also to be a Nazi sympathizer.

There has been a rise in the Belgian communist movement, especially in the cities of Brussels, Antwerp and Liége. Why? I asked, is it because Russian propaganda is more effective than western capitalists? No, I was answered, it is simply that Germany denounced Russian bolshevism more than democratic capitalism, therefore they concluded that communism is more desirable.

Other dissident political parties are embroiled in the general clamor. The local army contingent is in favor of retaining King Leopold for the purpose of providing an immediate framework for reorganizing parliament and the national post-war economy.

September 21, 1944.

All the replacements we received today are men returning from hospitals, many of them wounded in the first few days of the D-Day invasion. We escorted them forward to assign them back to their old companies.

Hitler's acclaimed superhighways were not in evidence where we entered German territory. We cut through the northern corner of the Duchy Of Luxembourg at the flag-bedecked town of Ulflingen, reentered Belgium again, then crossed the border into "Der Faterland" on a narrow road which we soon left to turn onto a narrower and bumpier dirt road leading to Regimental Service Company. Several loud artillery blasts greeted us. They were our own.

When we left Service Company for Regimental CP we got a taste of the enemy's. The Germans are hardly using anything in artillery as small as 88s on the Siegfried Line; it is big stuff almost exclusively. From atop a heavily wooded hill they have good observation of a bare stretch of road that we have to use. The stretch extends about two miles and is called by our troops Purple Heart Ridge.

As do all our vehicles, we ran this bumpy stretch at no less than fifty miles an hour while shells whined overhead and burst violently within several hundred yards of us fore, aft and to leeward. The German artillery so harassing is a clever and elusive beast. Every time our reconnaissance planes spot him he retreats to a hideout before our artillery can zero in and returns soon at a slightly different location.

Few prisoners are taken by either side in this campaign. One that we took was a member of the S.S. elite corps. He was brought before a battalion commander who ordered him to dig a hole in the ground.

That done, the lieutenant colonel said, "I want information from you; if you don't give it to me I am going to shoot you. And if you give me the wrong information I am going to shoot you."

He asked the SS trooper to detail the German strong points, then tested the information and found the facts exactly opposite. This SS soldier no longer lives.

September 25, 1944.

To keep us supplied, a mass of men and materiel must cross France for several hundred miles in a sustained stream. This could not be achieved as rapidly as we advanced, and for a time we experienced a slowdown in receiving supplies and troop replacements. Now the flow is fairly steady again. We are receiving an ever-increasing number of "Limited Service" personnel, men who had been wounded and are now obviously not fit for front line duty. One man returned with only one eye, another with bad hearing, and one with a crippled trigger finger.

We are trying to absorb as many as possible in rear echelon assignments, but most have to be sent to the front where their physical handicaps may jeopardize their own lives and others. Sometimes a battalion medical aid station will take upon itself to declare one unfit for duty and sends him right back for rehospitalization, except he is likely to land in a replacement pool which again sends him to the front division, this merry-go-round procedure to repeat perhaps three or four times. This is especially strange when we hear that the replacement pools are presently glutted with healthy, untried men.

Our regiment is now in a holding action a few miles inside Germany, if such it can be called with days and nights filled with the turmoil of a marathon artillery duel. Yesterday was rough, the Germans again having zeroed in on our regimental CP while I visited. Twice a shell fell uncomfortably close; the first time I crawled under a jeep, the second ran into the cellar of the house occupied by the CP. A raincoat and several blankets near the entrance were full of shrapnel holes.

The German civilians in this tiny village were ordered to leave. In other villages they remain and carry on normal farm activities. One of our interrogators told me these people were very much afraid at first, having been warned by retreating German soldiers to expect their farms to be plundered by American Jews, their cattle wantonly destroyed and probably themselves. Now they are anxious to please; they offer to wash clothes and cook.

It is against army orders to take and butcher local cattle or poultry; nevertheless every company is eating fresh steak three times a day. The farmers sense that this is against army regulations; one sees an elderly couple standing out in the pasture with their cows to watch over them, knowing the Americans will not kill the cattle while even one German farmer is looking. The farmers are laying in the harvest against the long winter, which helps us as well as themselves. They are not complying with Hitler's orders to pursue a scorched earth policy.

September 27, 1944.

Among factors delaying our progress on the Siegfried Line is the weather; it has been raining more consistently than in the first few weeks in Normandy. This morning the sky cleared and we were to have "jumped off," but for some reason it was called off. At the regimental Command Post I saw Assistant Adjutant Mr. Flannagan, recently promoted from master sergeant to warrant officer. He has difficulties other than from shells which he has grown used to and doesn't let interfere with his duties. He has plenty to keep him busy.

In the short time I spent at the CP today he dealt with the following matters: An MP brought in an enlisted man who claimed to be a member of the regiment but had been picked up fifty miles away. He spoke with a thick Slavic accent and had been held as a possible

German spy wearing an American uniform. Mr. Flannagan determined by cross-examining that he was AWOL from a replacement pool far to the rear for the reason that he was anxiously trying to join a front line unit. There was no choice but to send him back to the replacement pool together with a letter explaining his case so he would not be picked up again and thrown in with German prisoners for another interrogation.

Next I brought up a question of three men we received from the 4th Engineers.

"Have they been assigned to any company yet?" I asked.

"Not yet," replied Mr. Flannagan." I don't want to assign them myself; these men were sent to us by the Engineers because they displeased somebody. This Somebody wants them sent up as riflemen. I know they aren't being shanghaied because of misconduct—one came in as a corporal and the other two as pfc's. These men don't know anything about infantry; one is 39 years old, another 35. The one 39 cried, saying he has a wife and child, doesn't know anything about being a rifleman and sending him up front would be sure slaughter. Hell, I'm only a warrant officer, not an executioner. I'll let someone higher than me assign them."

He ran to answer the field telephone for the half-dozenth time in a half-hour.

"Hello,—you haven't been notified? I sent down the message this morning. There will be Jewish Yom Kippur services in one hour, at 3 o'clock, See that the men get there."

A few shells came down from a German tank that had ventured to the crest of the wooded hills, lobbed a few shells and retreated. The walls of the CP house are thick and the men inside feel fairly secure. On our trip back we stopped at a battalion CP where four American aviators had just been brought in. They swaggered nervously, a captain and three enlisted crewmen. The captain limped from antiaircraft flack wounds.

One of the crewmen told us what had happened, "Our B-24 Liberator was hit and the ten of us had to bail out. I landed in a field, looked around, spied a woman and cautiously went up to her, thinking I was in Germany and worried because I had no escape kit. I asked her how far I was from the Siegfried Line. She looked at me queerly and said, 'about four kilometers.' She tried to tell me I was in Belgium and I didn't believe her. I speak a little German and that's what fooled me when I questioned her—I didn't know they speak German in this part of Belgium. Then I talked with a kid and he verified the information she gave me. Finally I met up with these three members of our crew. We've been on 22 missions over Germany. It's tough; the Germans still pack a wallop. We all agreed that when we get back to England we will tell them that we escaped from Germany, then they'll send us back to the States."

September 30, 1944.

We expected our section will move into Germany, but because of a prolonged stalemate we moved instead to St. Vith, Belgium, eight miles from the German border. The last week of our stay in St. Hubert had been quite pleasant. The Belgian townsfolk had become accustomed to us and were very hospitable, inviting us individually for meals and to sleep in their homes when they saw that our pup tents had become waterlogged. We did any of this clandestinely and in violation of army orders not to fraternize with civilians. Had we complied with such orders we would have left St. Hubert after two and a half weeks with the people utterly frozen by our aloofness. We left them instead solidly pro-American. I believe this was achieved without revealing military secrets. Our officers in moot agreement looked the other way.

One person I met was a Brussels business man, a building contractor taking a vacation until his country will be on firm economic footing and ready to build again. In Brussels, he said, the Germans had not been extremely oppressive during their four year, four month occupation. They generally kept out of people's hair except when they wanted things. It was only their arrogant manner that kept the Belgians aware of their conquerors. They came once to this contractor to buy supplies from him.

"We are taking your stock," they declared crudely, and needlessly so for they paid him a good price. As in Paris, which Brussels is said to resemble as a place of gaiety, German soldiers had not been made welcome in cafes and restaurants and soon became discouraged from patronizing them.

October 3, 1944.

One receives the impression that western Europe is well provided with lumber from its ample forests, and is able to raise a good supply of wheat. Crossing France eastward from Normandy, the country that journalists habitually call "highly industrialized Belgium," and Luxembourg, I saw large tracts of land covered with rich stands of wheat now maturing and being harvested. There were extensive forests of pine and fir planted by man as a crop and in ripe or almost ripe stages.

My conception of Europe had been of a land with too many towns, settled took close to one another, crowding out forests and farmland, and the farmers that exist eking out meager crops from soil depleted of vitality due to centuries of unscientific cultivation. To the contrary, I observe farms spaced far apart as in, say, Pennsylvania or New Jersey, and if farm production is low it is because of a war-time manpower shortage. I theorize that postwar Europe will be substantially self-sufficient in growing its food.

The town we are in, St. Vith, is in the province of Kreis Malmedy, a section that Belgium had taken from Germany after World War I and Germany reincorporated as its own in 1940. Now it is again part of Belgium. The people speak German, and with no Belgian flags hanging from their homes as in the rest of Belgium, they are making a poor show at hopping on the Allied bandwagon though they claim to be loyal Belgians. French-speaking Belgians regard them as having been notoriously pro-German.

St. Vith is a strategic crossroad through which is now streaming probably as great a cavalcade of soldiers and weaponry as this or any previous war has ever seen. Today a roundup began of Nazi sympathizers suspected of transmitting information to the enemy. Civilians caught leaving town are incarcerated, and many are being rounded up from lists furnished by the underground. This action is doubtless in prelude to a renewed offensive. The other day a German patrol infiltrated our lines, placed a log across the road outside of town and sat back out of sight. Soon a victim came along, a colonel of the 28th

Division. He stopped his jeep to investigate the road block and the Germans opened fire with a machine gun, killing him.

October 8, 1944.

Our regiment withdrew from the front to an assembly area two days ago. The regiment started the Siegfried Line campaign three weeks ago with an assault lasting several days, then retreated a distance from its point of deepest penetration and went into a holding action.

Recently I saw a newspaper clipping from the States of a widely circulated article crediting our regiment with being the first to enter Germany. The account described our commanding officer Colonel Lanham as leading his men into battle singing. This sounds most unlikely. I asked participants in the action and was told that one thing the colonel and his men certainly did not do was sing. The action was one of the grimmest experienced by our regiment. In concept and execution the colonel's strategy is said to have been masterful. Realizing the regiment was weak and had nothing backing it up, he knew the Germans must be led to believe we were strong. Had we hesitated, the Germans might well have perceived our weakness and bowled us over in a counterattack. Therefore we attacked, and in addition to hoodwinking the Germans gained positions well into the crust of the Siegfried Line.

We have seen since D-Day Normandy that the only reliable barometer we have of major events on the western front is the action participated in by the 4th Infantry Division. Thus, when we assaulted, the whole front made important gains and when we were still any successes thoughout the Theater of Operations were of localized significance. Sensational newspaper headlines to the contrary, recent action along the Siegfried Line has been essentially confined to preparing for another offensive.

Today both Regiment and Division moved back on line from the assembly area. The 9th Infantry Division is on our left, the 2nd to our right. The 2nd Division has just been brought up from Brittany where it took part in the siege of Brest where the Germans resisted stubbornly, the troops having been told that they had the Allies surrounded and need only push them into the sea like a second Dunkirk to defeat the Allied invasion of France.

In a preliminary offensive action yesterday, the 22nd Infantry Regiment was assigned an objective to be taken within three days. We had it by 2 o'clock of the first.

Meanwhile our section moved to the Belgian resort town of Spa, half-way between Liége and Malmedy. St. Vith is the only town we ever left that the people made no show of waving and cheering as we rode out. Also, St. Vith is the first place we saw in which young Polish and Russian slave laborers had been imported to work directly for civilians. Their treatment by the community was worse than for slaves—as formal slaves they might have been accorded some little consideration. Those I spoke with had little good to say of their "Belgian" employers.

In Spa we are again in a French-speaking, liberation-enthused community. The prosperous resort aspect of the 9,000 population town is intact, with its fine scenery, soccer stadium and dormant gambling casino well preserved. We share the town with 12,000 other American troops. Here we eat and sleep (on the floor) in buildings as well as work in them. We are still not supposed to talk with civilians. Despite restrictions, we managed to buy ice cream cones, the first since leaving the States.

October 14, 1944.

The campaign has simmered down to an immobile mud and blood affair. The front is a morass of mud. Combat patrols are encountering more land mines than ever before. The men up front are sick of it all, wearier than ever; even the General reportedly said the division has had enough and it is time for a real rest.

The 4th Infantry Division is said to have put in more combat hours than any other American division including those which fought in Africa, Sicily and Italy as well as France. To top it off Army Chief of Staff General George C. Marshall visited our regiment the other day and said the boys should not feel too badly about spending the winter here if they have to.

Kids of 18 and 20 are suffering from rheumatism. The men pray for "million dollar wounds." Some men recently sent from hospitals for limited assignment duty included one suffering from a duodenal ulcer requiring a special diet, and certainly to avoid eating canned or packaged field rations. He together with several afflicted with "Psychoneurosis, moderate severe" were certified "Fit for general assignment" by our division medical board consisting of two majors and a captain. Their records were marked accordingly and they were sent to the front for regular duty. Within three days all of them had to be evacuated.

The strong men who have come through since D-Day, a mere handful, are haggard and jumpy, and the "battle-wise" soldiers are vulnerable as ever. One recently went up to a well-concealed observation post just to have a long-distance look at the enemy through field glasses. A bullet caught him square through the head a fraction under his steel helmet.

The front is a perpetual nightmare in which the men converse in a language all their own, understood only by those who continuously wallow with them on this border of hell. The rest of the army including those who experienced "close shaves" do not speak that language. They speak of their buddies who have come and gone, of officers good and bad who led them, of cold, wet, pitch-black nights, of gory sights and funny things that happened, Only they know precisely what they mean.

October 17, 1944.

I stopped into a shop in Spa to buy a pipe that attracted me. The owner invited me to go home with him for supper. He had spent three years in England and spoke English fluently.

"Very well," I agreed, "but I cannot be seen walking with you; I'll follow behind you."

His home was nicely furnished, middle class, and like the rest of Spa showed little effect of the war.

"I suppose you are not permitted to mix with civilians on account of the danger of imparting information to spies," he observed.

"Maybe, but I doubt that is a good reason," I replied. "A good spy would not waste time talking with soldiers. He would keep his eyes open and see more that way, with less risk, than he could learn by asking questions."

My host brought out a bottle of champagne that he said he had been saving for such an occasion. I asked how the Germans had treated him.

"They were very correct," he answered. "I often felt that individual soldiers would like to be friendly, to be invited into my home, but I went on about my business with no more to do with them than necessary. The only ones we really feared were the Russian and Polish soldiers in the German Wehrmacht. They were less restrained than the Germans and would act like hoodlums. We were glad there weren't many of them. It was only in the last weeks that the Germans started committing atrocities."

I asked what he thought German plans were for Belgium if they had remained permanently. Their whole aim was to make Belgians work for them, he replied. They wanted to become a nation of wealthy overlords and would not have bothered annexing Belgium to be a part of Germany.

"How does the situation look now?" I asked.

"I think we will be able to get on our feet again," he said, "The government made a good start by solving the problem of currency. We were, you know, flooded with German-made francs designed to corrupt our economy by fostering inflation and a black market. Now our government has designed new currency and declared all existing money invalid. The people may convert up to two thousand old francs into new without questions being asked, and more if they can prove they earned it legitimately. Belgian businessmen are very shrewd, you know; they foresaw that the working class was going to fight for better working conditions when the time comes that they are free, even if they have to go Communistic to do so. The manufacturers and other employers have taken the wind out of Communist sails by voluntarily giving their workers better conditions than they ever had before."

October 23, 1944.

More branches of First Army Headquarters moved into Spa and we had to leave to make room for them. We moved ten miles to Stavelot. The Germans have started sending over buzz bombs in wholesale quantities. We are on their direct line of flight, though apparently not their target for they keep on going—if they manage to clear the hill rising above Stavelot. About a dozen came over today, one plowing into the hill with a powerful blast.

The front is rather quiet, and still very muddy. Only one battalion at a time is staying right up on line, alternating with the other two every three or four days. New orders permit men to go on a pleasure trip to Paris for three days plus travel time, in segments of three from each company. The men on line the longest are given first preference.

The big question to everyone is: are we bogged down for the winter? It was good to hear that our forces invading the Phillipines equalled in numbers those landing in France on D-Day, indicating that the war in the Pacific is also getting somewhere.

Last night I visited a Stavelot family. The father came in from work as a town policeman wearing a dark blue uniform. He retained this post under the German occupation until six months ago when he fled to hide out in the woods along with a thousand other Stavelot men. The town's population is a total of 5,000.

Didn't the Germans look for them? I asked. He explained that the men had individually received passes to go to work in Germany and instead went into hiding. Whenever the Germans came to check with a man's wife she would put on a big act, say she has not heard from her husband in months and thought he was working in Germany. Maybe he is dead from the bombings, she would moan. Sometimes they took a woman to Gestapo headquarters to sweat out information from her on her husband's true whereabouts. People living in the vicinity of Gestapo headquarters frequently heard terrible screams emanating from it.

The whole town carried on a passive resistance in subtle ways. The 23-year old daughter in this family had received an offer of twenty thousand francs and special privileges if she stool-pigeoned for the Gestapo against her neighbors. She managed to decline. They know of only twelve such collaborators in the town, all now in jail.

One thing that distinguishes the French-speaking Belgians from the French is the language they speak among themselves. It is called Walloon, and is a language as old or older than French. It has survived as an auxiliary language spoken only in intimate family circles. It is a Latin-based jargon not taught in schools, except it has been accorded a niche in the philological department of the University of Brussels. It originated at the time of Julius Caesar whose armies occupied Belgium for many years, leaving a Latin influence on the country.

November 5, 1944.

The buzz bombs don't fly on schedule, but they can usually be counted on to wake us for breakfast and thereafter to streak through the air a dozen times a day. They arouse more curiosity than alarm, because the town is situated in a cup-like valley and the bombs seem to have little chance of dropping on us. But the Germans apparently spotted the heavy ordnance repair company in our midst, for their planes dropped a couple of 500-pound bombs which missed by three or four hundred yards, hitting instead an outlying house and wounding a bedridden elderly woman.

The lull on the western front has induced a deflation of spirits; nobody talks much even about the United States presidential election three days from now. Yet there is much evidence that our long-delayed drive will soon resume. Behind the lines activities are constantly churning; units are withdrawn from one sector, put in another until again moved to still another, as though without rhyme or reason. Our division has made several such moves and is about to make another, but this time attended by a greater aura of secrecy and expectation.

Our casualties are almost negligible during this period. Recently we had almost as many cases of venereal disease as battle casualties. With the slowing of the campaign our administrative processes have taken a normal pace. This means among other things that the strenuous game of regimental politics among officers has started up. The Colonel is a great believer in "reclassification" and will at the proverbial drop of a hat send back an officer to be reclassified, meaning his battlefield performance is considered unsatisfactory. Actually it is a break for him, for he is almost always sent to a non-combat post with a promotion in rank.

By contrast, enlisted men are "reclassified" with a reduction in rank to private if a noncom, and sent to an active front. He is at the mercy of any whim that might strike one of his frequently changing company commanders. One tried and esteemed mess sergeant for eighteen years somehow displeased a new company commander and was reduced to private for "inefficiency."

One sees much to support a popular theory that the army is composed of gradations of hierarchies from bottom to top. Each commander rules his dynasty, whether large or small, to suit his particular ambition which may be to attain glory, or competence, or to afford him the joy of sheer tyranny. He has the power to reign as a near-autonomous monarch while keeping within legal and prudent bounds.

November 15, 1944.

The first snow fell, blanketing the wooded hills in the Aachen sector with a sizable layer of snow. The ground remains muddier than ever. Our regiment moved to a forward assembly area southeast of Aachen, close to fighting which is one of the most intensive yard by yard battles since that preceding the St. Lô breakthrough. Part of our division, the 12th Infantry Regiment, was committed to action in the first few days and mauled severely. The 28th Infantry Division spearheaded this offensive in the Hurtgen Forest and suffered a withering rate of casualties. In this sector we are quite deep within the Siegfried Line. We occupy a large number of damaged and undamaged pillboxes, many small towns, and a broad section of grotesque "dragons' teeth," a series of closely-set concrete blocks designed to stop an invasion of tanks.

Our objective is to break out of the Hurtgen Forest hills and onto the plains of the Ruhr Valley leading to the Rhine River. Only a few thousand yards separate us from this all-important objective. The Germans are resisting with the desperation and resourcefulness of a cornered tiger. Both sides are using artillery with unprecedented intensity. I arrived on the scene yesterday a few minutes after the Germans had ceased shelling and our guns had just opened up. For the next two hours I heard and felt the concussion of massed artillery firing in devastating, incessant volume; big 155s and 240s set off in a consistency like concentrated rifle fire.

It seemed that every inch of German-held terrain had to be saturated with the shrapnel and concussion of the big shells; yet the Germans were subsequently able to retort in kind, probably accomplishing more with one-fourth the artillery, for we were on the attack and thus more exposed. They would hold their fire until our infantry came in close to attack their pillboxes, then, knowing the precise range of the pillboxes they would send salvos of artillery and mortar shells and "the kitchen sink." They might thereby do injury to their own men inside the pillboxes, but woe to the Americans outside.

One of our artillerymen made a discovery that barely averted a major calamity. He was assisting in loading a heavy shell into the breech of his piece when he noticed the word GAS imprinted on the casing. They removed the shell, inspected the others and found they had been shipped several gas shells, ostensibly to have on hand to retaliate in case the Germans started using gas. The matter was quickly reported to other artillery units and America narrowly averted starting poison gas warfare in this war.

November 20, 1944.

Our long-awaited grand assault on this part of the 460-mile western front is now in full progress. My regiment went into action four days ago, on November 16. We gained 75 yards on that first day, and thereafter our rate of advance improved but modestly and at very high cost.

Fate seems determined that our last few men who survived at the front since D-Day shall not escape. Lieutenant Colonel Teague is the last battalion commander in the 4th Infantry Division who started on D-Day. He was finally hit and evacuated, as were two of my ex-assistants, both hit in the head. Among strange circumstances that arise in combat is one experienced by one of our line company first lieutenants.

In between battles he is second in command with the title "Company Executive Officer." Repeatedly on the first day of battle his company commander gets killed and he takes command until the battle is over, then a new replacement arrives with the rank of captain and he is pushed back to second in command. This is the third time it happened.

The two-month stalemate has given Germany time to organize a "People's Army." We captured a 75-year old fighter, one 65, and some women.

Our men appear to have developed fully a requisite psychological attitude toward battle. They are killers. They hate Germans and think nothing of killing them; or, in fact, anyone who incites them. They regard their lives as cheap. Worse, they believe they are regarded as cheap, low-grade soldiers, else why would men discredited in rear echelon outfits be punished by reassignment to the infantry?

"I guess we are criminals," say those who have never been other than infantrymen.

A month ago, one of the men went into a nearby town while his battalion was "at rest" 400 yards behind the line, came back tipsy and was ordered by his squad leader to go on KP. He took out his gun and shot the squad leader on the spot.

A lieutenant ran toward him and was told, "Stop where you are or I'll shoot you too." The lieutenant stopped, while others crept behind the man and disarmed him, after which a friend of the felled squad leader walked up and shot him between the eyes. For this he was court-martialed and sentenced to six months imprisonment because he shot the man after he was disarmed; but someone failed to have him evacuated to serve his sentence and he was killed in action on the first day of the offensive. The lieutenant was also killed.

November 21, 1944.

Army-avowed policies are one thing and implementation another. So it is that among the replacements we receive are men over 37 years of age whom both President Roosevelt and General Marshall had declared not fit nor shall be assigned as combat infantrymen. One man said several Army doctors told him he positively was unfit to be a rifleman and he assuredly will be assigned to duties he is physically able to perform. None of the doctors bothered to pull him out of the replacement center assembly line that led inevitably to the combat infantry.

Today we received a man returned to duty from a hospital where he had been recuperating since D-Day when he was evacuated with two bullets in his stomach. His life had hung on a thread as he underwent a series of delicate operations that eventuated in a miraculous recovery and a tribute to the great skill of Army surgeons. We were certain he would be returned to the States when his condition permitted, and were amazed to see him returned as a front line replacement. He was weak and obviously unfit for anything strenuous. Nobody along the way had interested himself sufficiently to at least designate him for "Limited Assignment." We happen to know him and are trying to find a reasonable spot, yet there are men with similar histories whom we don't know personally and given their numbers could not help if we did, except to offer illicit advice on how to beat the game. We can only gasp incredulously that the Army sends such men to fill in at crack infantry divisions. We attribute this to ineptness or callous indifference of those in authority.

November 23, 1944.

We had an excellent turkey dinner this Thanksgiving Day, but the holiday was less than festive. Every infantry charge we make is pounced on by German artillery and practically stopped cold. In one assault we reached half of our first day's objective at the end of the fourth day. Instead of preoccupation with eating turkey the regiment has the problem of trying to regain contact with the 2nd Battalion which has been out of communication reach for 24 hours.

That battalion is led by a man who is obsessed, it is said, with the idea that he can crash through clear to Berlin with whatever the size force he commands. He spares himself no more than he spares his men and has the luck never to have received more than trivial wounds over the months that men all around him went down like flies. In his passion for achieving high power in his assaults he has no compunction in urging on his men at the point of a pistol. To illustrate his seriousness he did once or twice fire it over their heads. Despite this image of ruthlessness there is no evidence to support the commonly held notion that he gains his objectives at a cost in casualties out of proportion to other battalions.

It has rained almost constantly in seven of the last eight days of our offensive. Many of our current replacements were civilians on D-Day. They were rushed through an abbreviated basic training, hustled onto ships and forwarded through several replacement pools on the continent. Most had been exempted from being drafted earlier for having fathered from two to five children. Several were killed during their first or second day in action. Considering the successful German resistance, we wonder if our offensive has not been too long in the making, giving Germany an opportunity to regain equilibrium and rendering our ultimate victory over-costly.

We think we can see "the big picture" and speculate that our delay in starting the offensive was unavoidable. 1st Sergeant Reed of 1st Battalion Headquarters Company expresses this opinion. He is a slow-moving, gray, soft-speaking soldier with 26 years service and one of the few remaining D-Day 1st sergeants. He had many close calls, the most recent yesterday when shrapnel cut his pants on opposite sides of his leg without touching the leg.

"How long can you go on, Reed?" I asked.

"Barring accidents I reckon I'll finish standing up," he replied.

Nevertheless he is tired, old and shaky, though usually he manages to conceal his shakiness. Nobody in authority is interested enough to see to it that this hard-working, hard-fought soldier is sent back for a long, well-deserved rest. Reclassification to a rear area is a salvation reserved for officers who find little difficulty in getting themselves permanently evacuated from the front by claiming to be nervous.

November 29, 1944.

It becomes clearer each day that this battle on Germany's western front is one of the mightiest battles ever fought by an American army. Behind the lines many lesser dramas go on. Buzz bombs are falling on Liége sometimes at the rate of one every five minutes. Spies are operating in Belgium on a wide scale. To complicate matters, internal Belgian politics are quite chaotic. This affects us in not receiving adequate Belgian support in detecting spies and potential saboteurs. The Belgian underground has been officially, prematurely dissolved and disarmed. The few American M.P.'s who police towns like Stavelot are insufficient to prevent many incidents that need not have occurred if these resistance forces had continued to operate.

The political rifts in this country are not merely war warts. They have been brewing for many years. The great majority of the people are passionately anti-Nazi; there is considerable friction between those who cooperated in the slightest with the Germans during their occupation of Belgium and those who did not. The Pierlot liberation government has been phlegmatic in trying to unite the people. There is a strong Communist movement, though it is not necessarily Communistic in the fashion conceived by Americans; it is, rather, a seeking for relief from an ancient, deep-rooted economic and social caste system. The country is divided almost evenly by the French-speaking in the south and the Flemish in the north speaking a German dialect. The 19 ministries of the government are a source of friction in that 15 transact their business entirely in Flemish and 4 entirely in French.

December 6.

Our division was pulled out of action three days ago. Not entirely out; one battalion of each regiment will be committed in a holding action at a static sector of the Siegfried Line that will be termed a "rest area." Few men are left who really need a rest. In the past 17 days of action my regiment had nearly a 100 percent turnover of its 3,000 authorized strength including men little affected in the rear echelon. Hurtgen Forest will not soon be forgot. At the end the regiment was groggy; squad leaders hardly knew the men they were leading; many men did not know their company commanders, and first sergeants were not sure which men were supposed to be in their companies.

The Germans launched a vigorous counterattack during the final week of action. We held, though we required even the Service Company to reorganize into rifle platoons for additional support.

Now the Army is executing a new plan: a quota of men will be sent to the States for 30-day furloughs. To qualify, one must have been hospitalized with wounds at least twice. 20 men in our regiment qualify. Two weeks ago there would have been 200, the other 180 again hit and evacuated. No man in the division's rear echelon envies those who qualify. The 20 came today to be processed and issued new clothing, then a minor technicality was discovered that questioned the eligibility of half. The matter was submitted to the division adjutant general, Lieutenant Colonel Castegneto. He ruled that all the men may go. It was one of the most dramatic incidents I witnessed in months. The men were asked to specify their destinations.

One answered tersely, "My home; when I get there I am going to knock at the front door, then run around to the back and catch as he runs out the sonofabitch who has been sleeping with my wife."

December 10, 1944.

The division rear echelon has disbanded for the duration of the rest period and all personnel groups returned to their regular units. Our section rejoined the regiment and we are again under direct regimental control for the first time in nearly eight months. We moved from Stavelot to Mondorf in the Duchy of Luxembourg. Among the companies with us in this town is Regimental Headquarters Company, composed largely of men rescued at one time or another from the "line" companies, some of them old-timers I've known from the time I first became a member of Company E in Camp Gordon, Georgia, and remain so officially. They are in unanimous agreement that the Hurtgen Forest battle was fiercer than any they experienced before. They are enormously relieved at sleeping in quiet again, though they all have bad dreams.

Corporal Upchurch described one he had, "I dreamt last night that I was being cut up alive, bit by bit into little pieces. I woke up several times in a cold sweat and I think I screamed."

The Germans, I asked—did they take as much punishment as we? Far worse, they agreed.

"The Germans were piled high ten to our one," said one.

Pfc Cohen related, "That battle became so unendurable that we didn't care whether we lived or died. One night we moved up to a new area and shells started coming at us. We tried digging in but every time we scooped out a shovelful of mud the hole filled with water and more mud. We said the hell with it and just lay down in the mud to sweat out the shells."

Once a news reporter visiting the front asked a sergeant to comment on the fighting.

"Dammit," responded the sergeant, "I don't want to tell you anything unless you print exactly what I say and don't add any romance. Will that suit you?"

"Well," hedged the war correspondent, "you know it will have to be censored."

"I see you want a certain kind of story and nothing else," concluded the sergeant; "you better talk to one of the other fellows."

December 20, 1944.

The rest period for the 4th Division ended swiftly when the Germans launched a massive counter-offensive in the quiescent Belgium and Luxembourg area. We had no inkling that Germany had conserved enough power to drive into our lines with a force of 15 full-strength divisions. Yet that she did, and we were shocked not mildly to hear that Malmedy and St. Hubert were in German hands, also part of Stavelot.

In Luxembourg they attacked at a front point where our 12th Infantry Regiment was thinly spread out. One battalion from our regiment has so far gone to assist. If the situation is alarming that fact is not evident to us except in increased air activity, artillery fire that we hear (ours) and frightened civilians.

The citizens of Mondorf already got word that the Germans are making life miserable or impossible in some of the Luxembourg towns they have recaptured. Normally a thousand people inhabit Mondorf, but it is a health resort center and in the summer months many visitors take up residence in the fashionable hotels surrounding the opulent health bath-houses with spring water reputed to have curative powers. I and a few others staked a claim in one of the "pension" hotels and for ten days lived in elegant, unaccustomed comfort. The proprietor lived on the ground floor with his family. Several rooms were occupied by evacuees from the nearby Moselle River region. We are close enough to France to throw a stone across the border.

The proprietor's family included a young daughter-in-law and her 2-year old child. A few months ago her husband had been caught in a German Gestapo net and held as a member of the Luxembourg underground. Others caught were promptly shot. Her husband was spared and sent to work in Germany. She received letters from him until last August. She professed also to have participated in underground activities. She estimated that 20 percent of Luxembourgers had cooperated with the Germans; nearly all were of German extraction. The remaining 80 percent were bitterly anti-Nazi during the annexation of their small country into Greater Germany and despite the similarity of their language. They were subjected to a powerful campaign of German Nazi propaganda and compelled to buy expensive trinkets such as Nazi-insignia lapel buttons. They successfully resisted indoctrination of either themselves or their children in the schools. Perceiving their failure, the Germans became severely vindictive.

We left Mondorf today, in a manner unlike any we had yet experienced. We moved merely a few miles away to the village of Hamm, 2 miles from the city of Luxembourg, but the Mondorf residents were tearfully under the impression that we were fleeing before the Germans.

December 26, 1944.

The most intriguing question of the war is to what extent did our high command expect the German counter-offensive. The entire situation on the western front has changed. We hear that the Germans failed to capture one of their early main objectives, the road between Stavelot and Spa that we had long ago blocked off from traffic and lined with huges stores of gasoline.

The 4th Infantry Division has now been officially tranferred from the First Army to the Third Army commanded by General Patton. This army is now choking the roads with armored vehicles heading toward the bulge the Germans made in our line.

For the past four days and nights there hasn't been a cloud in the sky and our planes are striking hard at the German assault columns. We felt for months that the Germans have been holding something back. Though we seem to have been insufficiently prepared, it appears that her rash action has presented us with a rare opportunity to get at her reserve power.

Our regiment never fully replaced the losses in the Hurtgen Forest battle, notwithstanding which our regiment is again engaged in action. Our personnel section is again functioning as part of the division rear echelon, and today we moved back to Mondorf. The people were overjoyed to see us. They had been living in terror that the Germans would return and were poised to flee with a few packed belongings at the first sign that the Germans were approaching.

January 1, 1945.

Field Marshal Von Runstedt's counter-offensive netted our regiment only a few days of hot combat, then the line stabilized with each side establishing outposts and occasionally sending out a patrol. General Patton wrote a letter to our division general commending the 4th Division for its action in the Bulge, and calling it our greatest achievement to date. Has Patton never heard of Cherbourg? St. Lô? Branscheid? Hurtgen Forest?

The German bulge in this sector had pushed us in six miles from the Sauer River. A couple of days ago we decided to push them back. This was not very difficult, as they withdrew almost without a fight but with many losses. Sergeant Wagner of Company A described the scene at the house his squad moved into. Dead Germans lay around the back yard, and pigs nibbled at their carcasses. Nobody cared much.

Prisoners brought to the company CP were grilled through an interpreter by officers who took turns in walking over and cracking one in the face with his fist to encourage him to talk. One prisoner brought before this venerable council of interrogators had walked in and surrendered unarmed after walking ten miles with a gaping shrapnel wound in his back. The interrogators proceeded to question him while a pfc medic sewed him up. Why had he run away to surrender to us? He answered that he was an officer's orderly who had been bullied and mistreated. Sweat ran down his face as the medic sewed and his face twisted in pain.

"Let's kill the sonofabitch," proposed an officer bitterly.

The motion was turned down for the time being and the questioning went on. How many artillery pieces had he seen on the way? The German thought a moment, as though he took notice of such things in his condition and while trying to duck shells on his way to surrender; then, seeing by the ferocious faces of his interrogators that some answer had to be given, he replied, "Ten."

An officer walked over, slapped him and said, "You are lying. How many were there?"

The man thought again and said, "Fifteen."

January 9, 1945.

The other day Master Sergeant Roth of the "IPW" interrogation team became Second Lieutenant Roth. His status was changed to commissioned officer for the purpose of going on an unusual mission. The Germans had called a truce and requested that a specified area not be shelled by us because a hospital was there. This message was relayed to our division general who directed we might agree only if permitted to inspect. The Germans so permitted and Lt. Roth went together with a captain on a tour conducted by Germans behind their lines.

Later Lt. Roth described the experience: "It was a hospital, all right. It was modern and had everything, including some of our men. They were given the best treatment, too, and without expecting a visit from us. I spoke to one who had been wounded in the arm. He didn't want to talk to me at first—he thought it was a German trick—but he finally believed me. I asked him how he was treated and he said fine.

"The captain and I stayed overnight. I slept three hours. They gave us an excellent meal of fried eggs, home-fried potatoes, fresh asparagus and Moselle wine. The hospital's chief surgeon said it would take at least six to eight days to move all the serious cases. We went back in the morning and reported this.

"Instructions came back to us from 12th Corps Commander Major General Eddy that we give the hospital 24 hours to move out or, as an alternative, that we be permitted to have a radio outpost inside the German lines to watch that there is no military traffic except medical. Well, that was stupid, and I told them at Regimental CP that I would be staking my life to go back to the Germans with that message. They managed to get the order changed giving the hospital time to move out.

"I'll tell you one thing: those jerries are not getting ready to give up. They look well fed and they have brand-new equipment. Ernest Hemingway was dying to go with me on this mission but he went only as far as our outpost. He never leaves the 22nd Infantry Regiment. He spends a lot of time right up front with the companies, but he is afraid of falling into German hands. He's positive they have it in for him on account of his writings from Spain during the Spanish Civil War when Germany supported General Franco."

January 10, 1945.

Our personnel section people are not meant to be infantry assault troops, but our proximity to the front which is almost the same as our regular line troops might make us such. In Mondorf we are three miles from the Moselle River, with nothing between us and the Germans but a few of our jeep patrols and the river, The fact that at this point the river is at its widest adds little to our feeling of security inasmuch as the Germans might readily decide that a wide river is less of an obstacle than a narrow one backed by frontline infantry. Therefore we naturally assumed a state of aggressive alert last night when a string of rapid-fire automatic gunshots sounded off at the eastern end of the town. They sounded like German machine-pistol shots. A second string went off five minutes later and a 12th Infantry Regiment personnel officer informed us that the bullets had penetrated his bedchamber.

Warmly dressed and armed to the teeth, we took up guard positions in front of our respective buildings and awaited further orders. A jeep rumbled to my position near the head of the street and I challenged with a loud "Halt!"

The driver slid to a stop on the snow-packed street and spoke the pass-word, "Gordon Setter."

Captain Brill walked over and asked the riders, "What's the dope?"

"Some Germans crossed the river and are in a village four kilometers away," replied a lieutenant.

This explanation seemed insufficient for gunfire that sounded so near, and we continued our alert in the cold, dark night. Soon the

"Town Major" came along, a first lieutenant wearing the "Supreme Headquarters" SHAEF shoulder path.

He explained, "One of our security jeeps hit a rut and accidentally set off its machine gun. The men decided to stay on the spot and inform anyone investigating the gunfire that it was accidental. They changed their minds fast when machine gun bullets started splattering around them coming from another of our jeep patrols who preferred to shoot first and ask questions later."

That concluded the incident and we went back to bed, though still unsure about the report of the Germans entering the village four short kilometers away.

January 12, 1945.

When 600 replacements joined us one day recently, our regiment was at a very low ebb in personnel. Besides an exhausting attrition from battle at the German Bulge which our rifle companies were fighting with a strength each of only 50 to 90 men, we had a perpetual outflow of men for reasons listed as "Non-Battle Casualty." Among these were frostbite, trenchfoot, and self-inflicted wounds.

Sometimes accidental wounds take a serious toll, such as last week when a rifleman jostled a rifle grenade hanging from his belt. As luck would have it, he had just come in from a patrol mission and neglected to put back the safety pin in the grenade as he hurried to get in line for a cup of hot coffee. The grenade fell to the ground and went off. Seventeen men were wounded and evacuated including the mess sergeant and most of the cooks.

Such numbers of new enlisted men and officers streaming in created an effect rather out of the ordinary. There were never so few veterans in the companies, and when noncoms were appointed they usually rejected offers of promotion. In one company a platoon leader assembled his men and said, "Who wants to be a squad leader?"

"What does a squad leader do in combat?" asked a man whose experience was limited to the proddings of squad sergeants in basic training.

"He leads his squad against the enemy; he has to go in front and be a real leader," answered the platoon sergeant.

"The hell with that," responded the men, until a few decided to volunteer, reasoning that they might as well fight with the rank of sergeant since they had to be there anyway.

January 18, 1945.

On this day one year ago we sailed out of New York harbor onto the high seas en route to England. By this time the war in Europe should have been over and I back home in Pittsburgh. But I am now in a sort of Pittsburgh, for we moved today to Esch, which is the Pittsburgh of Luxembourg. This city of 30,000 is the second largest in the duchy, and has steel mills and other industries.

We moved into a schoolhouse near the town hall. Militarily, we share the city with Third Army Headquarters troops. It is the most populated place yet that we have been stationed in and is not "off limits" for us. There are many stores with a considerable variety of merchandise at prices far below France or Belgium. A strict curfew at 8 P.M. is in effect for both soldiers and civilians.

The town presents a depressing mien. Many people look seriously under-nourished. The poorest and least proud stand in a crowd outside the cafe that now acts as our mess hall. They stare hungrily at us and the remains in our mess kits, which we dump into their pails to ostensibly feed their hogs. Talking with them reveals endless, now-familiar tales of woe. Their sons and daughters had been drafted into the German Army and those who ran away sacrificed their families to the fury of the Gestapo. The food situation was fairly good until the German counter offensive cut off the industrial southern half of Luxembourg from the agricultural north. But as in other places where meat and bread rations seem ample, something lacking in their diet gives these people a sickly appearance. In any case they are intent more on berating their conditions than in glorying at liberation from the Nazi yoke.

"These are bad times," lamented a spindly matriarch, her tone seeming to betray, of all things, resentment toward her liberators—we Americans!

January 27.

Esch has a center for service men, operated by the Luxembourg Red Cross with supplies from our Army Quartermaster Corps and staffed by civilian volunteers. Heading the staff is a young high school teacher who speaks English fluently. As a teacher during the occupation he had traveled some in Germany, sponsored by the Germans on the theory that having Luxembourg teachers visit the Reich would influence them to accept German ideals. He had studied German propaganda during this period, and now he was applying himself to gain an accurate perspective of Americans. He was especially interested in American Jews, because the Germans had constantly hammered on that theme.

One American he spoke with told him that the trouble with Jews is they consider themselves Jews first and Americans second. Another American soldier told him there is prejudice against Jews in America, and they cannot buy homes in certain neighborhoods.

Are these things true? he asked me. Half-truths, I replied, and he proceeded aloud to work out in his mind the anomaly of racial and religious friction in a free democratic country.

He seemed to understand that America is still in the process of assimilating her diverse population, and that the biggest problem in doing so is with Negroes.

"I want to understand these things thoroughly," he emphasized, "so I talk to Americans rather than read about them in books. I want to know at least as much as my pupils know, for they have learned much in mixing with you Americans."

I asked him how successful German propaganda had been in influencing the people of Luxembourg. Not very, he thought, particularly among the majority who are deeply rooted Luxembourgers. Some of the newer ones of German descent retreated with the Wehrmacht. The Germans were aware of the general attitude and upon retreating a lieutenant flung a remark at a group of girls, "You can go pick flowers now to greet the Americans with; they will be here soon."

February 4, 1945.

John S. Zagorodny, in short order nicknamed "Zaza," had joined our outfit just before the Hurtgen Forest campaign ended. Before that he was a member of the 83rd Infantry Division from which he was evacuated to a hospital with a fever he contracted at St. Malo on the Brittany peninsula in France. With the 83rd Division he had been a draftsman in a regimental antitank company and when necessary, a Russian interpreter. Zaza's destiny may have been determined by his attachment to a violin.

He had completed two and a half years at Juilliard School of Music in New York when the Army got him, and by the third note I heard him produce on his violin it was clear that he was near to being an accomplished musician.

He was very disappointed at being assigned to the 4th Division instead of returned to the 83rd. One day when our regiment was about to leave Hurtgen Forest for a rest area in Luxembourg he spied some vehicles of the 83rd coming up to relieve the 4th on line. He grew excited and wanted to visit friends in the 83rd but it was time to move out.

Upon reaching the rest area in Luxembourg he went "over the hill" that evening and made his way back to his regiment in the 83rd Division. There he seriously intended to remain, indifferent to the formality of being now a member of the 4th Division. He declared this intention to his former company commander he was visiting. The matter was communicated to the regimental commander who sent back a message recommending but not insisting that Zagorodny had best return to the 4th Division.

In the midst of deciding Zaza suddenly remembered he had not brought along his violin. That settled it for him, together with the second thought that the 83rd was just going into combat after a three month layoff while the 4th was just going out of it.

When he returned next day to his company in the 22nd Infantry Regiment the first sergeant said to him, "Where the hell were you?"

"Visiting my old outfit," replied Zaza, and the first sergeant let it drop.

Now Zaza is content to be the company mail orderly and in off moments entertain with his violin, playing mostly lively Russian folk tunes and occasionally a snatch of classical music. In addition, he sometimes animates his lengthy form in a tempestuous Russian folk dance, for at odd times in his young career he had also been a dancer with the Don Cossack Chorus in America.

February 6, 1945.

Our regiment went into action near Branscheid, Germany, where last December we first penetrated the Siegfried Line. This time, in three days of fighting we advanced beyond the deepest point of our previous penetration, and against less opposition. We encountered little artillery, only small arms and some mortar fire.

Today and yesterday the regiment captured 800 prisoners. B Company alone took 300. A captured German colonel said he'd like to use his own trucks to haul American troops to Berlin and get there before the Russians.

Today our section left Esch, traveled by truck through the heart of Battle of the Bulge territory and settled in a half-dozen ramshackle farmhouses in the hamlet of Hautbellain at the northern tip of Luxembourg. Not since Normandy have we seen such devastation as in this area engulfing the German breakthrough. It is evident that the German withdrawal is forced rather than voluntary, for every inch has been visited by the scourge of fierce battle. Few places have been spared at least partial destruction. Road surfaces are rough from exploding shells and bombs. Large numbers of American and German tanks and other knocked-out vehicles dot the landscape; and now after nearly three weeks since the Germans departed dead carcasses of German and American soldiers still lie uncovered along the banks of the road.

The hotly contested town of Bastogne, Belgium, is considerably battered but not to the extent of most towns in Normandy. German demands of civilians during this brief reoccupation were mainly for food and clothing, and this time they did not bother to promise remuneration. A farmer told us he knew some civilians who were forced to accompany the Germans to be used in a labor battalion.

February 8, 1945.

The farmer in whose house I am billeted with a few others is named

Rassel Michal. He owns six acres of land in this section which is one of the most fertile in Europe. The house is innocent of ornamentation or furniture except of the crudest imaginable. He could never afford better. He never owned a radio. Yet he is considered one of the prosperous in the village, for his house is wired for electricity, a well is rigged up to draw water right into the kitchen, and the privy is practically indoors. In construction typical of the area, his house and barn are together in one building, separated by a wall with a door that opens to the kitchen.

The barnyard smell does not extend beyond the kitchen and dining room which are presently the quarters of Rassel, his wife and child. We solemnly respect their privacy. Rassel is 38 years old, of medium height, rosy cheeks and rotten teeth. His manner is shy, his wife's forward, but he is very much the master and her attitude toward him is docile, attentive, almost reverent. He married at age 32. Until then he worked on his father's farm raising pigs, potatoes, wheat, oats, six cows and a few chickens.

He has never been to Paris or Brussels, but has once or twice visited Liége and Luxembourg City. On Saturdays he used to take his family to Ulfingen three miles away where they purchased a few articles and sometimes saw a movie. The movie house and much of the town is now destroyed. Rassel's village fared less poorly than other places during the Germans' six-week occupations.

His house had accommodated SS elite troops in the living room which contained the only stove in the house besides the cooking stove in the kitchen, and regular Wehrmacht infantrymen in two of the three upstairs rooms. The third was allowed for the family.

The SS and regular troops showed great dislike for each other and did not mingle; and neither was one less domineering toward the civilians than the other. If anything the regulars were worse than the SS, prying and plundering with less restraint. The most precious of the articles they rooted out was the soap that Rassel's wife had saved, given to her by American soldiers as part of her compensation for doing their laundry. Rassel had imprudently hidden the soap in one place instead of splitting it into two or three caches.

February 12, 1945.

Several months ago, in Normandy, General Barton told the men, "When I've had enough, you've had enough."

Well, he returned to the States in December, and the men who "had enough" are still here. It is maddening to see the few remaining who heard him say that—a mere handful—whittled down in every action. Lord, these frontline veterans of Normandy and all the action since—have they not had enough? In the last few days I have seen more of them killed, men whose days in combat far exceeded any reasonable chance of surviving.

Typical of this group is Corporal Raymond C. Schmoltze who landed on D-Day and was killed this month after about 250 consecutive days in action. He was a jeep driver for Company E, and finally got his by hitting a land mine with his jeep.

He used to go out and pick up wounded in his jeep where most medics feared to go. His duty was always at the front, hauling rations and ammunition for the men in his company, doing every job he was given to do and never complaining. He had numerous close shaves, and some light shrapnel wounds never bad enough to warrant evacuation to a hospital.

The Army in authorizing 90-day furloughs to the States has recognized the need of relief for such men, but the quota for our regiment is only eight per month. Major Blazzard is leaving today on this furlough. He is a D-Day man and had been hit six times, never seriously. He has been awarded one or two of nearly every decoration there is for bravery in action.

The regimental commander had said to him: "Take your choice—do you want to go on this trip or be promoted to battalion commander with the rank of lieutenant colonel?"

He made his choice without hesitation: "I'll probably get the opportunity again to make battalion commander when I get back. I've been lucky, getting hit six times but never badly; my luck just can't go on like that. The next time might well be my last."

He told us later, "When an infantryman takes an objective, usually a hill, he has nothing to look forward to except assaulting the next hill. Getting wounded usually gives him only a brief stay of execution.

His only chance for not getting killed is to go insane or lose a limb, unless he is one of those rare men who uncannily don't get hit. Getting hit is one hundred percent a matter of luck, not knowledge or experience."

Our present action in the Schnee Eifel hill region has become savagely violent after the first day or two. We captured Pram, an important communication center, after an expensive in casualties bloody battle that left the town in total ruins.

February 17, 1945.

Whatever future appraisal will be made of our strategy on the western front, mud may legitimately enter into consideration as a major obstacle. Now with more than half the winter gone the weather has turned mild, sporadically rainy and the ground soggy. Our offensive near Prum is handicapped by road conditions so bad that supplies for the division are being dropped by parachute.

Since taking Prum our regiment has somewhat relaxed, except one day when the Germans vigorously counterattacked, They accomplished little more than to interfere with our much-needed rest. German tactics are to counterattack whenever possible, even if there are only two men left to do it with.

The decline in fighting is quickly reflected on A and D (Admission and Disposition) sheets which are published daily by mimeograph and distributed to personnel sections of the division. The lists give complete, tersely-stated data on every individual in the division who passes through a medical aid station. Most are shown as men lightly or seriously wounded in action, men injured in action, non-battle casualties of various kinds, and men treated who do not require evacuation. Casualty reports are made containing this information and sent to higher headquarters who subsequently notify next of kin by telegram in case of death.

The A and D sheets do not show KIA (killed in action) or MIA (missing in action), which reach us by other means. The severity of a battle is revealed to us most quickly on the A and D sheets which provide an infallible barometer of its intensity. When the previous day's tally of battle casualties lists between 15 and 30 for the regiment we know there is a fight going on but not a bad one. Between 50 and 80 the fighting is severe, and at 100 to 150 it is a terribly bloody battle.

Ninety percent of the casualties are caused by shrapnel, listed as "shell fragments." Other causes are concussion, white phosphorous burns, frost-bite, gunshot, etc. "Exhaustion," "battle fatigue" and "shell-shock" are listed as non-battle casualties. Reports of so-called momentous battles are suspect until put to the acid test of seeing the A and D sheets.

Our part in the Battle of the Bulge, which General Patton called the 4th Division's greatest achievement, had only a few companies of the division substantially engaged. Three companies of our regiment were in the thickest of it, yet there were only two or three days that showed casualties on the A and D sheets at 60 or 70 per day, far from the worst category.

In the Hurtgen Forest action which yielded no bonanza of commendation but was described by General Patton as "an epic of stark infantry combat," we had many days of battle casualties numbering 150 and up, plus a huge toll of killed and missing. It is hard then to accept General Patton's assessment of our "greatest achievement," unless he perceived some mysterious tactical brilliance in holding our part of the Bulge line in Luxembourg. In terms of sacrifice, no battle has approached the intensity of Hurtgen Forest since World War I's bitterest moments of trench warfare, and here we were without benefit of trenches.

February 22, 1945.

Presently life with the division's rear echelon is comparatively tranquil. Little of a violent nature occurs in the regiment for days on end to disturb us in our clerical duties whose nature provides so much of our insight in tides and events. We have a brisk traffic with front line men visiting us on one business or another—company mail orderlies, first sergeants, men on the way to or from 3-day passes in Paris or furloughs in the States. They usually stay overnight, laying out their bedrolls on the floor and leaving right after breakfast.

In the evening, after work, we listen to their tales of experiences in battle. With us they are at ease and inclined to bare details of every occurrence they can think of. Their tales are never lacking in interest. They express themselves without inhibition in a way they never can or will at home after the war. We are, consequently, a sort of division community center for an exchange of grapevine gossip and battlefield lore.

In Hautbellain we are near the front, yet far enough away not to be continually conscious of it. Artillery fire from our guns is sporadic and, rather than intrusive, blends inconspicuously with other non-threatening sounds one grows accustomed to hearing in a war zone. But our sense of immunity from harm in being at the "rear of the front" is sometimes breached when, as today, we are informed by a G.I. visitor that some of the explosions we heard were not from our guns but German shells falling at a nearby road junction.

Also today, a heavy two-hour shelling by our artillery this morning informed us the enemy is being softened for our 90th and 87th Infantry Divisions to "jump off" toward the high ground beyond Prum.

Yesterday a member of our field kitchen crew went on a souvenir-hunting mission in the surrounding fields and never returned. A mine blew him to smithereens with a loud explosion. All that was ever found of him was a shredded field jacket.

We thought nothing much about another explosion that shook our house until, a while later, a jeep drove up and an officer asked, "Where are the remains of the six Signal Corps men who were just blown up?"

Recently a visiting rifle company first sergeant shot himself accidentally while cleaning his carbine. As a civilian he had worked as an arms inspector in a gun factory. The bullet penetrated his shoulder and passed between two of our clerks.

Last night just after dark we were startled by five brilliant light flashes in the sky. They looked like giant flash-bulb cameras going off at ten-second intervals, illuminating the entire countryside.

February 27, 1945.

In conjunction with other units, our regiment will jump off tomorrow at 5 o'clock in the morning to attack the high ground past Prum.

Prum itself has hardly been a profitable conquest. "Jerry" has such good observation from atop the hill that his snipers hardly bother to shoot at any rank below second lieutenant. Our troops can't move in or out of town except at night when the enemy has to guess at where to fire their artillery.

In taking the town, our K and L Companies were virtually obliterated when they stormed across an open stretch. The Germans held their fire until we were up with a withering fire such as American news communiques from the Pacific describe when Japanese "suicidal attacks" are repulsed.

We are fairly well padded with men for the new push, having absorbed a substantial gush from the bottomless replacement pools. Our latest contingent of 100 who arrived yesterday were Air Corps men retrained as infantrymen. Nearly all had been recently court-martialed and sentenced to six months at hard labor, but were given an alternative choice of joining our illustrious ranks. We received in addition many returning from hospitals intended for "limited assignment duty" which remains a dubious category but doubtless enables some higher authority to relieve his conscience.

There is little place for dead weight in our regiment, and most must go to the front. Individuals have come to us with wounds still raw, with arms and legs partially disabled, and there was one just nine days out of the hospital with an appendicitis operation. Our impending push to the Rhine River in concert with the First and Ninth Armies holds promise to be fruitful at last, and we pray that it will be for the war is lasting too long, our strategy turned into a stationary slugfest with the last-ditch stand put up by the Germans.

March 2, 1945.

Colonel C.T. Lanham, West Point 1924 graduate, came into command of our regiment a month after D-Day. In the month of combat before he took command two others were given that exacting post but were soon relieved as unsatisfactory. Today after more than seven months as our regimental commander Colonel "Buck" Lanham is leaving us to become assistant commander of the 104th Division with the rank of brigadier general. The only direct contact most in our section had was when he addressed us shortly after he took command and told us, "You musn't mind if I seem grouchy; I'm getting to be an old gray son-of-a-bitch."

Indirectly we've had a good deal of contact with him and found his self-characterization to be quite accurate. One who worked in close proximity to him describes him to us as "very brilliant and crazy as hell." He is widely reputed to be a sound tactician and a commander who never fails to take an assigned objective. His combat creed is best revealed in notations he made on the efficiency reports of his officers. He remarked of one lieutenant colonel: "He is a near-perfect administrator but lacks ruthlessness and determination essential to command."

Of another, battalion commander Lt. Col. Teague, he wrote: "He could command a division with distinction. He has a miraculous eye and feel for terrain, and is the most competent leader in battle I have ever known."

In appearance Col. Lanham is slight of build, medium in height and has iron-gray hair. He is 42 and looks 60. In a civilian setting one could visualize him as a kindly grandfather indulgently taking his young grandchild on a peaceful Sunday stroll. As a soldier he presents an aspect of daring that verges on foolhardiness, sometimes jeopardizing needlessly both himself and others. He is shrewd, and calculating in that he never fails to capitalize on his ventures into no man's land by seeing to it that each heroic act he may perform is observed by a fellow officer who will promptly write it up for a battlefield award. Thus he is a much decorated man.

Different stories are told by lesser witnesses of his part in the action for which he was awarded the very high Distinguished Service Cross, but since they are varied and inconsistent they cannot stigmatize his worthiness for honor.

I suppose it is a trait of his profession that he also displays no humility by pouncing on an award citation written about him that reaches his desk and he revises the wording to embellish it with his own descriptive flourishes. It happens that the action for which he received the coveted DSC yielded in addition a rich harvest of awards for several other officers, and perhaps it is irrelevant to point out that the incident from which arose all this exalted recognition involved nothing more climactic than is experienced every day by the average foot-slogging rifleman whose recognition for committing deeds of valor is at best sporadic.

Col. Lanham (soon to be addressed as General Lanham) professes adherence to no particular religion. Written on his service record under the heading "Religious preference" is the word "None."

He is an astute judge of field officers and, tolerating little inefficiency, has sent out more officers for reclassification than both other regiments of the division combined. That this is for the good may be compromised somewhat by the fact that he is petty and untrusting of his subordinate officers. He minutely peruses administrative details and takes niggling exception to the judgment of responsible officers, thereby inhibiting them from taking any constructive initiatives.

One of his least admired decisions came in the awarding of the Combat Infantryman Badge. Congress had authorized that it be awarded retroactively to 6 June 1944, D-Day. Lanham rejected this date and made it effective no earlier than 14 Aug 1944, which deprived the men of an additional $10 per month for the full period in which they fought.

His reason: "Whatever happened in this regiment before I took command does not concern me."

Because he is cantankerous and unpredictable most officers and enlisted men of the regiment are relieved at his leaving, but for his ability to get results in combat they are sorry to lose him.

March 9, 1945.

Our section moved today to Prum, Germany, in the wake of our fastest moving offensive since last September. Prum is a city of ruins, with a room here and there habitable for military purposes. Of the regular 30,000 population, there is not a civilian in sight. We took up residence in a schoolhouse that had been spared except for a portion of the roof, all of the windows and here and there odd chunks of concrete.

It is easy to see why both sides contested so determinedly for possession of Prum. It is a strategic road junction controlling a pivotal network through the hills. The German front collapsed here, achieved by our division assaulting a steep ridge in a wedge formation that bored clear through the German defenses. This enabled the 11th Armored Division to ram through the breach with its tanks and race for the Rhine.

To do this our regiment first had to go through thickly-sown mine fields, which took a severe toll in legs and lives, then rush into the fire of machine guns fixed in do-or-die positions. Our casualties were high for three or four days. After the 11th Armored galloped off we followed through rapidly, mopping up small pockets of resistance which is not a pleasant job, but not very costly. It has been a grueling, bitter winter of combat, and now we see the first encouraging signs that the German might is really deteriorating.

March 14, 1945.

At last the 4th Division has been taken out of action for a rest. We were transported by rail in "40 and 8's"—40 men or 8 horses—to a rest area near Luneville, France, 30 miles southeast of Nancy. We are now part of the 7th Army under General Patch. Our section is now operating with the regiment in a small village called Marignieres, a few miles from Luneville.

For the first time since the 5th of last June everyone in the regiment is out of earshot range of artillery. We are eighty miles from the front and need not carry rifles or wear steel helmets. Here we may train our new men in peace. What recreation and diversions may be available is problematical, for wine and women in this part of France are scarce. It is a poor locality by our standards, grimy and manure-laden, but the countryside is pleasing to the eye and spring is in the air. The quiet and warm sun should do much toward healing our combat-weary men of frayed nerves and shell-wracked ears.

March 21, 1945.

The division's sojourn in a rest area terminated abruptly after a mere five days. Our regiment suddenly pulled its shallow-rooted stakes and went by truck 80 miles eastward, settling in a forward area near Haguenau but not back in action. We had only three casualties during the rest period, occurring when a mortar shell fell short on a practice range.

Our section rejoined "Cactus Rear" and moved to the city of Luneville, which is a focal point of the defunct Maginot Line that was to have stopped any attempt by Germany to invade, and the historic site of the Napoleonic Battle of Luneville. It is for all that a shabby, sprawling town of some 22,000 souls, now crammed with 7th Army Headquarter troops, MP's and troops of the First French Army wearing American uniforms.

March 22.

Our stay in Luneville lasted only one day, then today we loaded gear and operatives onto trucks and set a course due east over a good highway that cut through the flat rich land of Alsace and its cities Saarbourg and Saverne. We arrived at the Alsatian city of Haguenau, ten miles before the Rhine, and set up shop in modern buildings that the French and German armies had used to garrison their troops and are now a bit tarnished with recent battle scars.

American troops first entered the city on the 30th of November, then on January 21 were pushed back by the Germans to the Moder River that runs through the middle of the city. From that time on until a week ago, March 16, we held the southwestern half of the city and the Germans the northeastern, which had suffered much the worst punishment from our superior artillery. Nearly all the 18,000 civilians had left and are now beginning to return. I spoke with a few and learned that their lot resembled that of Luxembourgers. Germany annexed Alsace in 1940, The Alsatian German dialect was outlawed and persuasive efforts were made to Nazify the people, with little success.

March 28, 1945.

Today we left Haguenau and traveled northward on a highway crowded with military vehicles rushing to occupy the territory opened up by General Patton's Third Army. We passed through the cities of Landau and Neustadt and stopped fifty miles from Haguenau in the town of Bad Dürkheim, which is in the heart of the Saar Basin, or

"Palatinate," a region that had been given the choice in 1935 of joining either Germany or France. It made the unfortunate choice and threw in with the Nazis.

The 10,000 population town of Bad Dürkheim is, like the other Saar towns we saw, largely ruined. Five hundred people are still unaccounted for, nearly all buried in cellars where they had sought shelter. The remaining are busy salvaging what they can from the ruins and orienting themselves to the condition of being conquered and controlled by an American military government.

In keeping with both spirit and letter of orders against fraternizing with civilians, our troops walk through the streets eyeing the bleak-faced citizenry with utter coolness while they, white surrender flags hanging from their few habitable buildings, regard us once with a conciliatory smile, again with humility and penitence, then with complete blankness. Hardest to ignore are the children, whom we are not supposed to gift with candy, chewing gum or biscuits but some soldiers do.

The people say they are sick of Nazism as well as the war. They are particularly angry with the German Wehrmacht who had promised to vacate the town so it wouldn't be fought over and ravaged by battle. The German Army did leave town, then changed its mind and returned to fight and gain time to prepare the defenses of Ludwigshafen and Mannheim, both on the Rhine River 12 and 15 miles to the east. The 4th Division is in the vicinity and still not engaged in any action more severe than drinking unlimited liters of local wine.

April 1, 1945.

Our division went into action, following behind the 12th Armored Division whose tanks surge ahead in search of the retreating enemy. The troops are advancing 30 to 50 miles a day in mop-up maneuvers and are finding almost nothing to mop up. Our section moved today, crossing the Rhine at the bomb-gutted city of Worms and traveling 35 miles through country flat as Detroit. We crossed the Rhine on an Engineer Corps-constructed pontoon bridge next to the huge bridge whose main span had been blasted into the river and created a minor rapids in the otherwise placid stream that put me in mind of the Ohio River.

We stopped 15 miles beyond it and unloaded in the town of Heppenheim which is situated exactly where the flat land rises abruptly to towering foothills. Wounded American soldiers were found in a German hospital in this town. They were nearly starved and their wounds had been neglected, a condition attributed to a fanatic doctor who despised American "guts." The liberating Americans met a single subordinate doctor who had been left behind. He was shot on the spot.

I find it hard to realize how in this pleasant resort town, plush with gracious frills and the fine arts of a most advanced western culture, barbaric behavior among its inhabitants could have occurred. We meet everywhere in this region liberated Russian, Pole, Greek, French slave laborers. They all tell stories of brutality heaped upon them, the details invariably lurid and debasing.

The Russians especially were considered a caste equal to dogs and to illustrate were forced to act like dogs by barking and walking on hands and knees at the end of a leash. The men were tortured for actual or imagined misdemeanors, and the women would not think of refusing the advances of a German soldier. The young and attractive women are all now seasoned if unwilling prostitutes, and nearly all are diseased.

We also see here many German men of ideal military age, obviously soldiers who had simply taken off their uniforms and put on mufti. Many remain in uniform and walk around freely, unarmed, waiting for the convenience of Americans to take them prisoner.

April 3, 1945.

We moved this morning 50 miles east to Buchen, where we found the best living and working quarters in many a day. This Franconian town of 8,000 is not wrecked. Even the electric lights work; but we are warned to avoid the spring water the civilians use. Tests reveal that it contains cholera-producing organisms and is dangerous even when treated with Halizone tablets.

We came upon another horde of released slave laborers, a bedraggled lot showing symptoms of starvation. They are supposed to be fed by a newly-approved burgormeister but meanwhile swarm near our kitchen and wait for us to finish eating and give them our leftovers.

Though it is quiet here we are on a strict alert and may not circulate freely; this in serious anticipation of trouble from so-called "Were-wolves." The symbol of this society is a large black shadow which appears painted on walls in the form of a sinister thug, and in the center of the black figure is a question mark painted in yellow. The reality of the menace is borne out by the discovery of discarded SS uniforms. Bands of fanatic SS troopers are at large posing as civilians but sworn to the purpose of murdering alien troops and any Germans who collaborate with our military government.

Several miles from here our regiment is exploiting a bulge in the German line south of Wurzburg. We are getting some casualties from stubborn if sporadic rear-guard opposition, and the Germans are using jet-propelled fighter planes to strafe our troops. They run circles around our much slower propeller-driven planes which try to stop them.

Our first group of men who went December 8th on furlough to the States has just returned. The men report that the United States looks good and essentially the same as ever. Only a few met with anything less than a deliriously happy reception at home. One found his wife "shacked up" with another man. Another discovered he was the father of 3-month old twins though he had been overseas for three years.

Nearly all tried to finagle transfers to outfits stationed permanently in the States but were prevented by a strict order from General Eisenhower not to interfere with their return overseas. One man with bleeding piles was told by a Camp Kilmer medical officer that he would have to wait for treatment until he sees his battalion surgeon. At least they are all happy to have attained a nearly 4-month reprieve from the front.

April 8, 1945.

The regiment is fighting a peculiar action against a foe whose tactics are almost guerrilla-like. The front lines are but a surmise. The bulge we are pressing forward at sticks out south of our newly-captured territory in central Germany. The German Army incongruously puts up a stiff rear-guard fight in one town and none in the next. The civilians in each town project an air of peaceful home-loving folks. They run out to meet the first American troops, their arms laden with watches, rings, cameras, and plead, "Please don't destroy our homes." Resembling our own kind in the States, it is hard to realize they are part of a unified nation whose soldiers shoot at Americans then run out with hands up shouting "Kamarad!"

Yesterday we took the town of Bad Mergentheim. Today Service Company and Headquarters Company moved in though just a few hundred yards from town the Germans still contest a castle atop a small hill and there is an occasional flurry of small arms fire as the Germans alternately leave and infiltrate back. Inside the town which has not had much damage, civilians stroll about in their Sunday finery, calm and seemingly unconcerned. At times they appear to regard us as liberators instead of conquerors. There are indications that their own army treated them poorly. By contrast the Americans are polite while demanding facilities from them, and when merely ignoring them there is a clear absence of hostility in the American attitude.

German civilians have been known to assist Americans who escaped from prisoner of war camps. Six of our men walked in yesterday who had been hidden and fed for several days by the people in a German village. The prisoners had volunteered to work on farms so they might eat better and escaped just before their scheduled return to the prison compound.

In the present new style of battle our losses are moderate in total numbers but the proportion of men killed is higher. The enemy operates largely as roving bands of snipers, selecting small isolated groups as their primary targets and shooting to kill. Recently an SS captain sent two young soldiers dressed as civilians into our lines with the information that the Germans were massing 100 tanks and ten thousand men for a drive to cut off our bulge. We put in a hasty call for tank destroyers and made ready for the attack which was to take place the next morning. Our regiment waited tensely for the dawn. Morning came and passed and nothing happened. Our interrogators then took the youths in hand.

"We were only kidding," they said. Later we captured the SS captain who had thought up the plan to throw us from an offensive to a defensive posture. Even so we received word from General Eisenhower to be prepared for a broad German counter-offensive.

April 12, 1945.

Today our section moved to Bad Mergentheim, our 31st move since crossing the English Channel last June. This town of 11,000 was once frequented by the upper classes for its health sanitariums, fine hotels and an overwhelming ratio of men to women. Our regiment jumped off from here two days ago and is now upwards of 12 miles away, to the south. We are settled in good quarters again, having taken over a hotel and one of the public buildings housing mineral baths.

As we travel in Germany we find plentiful stocks of equipment we can use. We appropriated several typewriters with the only difference from our standard keyboard being the Y and Z reversed. We have now also a good radio, a large mobile generator that can light a large building but has to be used sparingly as it consumes liberal quantities of gasoline, and champagne that is not aged enough, but serviceable.

We just received the news of President Franklin D. Roosevelt's death. It came as the most unexpectedly shocking news since the Japanese attack of Pearl Harbor.

April 14.

Our regiment changed course from south to east in advancing 18 miles. The regimental CP moved two or three times and four of us set out by jeep to find it—Captain Brill, the driver Corporal Stevens, myself, and Lin Streeter who tagged along to pick up ideas for his locally-famous cartoons in *The Ivy Leaf*. After detouring a few times for blown-up bridges, we arrived at the CP's supposed location in Laudenbach and found it had moved forward a few miles. We finally tracked it down in a small farming village 4 miles west of Rotterbach. On the way we passed a jeep blown apart so badly that only a small section remained, on it inscribed the name of the jeep, "Devil's Own."

For the first time in weeks, our artillery is firing in concentrated force. The colonel, blazing mad that we had suffered too many losses in taking the previous town, vowed not to spare artillery shells in preventing it from happening again.

In the town just before Rotterbach a battalion of SS troops had declined our surrender ultimatum. We usually try in advance of entry to contact the burgomeister of every town and demand the townsfolk hang white flags in front of their houses and pile all their weapons in the town square. Many towns comply and hardly a shot is fired. This town decided to hold out so the colonel called on the field telephone for all the heavy ammunition he could get and proceeded to blast the place to rubble and ashes.

The campaign is progressing swiftly in Germany and the end seems near, but this is a touchy subject with the men on line. To them every instant of fighting exposes them to as much danger as ever, and there is a bitter awareness of possibly being hit two minutes before the end of all hostilities. One man returned from a furlough in the States was killed the next day.

April 17, 1945.

Tech-Sergeant George Kraus had twice been offered a battlefield commission to the officer rank of 2nd lieutenant and refused each time. I met him recently when he came back to be transferred to the 83rd Infantry Division. He stayed with me before entering the notorious channel through replacement pools. He orginally came to France as a member of the 83rd Division, arriving with the division advance party on D-Day plus 3 though the division did not go into action until July 4.

On that date, Kraus told me, the 83rd went into a series of engagements that may well rank among the worst American combat failures of the war. Led by incompetent commanders, each regiment engaged in action after action grossly ignoring all principles and knowledge of modern war science. Time after time they assaulted enemy lines with little effort at subterfuge or finding protection in the recesses of a studied terrain.

In consequence they consistently suffered a rate of casualties far out of proportion to gains in comparison with other divisions. After 5 or 6 weeks the division was taken out of action and all three regimental commanders were relieved of command. A program of reorganization was instituted that kept the division out of action perhaps longer than any other division. Afterward it is said to have become a good division.

Kraus recalled one battalion commander, a lieutenant colonel, who became so aroused by the incompetence of his CO that he went to him holding out the lieutenant colonel insignia he had stripped from his collar and declared he was reclassifying himself at once.

Kraus had been wounded at St. Malô. His hedgerow-fighting experience in Normandy was in the capacity of anti-tank acting platoon leader. Upon return from the hospital, he was sent to the 4th Division four days after the Hurtgen Forest battle began and assigned to the antitank platoon of 2nd Battalion Headquarters Company instead of being returned to the 83rd Division. He arrived amidst a heavy German counterattack.

His new company commander immediately said to him, "Sergeant Kraus, both the platoon officer and platoon sergeant of your platoon have just been hit. You are now in command." And he started walking away.

"Hey, wait a minute, where is the front?" asked Kraus.

"You are on it," replied the captain.

Kraus has led the platoon from then on in every action of the 2nd Battalion. For a short time an officer was over him, but didn't know the 57-mm gun and placed himself under Kraus's direction until he was transferred to a company with guns that he knew where he proved himself a wise, competent commander.

Like every soldier who ever survived Hurtgen Forest, Kraus considers it incredible that he had not been hit there. He has never been able to reason out a justification for our lengthy suicidal attack in that small forest. He is ambivalent about returning to the 83rd Division. He made many friends in the 4th, and finally decided to transfer out because the 83rd had gone to some trouble to get him back.

April 26, 1945.

We pulled up stakes from Bad Mergentheim and moved 60 miles south to a small town in the province of Wirtemberg called Oberkochen. Here we are 20 miles from the Danube ("Donau" in German) River which our regiment crossed yesterday in advancing half-way to Augsburg. In the past three days the A and D sheets have shown no battle casualties for our regiment and very few for the others.

Listed frequently among non-battle casualties is "gonorrhea, new," though the program of pleasure trips to Paris has been discontinued. The men say they are not violating rules against fraternization but are merely utilizing the natural resources of the region.

We passed one town that had attempted to impede our progress, a sizable one called Crailsheim. As usual, the burgomeister was contacted in advance and asked to surrender. He agreed, and white flags were hung from the buildings. Then 1st Battalion Commander Lt. Col. Goforth sent Lt. Geoffrey Jones into the town to see if it was clear. Jones was shot in the back as he entered town and died instantly.

A man was seen committing this post-surrender act. He was in civilian clothes and no one pursued him. Instead Colonel Goforth, extremely provoked, called for air and artillery action. He asked them to level the town. This is the largest town I have seen that was destroyed primarily for a vindictive reason. It was not an unpopular decision.

November, 1995 UPDATE TO ENTRY OF APRIL 26, 1945:

The Town of Crailsheim had once been home to Dr. Armin Ziegler and his family. Half a century after the event described in this entry, Dr. Ziegler undertook an investigation that corrected the record of what happened on April 20, 1945. Both my entry and the memoir of our regimental Chaplain Dr. William Boice indicated that the citizens of Crailsheim had acted in a dishonorable fashion. Dr. Ziegler obtained full documentation from United States Official Army records that proves otherwise. Lt. Walter E. Jones was shot not in the back but in the throat. No white flags of surrender were displayed because the residents were forbidden to do so by diehard German SS troops who threatened death to anyone who defied their orders. I heartily welcome this new information. No sane person would willingly cause more death and destruction when the war was so near the end.

April 27, 1945.

Oberkochen, population 1,800, is situated at the base of several high densely wooded hills. It contains two modern factories, one owned by the government producing airplane parts, the other a privately-owned tool and die plant. Our section took over the office of the smaller, privately owned factory. As we arrived the short, barrel-chested director was hastily locking up papers and blueprints.

"How many workers do you employ?" I asked.

200, he replied.

"And how many slave laborers?" I pursued having seen the familiar shacks fenced in nearby with double barbed-wire barricades.

80 Russians and 9 Frenchmen, he answered, then took a last anxious look around the premises and mumbled something concerning the preservation of his facilities.

"Don't worry, we won't ruin anything," I commented.

"Yes I know," he said quickly, "but those Russians, they might try to break up everything."

I chose not to follow up on the subject of the Russians. Both he and his kindly-looking elderly secretary who requested we water the ferns adorning her office did not seem embarrassed at being the employers of slave labor. Later I spoke with some of the French and Russians, the latter through Leo Gorelick who speaks Russian. The French had not been treated badly but the Russians were fed a diet just short of starvation. Anyone who got sick declined rapidly.

A 23-year old girl stricken over a year ago with appendicitis was hospitalized for three months. The doctor said her blood was too poor for a complete recovery. She got well enough to work and in violation of the doctor's orders was returned to a full heavy-duty routine. Complications soon set in. The director wanted to send her away to a place where sick workers are usually sent and never heard from again. The girl begged to remain and he relented after she offered to sew the clothes of the other Russians which were constantly in serious need of repair.

Working hours for the Russians were longer than for the French, from 6 A.M. to 7 P.M. daily and off Sunday, except there was usually an excuse to work them on Sunday as punishment for alleged misbehavior. They were paid 40 to 50 marks per month, part of which had to be deposited in a bank for safe-keeping until 1950. Workers over 17 years of age were seldom beaten.

There is a small pond stocked with rainbow trout behind the factory. From it we fished out a box of Nazi swastika banners marked with the names of Nazi party members who held key positions in the two factories.

Every business letter I saw ended with the salutation "Heil Hitler." Now that they are liberated, the Russians instead of taking advantage of new conditions are going through a stage of reacting meekly. Knowing there are large food stocks in every home, they yet go about timidly scraping together meals that are hardly an improvement over their customary fare, except for a few leftovers we give them from our kitchen.

April 28, 1945.

As usual when the regiment is moving fast, we were not sure where the regimental command post would be. Three of us went to look for it, Lt. Hoehn—Captain Brill's assistant—Corporal Stevens and I. We crossed the Danube River at Lauingen, over a pontoon bridge bearing a sign reading: "Waltz over the Danube to the tune of Company C, 536th Engineers." The river appeared half as wide as the Rhine and instead of blue looked to me very green.

Five miles farther we came upon Service Company waiting for trucks to transport them closer to the regiment. Our swift advance has left many German prisoners in collection clusters awaiting transfer to the rear. We arrived at Service Company just as two civilians were being questioned by the first sergeant. Two men from the company had gone out duck hunting and on the way met two liberated Poles who asked them to take custody of two civilians they were holding on suspicion. These were the two that the first sergeant was examining. Their identification cards showed them to be SS troopers in disguise.

"Throw them in with the others," he directed.

We learned that the regiment was forty miles farther and we continued on our way. We drove on back roads for miles without seeing other Americans. The people in villages gaped at us as though we were the first Americans they had seen. Likely the territory had been by-passed and not yet officially secured. Three hours later we came upon the 1st and 3rd Battalions, then the regimental CP. Our 2nd Battalion had gone on ahead together with the 8th and 12th Infantry Regiments in hot pursuit of the enemy.

"This is a rat-race like our run through France," observed warrant officer Mr. Flannagan.

The CP staffmen were weary from the continuous traveling and had been unable to complete some reports that were awaited. It was after 6 P.M. before we headed back on the 70 mile return trip. To make time we took a different route for part of the way, riding for a few miles on the "autobahn" superhighway that goes from Munich to Augsburg an Ulm. The road was in perfect condition and had been used by the Luftwaffe as a runway for jet-propelled planes. I counted 16 knocked-out planes that failed to make a getaway from their camouflaged hideaways in the woods lining both sides of the highway.

Soon after leaving the superhighway we were waved to a stop in a small town by a sentry whom we recognized as a liberated prisoner but could not make out the country his uniform represented.

He told us in German, "I am a Yugoslav. There are five of us armed with pistols and checking all civilian identification papers. We have two men here with no identification papers. Please instruct us what to do with them."

I translated this to Lt. Hoehn, and he said, "Tell them to hold those civilians until a Military Government patrol arrives to question them."

I relayed the message; the Yugoslav saluted smartly and we continued on our way without further incident, except for a flat tire and a brief hailstorm.

April 29, 1945.

At breakfast I carried my cereal, flapjacks and coffee-laden mess kit to a table partly occupied by three men in British Army uniform.

"Are you radar men?" I asked.

"No," replied one in a thick Scottish brogue, "we're ex-prisoners of war; we've been prisoners of the Germans for five years."

Their stories were amazing. They had watched the German war machine as it developed since 1940, and observed the psychological transition of the German people. Some would pour out their troubles to war prisoners, tell them things they would be afraid to say among themselves. In the past year, said the Scot, the people were disgusted with their leaders and sick of the war.

This did not keep them from exploiting slave labor, and they had shown genuine hatred for the Jews when they were still around by spontaneously lynching them. Nazi party members got all the good clothes and food looted from invaded countries. The nice-looking clothes we see are often made out of processed paper.

The prisoners of war were able to survive mainly because of Red Cross packages they received. They would trade secretly with civilians, exchanging chocolate and butter for bread.

In recent months they tramped through Poland, Czechoslovakia and Austria. Once the Russians came within three miles of them, then swerved the other way. For three days before he was freed, said Scotty, he had escaped and hidden in the woods. He saw an American column approaching and signalled the lead car to stop.

"Don't shoot," he yelled, "I'm British!"

He told an officer that if they would change course a little t' would reach a camp of 10,000 American prisoners of war 70 away. The officer immediately assembled all the jeeps in the c armed the men in them with submachine guns and raced to th reaching it in time to prevent the POW's from being with the mountains in the south.

"Then one hour later," said Scotty, "I was watching ? movie. A bloomin' Yank comes over and says, 'Hey Sc the movies.' I says, 'What do you mean? There's still on around here, how can there be movies?' He show though, and there we were, fighting going on a' seeing a bloomin' Yank movie!"

May 6, 1945.

We moved 80 miles today and joined the regiment at Limbach, just outside Schwabach and ten miles from Nuremberg. "Cactus Rear" is now dissolved, probably for good, and hereafter we will operate with the main body of the regiment as in pre-combat garrison days. In fact our regiment has begun to operate in garrison fashion adapted to an Army of Occupation situation.

Our division is now again part of the 3rd Army under General Patton. The 4th Division combat career in Europe virtually came to an end a few days ago when we swept south of Munich into Austria. We suffered few casualties in that action, took many prisoners and avoided taking more because we couldn't handle them.

Some of the German soldiers who had changed into civilian clothes are carrying official honorable discharge papers made out by adjutants a few hours before they would be captured. These men are being ignored for the time being except in one instance when a civilian was brought in by an excited group of Ukrainians who passionately declared him to be the SS officer in charge of one of the notorious concentration camps.

At Landsberg, west of Munich, several of our men had occasion to see one of these camps with its full regalia of torture chambers, incinerator death-houses and a large number of corpses in a variety of ghastly poses and stages of disintegration. The men say the horrors they witnessed were not exaggerated in the reports they had heard before going there. But it must be seen in the condition in which they saw it to be really believed.

May 8, 1945.

Today at 12:01 A.M., May 8, 1945, the war in Europe officially ended. Through the entire term of combat our regiment had three complete turnovers in authorized strength. Over 1,400 men were killed. The mean average age of the men in the regiment before we went into combat was 26 and a half. Today it is almost the same, 26 and a quarter, though now we have more men aged 18 and 19 than we had before. Of the 3,000 men in the regiment, over 500 have been in the Army four years or more and never left the regiment; which illustrates

where the casualties occurred. Being among the early draftees obviously paid off richly for these men whose specialist jobs kept them just back enough from the battle lines to give them a reasonable chance to survive.

The nine rifle companies who usually fought with less than 150 men apiece, each had about 1,000 casualties. The other two regiments of the division are statistically similar. Along with the rest of "Cactus Rear," our personnel section suffered only a few casualties, mostly through road accidents, sickness and guns accidentally discharged. Other divisions' rear echelons have been less fortunate; some have had to requisition entire new finance sections, adjutant generals and regimental personnel sections.

June 6.

At Heilsbronn, a village 15 miles west of Nuremberg where we moved on May 15, we have been concluding business left over from combat. Among other things we court-martialed six medics for alleged mutiny, on slim conflicting evidence for which they got 10 years each and a dishonorable discharge—the sentences would have been longer but for their battlefield decorations for heroism.

We selected a man from California who had qualified for discharge at this time on "points," to accompany General Patton on a native-son hero's return to California. To prepare him, the powers that be awarded him all in one day a Silver Star for bravery, a Bronze Star, a Purple Heart, and promoted him from "buck" sergeant to staff sergeant. Ordinarily he would no doubt have received, after some red tape, the Bronze Star for group participation in action and the Purple Heart. Then we wrote up at last Colonel Tribolet, who had been relieved of the regiment's command shortly after D-Day, for award of the Legion of Merit and the Silver Star.

To date the division is eligible for its men to receive three Bronze Service Stars for the time they individually participated in action, and two more are expected to be authorized. We were informed that our division stands 5th in casualties among all divisions in the U.S. Army. The first four include casualties they received fighting earlier in Africa and Italy.

From D-Day to now, the 4th Infantry Division had more battle casualties than any other division in the Army. Now everyone is concerned with points. The more he has the earlier he will be in line for discharge back to civilian life. We are sweating out the current crop of rumors, which are to the effect that we will be back in the States within a few weeks and are to leave here in a few days for a marshalling area near Cherbourg preparatory to getting on a boat for home.

Continental Odyssey of "Caisson" Personnel Section

1	June 23, 1944	Landed, "Utah" Beach, Quinnéville, <u>France</u>
2	June 23, 1944	Huberville, Outside of Valognes, <u>Normandy</u>
3	June 29, 1944	Cherbourg Airfield
4	June 30, 1944	Amfreville, West of St. Mère Eglise
5	July 3, 1944	Huberville
6	July 11, 1944	Blosseville, South of St. Mère Eglise
7	July 30, 1944	Marigny, West of St. Lô
8	Aug 7, 1944	La Trinité, North of Villedieu
9	Aug 15, 1944	Los Landos, East of Mortain
10	Aug 20, 1944	Champfremonte, East of Alençon
11	Aug 24, 1944	Chateauneuf, South of Dreux
12	Aug 27, 1944	Villiers sur Orge, South of Paris
13	Sep 1, 1944	Nantouil, Northeast of Paris
14	Sep 7, 1944	Tremblois, Forest of Rymond, West of Charleville
15	Sep 13, 1944	St. Hubert, <u>Belgium</u>
16	Sep 29, 1944	St. Vith

17	Oct 7, 1944	Spa
18	Oct 21, 1944	Stavelot
19	Dec 8, 1944	Hamm, Luxembourg, Outside city of Luxembourg
20	Dec 9, 1944	Mondorf
21	Dec 20, 1944	Hamm
22	Dec 26, 1944	Mondorf
23	Jan 18, 1945	Esch sur Alzette, Southwest of Lux. City
24	Feb 6, 1945	Hautbellain, Northern tip of Luxembourg
25	Mar 9, 1945	Prüm, Germany
26	Mar 14, 1945	Marignieres, France, West of Lunéville
27	Mar 21, 1945	Lunéville, Southeast of Nancy
28	Mar 22, 1945	Haguenau, North of Strassbourg
29	Mar 23, 1945	Bad Dürkheim, Germany, East of Kaiserlautern
30	Apr 1, 1945	Heppenheim, East of Worms
31	Apr 3, 1945	Buchen
32	Apr 12, 1945	Bad Mergentheim, South of Würzburg
33	Apr 26, 1945	Oberkochen, North of Heidenheim, East of Stuttgart

I arrived in New York from overseas July 11, 1945. Had departed from Le Havre, France aboard a U.S. Liberty 10,000 ton troopship. Date discovered in 1993 from an old telegram.

Name of ship: USS *James B. Parker*. Honorable Discharge from Army at Camp Butner, NC, September 28, 1945